Pirate Novels

Pirate Novels

Fictions of Nation Building in Spanish America

Nina Gerassi-Navarro

Duke University Press   Durham and London

1999

© 1999 Duke University Press

All rights reserved

Printed in the United States of America

on acid-free paper ∞

Designed by C. H. Westmoreland

Typeset in Palatino with Oxford display

by Tseng Information Systems, Inc.

Library of Congress Cataloging-in-Publication

Data appear on the last printed page

of this book.

a mi madre,

Marysa Navarro

Contents

Acknowledgments

This work grew out of my dissertation at Columbia University and is the result of a long endeavor that was sustained throughout many years by the support of institutions, friends, and colleagues whom I wish to thank.

I am grateful for the support I received at Columbia University and for the Mount Holyoke faculty grants I received to continue my research over the years. I am also thankful for the assistance I received from the Archives and Special Collections at Mount Holyoke College, the Beinecke Library at Yale University, and Alessia Stevani at the British Library.

I would like to thank my dissertation director, Jean Franco, for her guidance and insights. Flor María Rodríguez-Arenas pushed me to expand the original scope of my dissertation and has continued to stimulate my work over the years. Josefina Ludmer, who has been a friend and mentor from the University of Buenos Aires, always provided me with excellent advice and support. Among my friends and colleagues at Mount Holyoke College who read different parts of my manuscript and whose intellectual insights were a significant contribution, I would like to thank Amy Kaplan, Elizabeth Young, and Awam Amkpa. Roberto Márquez was particularly helpful in revising my translations; I am grateful for his thoroughness and keen suggestions. I also thank Cynthia Stone and Luis Fernando Restrepo for their readings. Reynolds Smith and Paula Dragosh at Duke University Press provided valuable assistance, and Bill Henry carefully worked on my prose, ensuring that my Spanish did not hamper the manuscript's readability.

Throughout the different stages of my work, I received support from many friends. Among them I thank Daniele Baliani, Shari Zimble, Ana María Amar Sánchez, Kavita Khory, Eyda Merediz, and Raquel Medina. I am indebted to María Elena Qués for lending me her 1917 edition of López's novel, which first sparked my excitement in this project. I especially thank Marysa Navarro for her careful readings and our numerous heated discussions; her inexhaustible constructive criticism, unwavering support, and encouragement throughout the years have been vital. And finally, very special thanks to Ernesto Livon-Grosman and our son Nicolás for making the last stressful phase of completing a book a joyful period in my life.

Introduction

Que es mi barco mi tesoro,
que es mi Dios la libertad,
mi ley la fuerza y el viento,
mi única patria la mar.
—José de Espronceda, "Canción del pirata"

Throughout the centuries, piracy has captured the imagination of historians and fiction writers alike. Portrayed as daring adventurers at sea, heroic rebels against authority, bloodthirsty villains, or comical Captain Hooks, pirates have sprung from facts and myths into legends that have fascinated readers of all ages. The enchantment continues even today. One has only to surf the Internet to explore the many Web sites filled with images of flags, treasures, and weapons, as well as brief biographies of some of the most renowned pirates, articles on their favorite torture methods, lists of Hollywood films, or a rundown of the latest pirate conventions being held.[1]

The history of piracy is as old as the history of trade. As far back as 5000 B.C. in the Persian Gulf, the Mediterranean Sea, and the Indian Ocean, maritime bandits, or "enemies of the human race," as Cicero called them, emerged to make a profit from preying on those who transported goods from one point to another. In the Caribbean, piracy was particularly widespread and vigorous, lasting almost three centuries. Shortly after Columbus's first trip, the French sailed to the New World in the hope of establishing their own stronghold. As the Spanish were quick to expel all foreign settlements from their newly claimed territories, raids by the French and the English, and later by the Dutch, soon began. Although officially terminated at the end of the eighteenth century, piracy in the Caribbean continued, albeit in a much more diffused fashion.[2]

As piracy became a staging of the past, a body of fictional portrayals of the pirate emerged in Europe. Walter Scott's historical novel *The Pirate,* Lord Byron's epic poem "The Corsair," José de Espronceda's poem "Canción del pirata," Verdi's opera *Il Corsaro,* Berlioz's overture *Le Corsaire,* and of course Robert Louis Stevenson's notorious *Treasure Island* are just a few of the most well-known works with a piratical theme. These works reflect a fascination with the pirate as they construct and define his voice and riveting image. The conceptualization of this genre could take place only once the spatial and temporal limits have been set, thus marking the frontiers of the object to be constructed.[3]

European romantics saw the pirate as their ideal hero: independent, audacious, intrepid, and rebellious. Defying society's rules and authorities, sailing off to the unknown in search of treasures, fearing nothing, the pirate became the ultimate symbol of freedom. The English poet Lord Byron captured this emotion distinctly in his poem "The Corsair," published in 1814:

> O'er the glad waters of the dark blue sea,
> Our thoughts as boundless, and our souls as free,
> Far as the breeze can bear, the billows foam,
> Survey our empire, and behold our home!
> These are our realms, no limits to their sway—
> Our flag the sceptre all who meet obey.[4]

As masterless outlaws, pirates often became national legends. In England, they not only embodied the romantic hero navigating across the seas to the unknown but also became great national heroes as their assaults against the Spanish empire during the colonial period were evoked. Referred to more often as admirals, privateers, and explorers than as pirates, men such as Francis Drake, Walter Raleigh, and Henry Morgan were even knighted in recognition of their "discoveries" and conquests. Assaulting ships carrying amazing treasures from Peru and Mexico, and colonizing whatever territories they could in the New World, these men—along with many others—created an overseas empire for England and challenged Spain's economic and geopolitical hegemony in Europe and the New World.

Although pirates aroused a sense of freedom and adventure among Spanish romantics, these seafaring bandits were rarely viewed as national heroes. The Spanish had been subjected to constant attacks in the

Mediterranean from the Barbary corsairs, the dangerous Berbers from the northern coast of Africa who were extremely active along the eastern Atlantic coast as well as throughout the Mediterranean. In 1575, they captured Miguel de Cervantes, who remained a slave in Algiers until he was ransomed by Trinitarian friars five years later. Having also suffered pirate attacks for almost three centuries in their American territories, Spaniards saw piracy as a brutal and violent force aimed at uprooting Spain's empire. But it was the English who prominently stood out for having defied Spain with such tenacity. Thus, in José de Espronceda's "Canción del pirata," perhaps the best-known example of Spanish romantic poetry dealing with piracy, when the Spanish pirate sets out in his vessel and dares to confront the dangerous sea forces, the English are sure to be among them. In fact, the greatest triumph will be precisely to subjugate the English forces:

> Veinte presas
> hemos hecho
> a despecho
> del inglés,
> y han rendido
> sus pendones
> cien naciones
> a mis pies.[5]

> [Twenty prizes
> we have made
> in defiance
> of the English
> and one hundred nations
> have surrendered
> their banners
> to my feet.]

In Spanish America, the portrayal of the pirate reflected a much more complex series of images. Having recently gained their independence, but without a consolidated project for their nations, Spanish American writers set out to create national legends and myths in the hope of defining their heritage and formulating a unified vision of their past. This did not prove to be easy. As writers looked back, conflicting images of heroes and enemies intruded on their spatial delimitations and exposed the contemporary political conflicts that disrupted their own national formation. Until the consolidation of the state during the last decades of the nineteenth century, most of the countries in the continent were immersed in civil wars, in which opposing political and economic projects constantly imperiled national unity.

During this period of national reorganization, a number of pirate novels were published, but rather than presenting an idealized vision, they cast the pirate simultaneously in two distinct and contrasting images: a fearless daredevil seeking adventure on the high seas and a dangerous and cruel plunderer moved by greed. Far from evoking escapist ideals of heroism and grandeur, when Spanish American writers looked back into their past to inscribe their national heritage, the pirate —with his provocative images of both terror and freedom—came to embody the difficulties many nations experienced in their quest for national formation.

Writers focused on retrieving the past, hoping to build an identity that would bond the fragments of their nations. However, the same ideological battles held during postindependence were transferred to the reconstruction of the past. Pirates had undoubtedly played a significant role in Spanish America when French, English, and Dutch forces had assaulted the Spanish colonies, bringing fear and economic distress to the population. But when writers reconstructed these historical events, their concern was less to present a historically accurate portrayal than to use the figure of the pirate to discuss the future of their countries. Hence, as writers used the image of the pirate to articulate their contemporary ideals of nationhood, historical events were constantly being resignified to set forth clashing images of each country's national heritage.

In *The Writing of History,* Michel de Certeau reflects on the changing ways of historiographic discourse in the West.[6] History seeks to transform the given into a construct, staging the past from the perspective of the present and apprehending it through language. De Certeau underscores the relationship between past and present and analyzes the different forms of knowledge that become apparent in the process of recuperating what has been lost, dead (the past), and how sense is made of that past with words. Each representation of the past legitimizes certain values that in turn organize and define the understanding of that past.

What the pirate narratives in this study reveal through their different stagings of the past is a disturbing inability to come to terms with the values that need to be legitimized for the well-being of the nation. Ambivalent images of the pirate illustrated whatever corrupt or heroic forces writers felt were necessary to highlight in the process of nation building. Consequently, pirates could be viewed as a dangerous menace, an emblem of progress, or even a symbol of independence. Francis Drake, for example, was simultaneously portrayed as a hero and a dangerous heretic. In contrast, in Spain he was and is still known as the worst pirate of all times. The determining factor in these reconstructions was not the actual event during the colonial period but how nineteenth-century authors viewed those events from their contemporary positions and related them to the future of their countries. As a corpus, these conflicting fictional reconstructions of the past expose the fragments of a complex culture trying to come to terms with its heritage that it is simultaneously breaking away from.

To discuss nation building in Spanish America by focusing on the image of the pirate can highlight significant characteristics and concerns that marked an important part of the literary production during post-independence. Obviously, not all nations in the continent shared the same process of nation building. Puerto Rico and Cuba, for example, remained part of Spain's American empire until the end of the century when the United States stepped in. In Central America and the Spanish Caribbean, the old patterns of European colonialism persisted much longer than in the rest of the continent. Yet regardless of the political course each country embarked on, during this time they all struggled in different ways over their national identity and how they were to define their uniqueness and seize control of their future. And literature played an important role in that struggle.

This book analyzes four historical novels written between 1843 and 1886, by well-known and accomplished authors from Argentina, Colombia, and Mexico. Except for the Colombian author, Soledad Acosta de Samper, these writers—Vicente Fidel López, Justo Sierra O'Reilly, and Eligio Ancona—were recognized as important actors in the political and cultural events of their countries. It is only recently that Acosta de Samper's work has been acknowledged and reconsidered.[7] Despite the time span and geographic distance separating these works, they articulate the debates over national identity as well as the reconstruction of the distant past through specific historical events in which the pirate plays a central role. The events are documented confrontations between two forces, either the Spanish and the English, or the Spanish and the *criollos.*

The defining trait of this corpus is the figure of the pirate, for he is the one who articulates and embodies the confrontation. The genre framing the corpus is the historical novel. Spanish American writers found this form—as an imaginary portrait of the past grounded on a certain accuracy or "truthfulness," presumably corroborated by facts—particularly attractive. It enabled them to present their fictional interpretations of the past within a frame of legitimacy. This was especially important for writers during postindependence, since they were also statesmen, politicians, and military men. Until the last decades of the century, literature was intimately linked to politics. It was an essential component in securing the founding principles of the nation and was seen as having a "civilizing" role. The historical novel was an ideal genre to embody this didactic task and became one of the main literary expressions through which people learned about their history and culture; thus the novel's distinctive role in the formation of national identities.

The positioning of the pirate in relation to the law presented a distinct attraction for Spanish American writers discussing their own national projects. Owing obedience to no one and loyal only to those sharing his way of life, the pirate knows no limits other than the sea and respects no laws other than his own. His portrait is both fascinating and frightening. In an insightful book on Anglo-American piracy during the 1700s, Marcus Rediker analyzes the development of piracy. Generally, most men were previously involved in some form of seafaring employment, either as merchants, members of the navy, or privateers, for it was not easy to adapt to the rigors and sacrifices of life at sea. Political and economic circumstances often turned seamen into pirates, particularly during periods of peace, when wages and the demand for jobs decreased.[8] Organized piracy seemed to arise during times of economic change in which classes or social structures began to shift. In much the same way as banditry, this kind of piracy can be seen as a form of resistance toward changes affecting a way of life as well as toward the political authorities enforcing these changes.[9] Thus piracy is, in a way, a "cry of vengeance" against shifting socioeconomic structures. To protect themselves from "arbitrary" impositions, pirates created their own social order, which was governed by a "democratic" selection of officers and an egalitarian system of bounty distribution, and this order was fervently defended.[10]

Pirates also represented "crime" on a massive scale.[11] Violence was their most distinguishing trait. They not only took possession of their prey through force, robbing and torturing their victims, but also were known to be extremely rigid with their own laws of conduct and punished their traitors severely. Refusing to submit to any political law, pirates could be stopped only by force. Thus piracy, like other forms of banditry, institutionalized violence.[12] Whether or not this explicitly appealed to writers in Spanish America is unknown. However, given their own political circumstances, it seems probable that writers would have felt a strong attraction toward the role violence played in the forging of the pirates' identity. The pirates' freedom to choose their way of life was possible only through violence. Writers discussing their future national projects may have felt an affinity with piracy primarily because Spanish Americans had been able to build their independent nations only through the use of violence. Violence would become the indispensable mark of freedom for the emancipation movements of Spanish Americans, in the same way it had been the initial stamp of the conquest.

Piracy was undoubtedly a brutal form of survival as well as a form of independence. Here lies the appeal for Spanish American nations envisioning their future. As pirates defied the law and refused to submit to any form of authority other than their own, so Spanish Americans defied Spain's authority and struggled to impose their own laws and regulations. The independent republics came into being by rejecting Spain's hegemonic power through violence. In this sense, violence was a powerful determining force toward the definition of the new communities and the transformation of power and social structure within the community.[13] Thus, when writers looked back on the past to retrieve a unifying image for their future projects, the pirate seemed to captivate their attention as a medium for the violence embedded in nationhood.

In this study, I read pirate novels as metaphors for the process of nation building in Spanish America. Although the authors do not explicitly refer to piracy as a means of highlighting this process, their texts, as a corpus, provide a new reading of the political and cultural paradigms that marked the literary production during this period. An emblematic figure of independence and boldness, the pirate captures the spirit behind the desire for political autonomy. But more importantly, these pirate stories reflect the extent to which the narratives of national identity in Spanish America are structured in relation to existing cultures, notably the European.

There is a symbolic analogy in the way in which pirates and the Spanish American republics came to exist. The pirate does not produce any goods, nor does he have a plan for how best to invest his prizes; he exists solely by preying on others. No matter how organized or "democratic" pirate society may have been, lives in it were not planned. Pirates lived day by day, their only project being perhaps the latest strategy to strike at a specific target. Independence in Spanish America did not come as a result of long-range planning. The rising *criollo* elites seized the opportunity to rebel against Spain's power, which allowed them little space for their own political and economic maneuvering. But the revolutionaries failed to elaborate well-developed plans for what was to come after their triumph. Hence, the political elites—for they were the ones who took command—found themselves scrambling to secure a direction for the future of the republics.

The pirate narratives expose this process and reflect the consequences embedded in each political project. Throughout the novels, which unfold as intense melodramas stamped with strong political overtones, the only successful projects are those in which the pirate is identified with Europe, as in the novels of Soledad Acosta de Samper and Vicente Fidel López. When the pirate is American (meaning Spanish American, as in Justo Sierra O'Reilly's and Eligio Ancona's texts), not only do his ventures fail, but the novel itself offers a dim future for those surviving the conflicts. Hence, what becomes visible in these texts is the extent to which the identity and independence of the Spanish American republics were seen as being contingent on existing European models. Spanish Americans faced the difficulty of creating alternative models that would take into account their own social, cultural, and political differences with Europe. Each reconstruction of the past inscribes the spatial and cultural settings of legitimacy while endorsing opposing values essential for the future of the nation. These novels underscore the difficulties of establishing political and cultural alliances, consolidating national projects, as well as addressing questions of race and identity.[14]

By exploring these historical narratives of pirates, my goal is to expand the literary corpus on which recent studies on nation building have focused when analyzing postindependence literature in Spanish America. As Benedict Anderson has argued, the emergence of print culture played an extremely important role in the formation of national identities.[15] Yet when studying this process in nineteenth-century Spanish America, literary critics have tended to focus on classical examples by authors such as Juan Bautista Alberdi, Manuel Altamirano, Andrés Bello, Tomás Carrasquilla, José Mármol, and, of course, Domingo F. Sarmiento. My study is part of an effort to move beyond these "foundational fictions," to include new texts and offer new perspectives in looking at the ways in which the "imagined community" was constructed.[16] Drawing from a considerable body of theoretical work on nation building, as well as from feminism, anthropology, and cultural studies, my goal is to break away from the traditional texts used in discussing the paradigms of nation building to generate new insights into the way in which the nation was emplotted through literature in nineteenth-century Spanish America.

Claiming the sea as his own and defying all national borders, the pirate is unrestrained by spatial boundaries. He is free to imagine his own place, constantly reshaping it as he sails the seas from coast to coast. His mobility is empowering, for it enables him constantly to reconfigure his space (depending on his needs) and allows him to establish alliances with whomever he wishes without endangering his own identity. So long as he does not confine himself to a fixed place, the pirate's identity remains intact. What is particularly menacing about the pirate is that he has no interest in being part of an imagined community that seeks legal recognition. Although he has his own laws of conduct, the pirate is perceived as lawless precisely because he respects no political or spatial boundaries. Yet he cannot be ignored because of the dangers he brings forth. So the pirate must always be resisted with violence, which paradoxically reinforces his power and importance.

The pirate's rootlessness enabled Spanish American writers seeking to define their imagined community to assign pirates extremely varied characteristics. Their positive or negative connotations depended on the authors' political and cultural positioning. Hence, an English pirate such as Drake could become a hero or an enemy. For authors such as

Acosta de Samper, who sought to reinforce her country's Spanish heritage located within its national territory, the pirate was cast as a dangerous foreigner lacking moral values and respect for the law. But for those authors like López who sought to transcend the confinement of their geographic and cultural boundaries, the pirate embodied the freedom of self-fashioning and could be recast in any form. These contrasting portraits reveal how the pirate's mobility articulated the disjuncture between national space and identity underlining the battle of nation building in nineteenth-century Spanish America.

This study is divided into five chapters. The first offers an introduction to the history of piracy in the New World from the beginning of the sixteenth century to the mid–eighteenth century. During this period, the categorization of the pirate varies significantly according to the international relations between Spain and the European nations that defied Spanish hegemony in America—namely, England, France, and Holland. From pirates to corsairs, buccaneers to freebooters, piracy is constantly being redefined. However classified, these violent plunders of the Spanish colonies not only undermined Spain's claim to an absolute, exclusive hegemony over its colonial territories but also redesigned the map of the American continent while exposing the social, economic, and political forces that would condition the debate of nation building in nineteenth-century Spanish America.

Many of the piratical attacks are recorded in the chronicles and epic poems of colonial Spanish American literature. The main goal of these testimonial accounts is to "document" the portrayal of the pirate—generally the English—as a violent heretic and to highlight the heroic actions of the Spanish. In "truthfully" describing the attacks and frightening deeds of the pirates, writers often convey a sense of amazement. This does not mean, however, that the pirates have any redeemable value among them, for as heretics they lack all sense of morality. Moral virtue in these texts is positioned above everything else and linked to Catholicism. Thus morality becomes the underlying force dividing the world between good and bad, heroes and enemies, Spanish and others. Nevertheless, at times, chroniclers seem to struggle to uphold the moral order they endorse as they relate some of the most astonishing assaults committed by pirates. If morality is to structure the world order, the question lies in how those devastating assaults are to be understood. In trying to resolve this quandary, colonial writers constructed a system of oppositions that separated the English from the Spanish and positioned the latter as the emblem of virtue, even when they were often stripped of their riches. The focus of the second chapter is to look at the ways in which writers addressed the contradictions of their world configuration and how they reframed those piratical events in accordance with their cultural and religious understanding.

The third chapter analyzes the ways in which nineteenth-century authors used the figure of the pirate to articulate a specific national identity. The discussion of national formation in these novels is expressed through encounters with pirates. The arrival of the pirate introduces the appearance of a new socioeconomic order within the colonial world, which is discussed in terms of its moral principles. Thus, following the continuum set up during the colonial period, the pirate is identified not only with a specific nation but, more importantly, with a specific ethos. However, he does not have a fixed identity that embodies virtue. The author's ideological outlook is what determines how the pirate's ethos should be understood. An English pirate may be cast as a hero when he opposes the corrupt Spanish Inquisition, or he may be a dangerous enemy because he threatens the well-being of that same community. Exposing the boundaries between insider and outsider, the pirate becomes instrumental in the construction of the "other." The "imagined community" constitutes itself in its opposition to the pirate, and only in relation to this opposition do the characteristics of each community become apparent.

The determining role history plays in these reconstructions is discussed in the fourth chapter. Employing documented events, these novelists seek to legitimize their particular reconstructions of the past. Their goal, however, is not to reconstruct historical events but rather to assign an event with a particular meaning that heightens their ideological project embedded in the fictional plot. By focusing on the narrative techniques used to emplot history and the link established with the fictional story, these texts illustrate the power of literature to authorize a "documented" construction of the past. How these forms of emplotment are articulated within the text and why the historical novel was so important in the consolidation of the national project in Spanish America are the central questions considered.

Finally, the last chapter focuses on the melodramatic structure of these texts and how this particular structure offers a political setting to address issues of race and how women should participate in the building of the nation. Using images of excess and hyperbole, the narratives transfer the debate among ideological projects within the home, where the conflict is articulated through polar concepts of good and evil. The battle between moral opposites, characteristic of melodrama, is resolved as virtue triumphs over vice and ensures a distinct societal order. As the conflict plays itself out within the realm of the home, the focal point becomes the family, and this is where the woman's role takes on an important part in consolidating a national identity. However, although decisive, women are simultaneously positioned at the margins of the ideological framework structuring the national project. The same occurs with race. In all of the pirate novels, race and ethnic differences appear as important factors in the conflict. In some novels, the ideological project endorsed proposes establishing a more European society, either Spanish or English but white, while in other novels the goal is to affirm a hybrid mestizo culture. Yet in both instances, the novels elude discussing the complexity of race in Spanish America by focusing on the consolidation of the family and subordinating these issues of difference to the confrontation between English and Spanish models. It is through the structural masking of melodrama, a genre that clearly articulates conflict while leaving little space for ambiguity, that the role women and race played and did not play in the plotting of the family and of the nation become apparent.

This study focuses on the ways in which the pirate was appropriated by nineteenth-century authors in Spanish America to discuss their future national projects. Although these authors reconstruct events that affected colonial society as a whole and use a popular narrative mode grounded in history, these texts are neither directed to nor reflect a popular audience. Instead, they mirror the conflicting images of the dominant culture debating its own projects. By highlighting the constant shifts within the texts and between political projects, this study seeks to expose the overlapping elements that Spanish American authors claimed as their own to construct a unified vision of the past and project a consolidated national identity—an identity, however, that remained uncertain until the end of the century.

CHAPTER ONE

Piracy in Spanish America:
A History

Un caso duro, triste y espantable,
un acontecimiento furibundo
una calamidad que fue notable
en ciertos puertos de este Nuevo Mundo
canto con ronca voz y lamentable,
que el flaco pecho de lo más profundo
embia por sus vias a la lengua
—Juan de Castellanos, "Discurso de el Capitán Draque"

On his return from Hispaniola, in a letter dated November 5, 1523, Diego Colón, son of Christopher Columbus, wrote King Charles I of Spain complaining about the number of corsairs roaming the seas trying to rob the Crown of its well-deserved and legitimate riches.[1] These first pirates, or corsairs—as they were generally called by the Spanish— were mostly French. The English and Dutch soon joined in the raids on the Spanish colonies in the Caribbean (as would the North Americans in later years). Their plunders were violent. The pirates seized Spanish vessels at sea and descended on villages and ports, raiding churches and homes, harassing the civilians for treasures. By the end of the sixteenth century, pirates had become Spain's most feared commercial and political enemies and would remain a menace to the Spanish colonies throughout the eighteenth century.

Pirates are by definition enemies. The word derives from the Greek *peiran*, meaning to assault or attack. Plundering the seas and responding to no other laws than their own, they are feared and persecuted by every

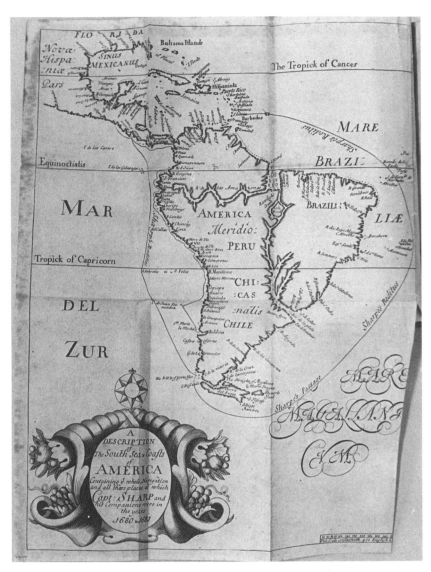

"Map of the South Sea and Coasts of America," in *The History of the Buccaneers of America from their first original day to this time, written in several languages and now collected into one volume,* by Alexandre Olivier Exquemelin (London: Printed for the Newborough, 1699). *Courtesy of the Mount Holyoke College Archives and Special Collections.*

society. However, throughout the three centuries of piratical activity in the New World, there were serious contradictions in the way pirates were classified as well as in the numerous terms used to define the attacks made by foreign nationals. These differences reflect the conflicting roles and significance piratical assaults had for the nations involved. For England, piracy was an instrument of national policy and received covert official support. With certain differences, the same was true for France and the Netherlands. In essence, piracy became an important vehicle through which these European nations battled against the Spanish empire, hoping in exchange to build or enlarge their own empires.

Although the terms "pirate" and "corsair" were often used indiscriminately during the colonial period (in fact, in English today, "corsair" is commonly defined as a pirate),[2] a crucial difference must be highlighted. Unlike the pirate, who plundered the seas or navigable rivers independently without any form of governmental authorization or support, a corsair (from the Italian *corsaro*) was a pirate or pirate ship sanctioned by the country to which it belonged. A corsair was the equivalent of the English privateer (introduced in 1651), a privately owned armed vessel with a commission, or letters of marque, from the government authorizing the owners to use the ship against a hostile nation, and especially in the capture of merchant shipping.

The transformation of piracy in Spanish America can be seen when at the beginning of the seventeenth century, two new terms appeared: *bucanero* and *filibustero*. These individuals, originally French and English cattle hunters living in the northwestern part of Hispaniola and the nearby island of Tortuga, became famous for their brutal plunders in the West Indies and South Seas. The use of terms, however, varied according to the language. The Spanish used *bucanero* and *filibustero* almost interchangeably, placing one chronologically before the other as the nineteenth-century Mexican historian Justo Sierra O'Reilly explained:

> The "buccaneers" . . . originally established themselves on the island of Santo Domingo from where they exerted thousands of bloody vexations on the Spanish colonies. Their pretext was to hunt cattle to sell the hides in Europe and make a good profit. France recognized them by sending them a governor in 1665, and under his protection they set out to execute all sorts of excess. Later came the "freebooters," more enterprising and daring than the buccaneers. . . . This gathering of pirates

and adventurers from all nations was famous in the seventeenth century for its terrifying and extreme cruelty against the Spanish government, or rather against its ill-kept colonies. The freebooters roamed the seas assaulting fleets, murdering crews, burning vessels, besieging forts, destroying everything that fell into their hands.[3]

The historian José Bravo Ugarte distinguishes four specific phases of piracy that correspond to the wars in which Spain was engaged. The first period, marked by the presence of French pirates, was quite brief (1521–1524) and coincides with the Franco-Spanish war in which Kings Charles V and Philip II of Spain opposed Francis I and Henry II of France. The second phase (1568–1596) belongs to the English corsairs and coincides with the battle between King Philip II and Queen Elizabeth of England. Hostilities between the Netherlands and Spain led to the third period of piracy (1621–1650) when Dutch corsairs attacked Spanish possessions, which officially ended with the signing of the Peace of Westphalia (1648). According to Bravo Ugarte, the fourth and last phase lasted almost a century, more or less until 1750, when all nationalities seemed to bond indiscriminately and "buccaneers, *pechelingues* and freebooters, controlled the strategic points in the Caribbean Sea."[4]

In French the term *boucanier* was more restricted to the cattle hunters of Hispaniola. By extension it also referred to any pirate in America. *Flibustier*—from the Dutch *vrijbuiter* or English "freebooter"—was a more general term used to refer to the pirates assaulting the Spanish colonies.[5]

In English, however, the term "buccaneer" was used synonymously with "corsair" or "freebooter," leaving "privateer" as the officially recognized armed ship or crew member. "Filibuster" was not commonly employed in English until the nineteenth century, when it came to designate a certain type of adventurer from the United States who, particularly between 1800 and 1850, led armed expeditions to the West Indies and Central America "in violation of international law, for the purpose of revolutionizing certain states."[6]

The first corsairs defined as such were those sent by the Barbary nations of North Africa to attack Christian ships and coasts as part of an accepted policy of their Muslim governments. Thus the term "corsair" originally referred to a conflict that was based on a religious division between Islam and Christianity. As the word continued to be used in the sixteenth, seventeenth, and eighteenth centuries, it retained—at least for the Spanish—a certain religious connotation. When the Spanish used "corsair," they were probably alluding to the attackers' "heretical" characteristics in addition to defining their political aggression. In fact, Francis Drake is known to have been extremely offended when the Spanish called him a *corsario*.[7] This would explain why the Spanish generally used the terms "pirate" and "corsair" when referring to the English, whereas they preferred the words "pirate," "buccaneer," and "freebooter" to refer to the French attackers.[8]

The difficulty in classifying these individuals according to the terminology used at the time is clearly illustrated by the particular situation of Francis Drake. While acknowledging that to a Spaniard, Drake would certainly have been considered a pirate, Philip Gosse, in *The Pirate's Who's Who,* calls Drake a "most fervent patriot."[9] Thus the categories of pirate and patriot undoubtedly depended on the point of view from which they were presented. For the Spanish, however, the distinction was moot: all foreigners in the Indies were national enemies, whether pirates, smugglers, or corsairs, and their ships were to be seized whenever possible.

European nations attacking the Spanish colonies often played up religious differences to justify their own economic interest in obtaining the precious metals and spices Spain had monopolized. Although religion was used as a means of justification, it was not the governing motive behind the attacks; securing a trade route and market was. Consequently, the conflicts were between Protestants and Catholics, as well as among rival Catholic nations, the most prominent struggle being between Spain and Portugal. Spain claimed and marked the boundaries of its territories in the New World by upholding the dividing line the papacy had drawn with Portugal. It had been the accession of Queen Isabella (1474–1504), who, moved by her own intense religious convictions and the need to avoid a new holy war, revived Spain's determination to conquer Islam and reclaim her kingdom under one religion. In 1482 a systematic reconquest of the Iberian Peninsula began. The defeat of the Moors and the expulsion of the Jews in 1492 would allow Spain to assert itself over the rest of Christian Europe. It would be in the name of religion that the rest of Europe would violently attack Spain.[10]

The fluctuating terminology used to classify the aggressors of the

Spanish colonies is conditioned by the complex political circumstances that marked relations between Spain and the rest of Europe, ranging from open acts of war to peace treaties or pacts with or among France, England, and the Netherlands. It was also quite common for corsairs to attack their own country's vessels at some point and thus become "official" pirates, further complicating the definition of piracy in the New World. In the words of Enrique de Gandía: "Most corsairs were also pirates, since it would be quite strange to encounter one that did not overstep the orders of his commission."[11]

Although Spain considered all foreign trade within its territories an illegal act and treated the individuals involved as pirates, not all foreign activities during the colonial period were true acts of piracy. In addition to the sea plunders there was the contraband trade of small-scale smugglers and slave runners.[12] Later, in the eighteenth century, as Spanish industry declined and the cost of shipment to the Indies through authorized channels rose, a strong unofficial trafficking between the colonies and other European merchants began to emerge. These merchants offered both cheaper manufactured goods and slaves in exchange for Spanish American hides and dyewoods, which in turn would reduce the production costs of the textile trades in Europe.[13]

However "piracy" is explained, it is apparent that the intense "envy" European nations felt toward Spain and its territories began shortly after Columbus's "discovery" excluded all foreigners from the New World.[14] On Columbus's return from his first voyage to America, the Spanish Crown obtained formal recognition of its new territories. The Treaty of Alcaçovas between Portugal and Spain had granted the Portuguese a monopoly of trade in West Africa as well as settlements in Madeira, the Cape Verde Islands, and the Azores; Spain had retained the Canary Islands. Now it was Spain's turn to assert its claims and what it thought to be the alternate route to the Orient, the strongly sought land of spices. On May 3, 1493, Pope Alexander VI issued the bull *Inter caetera*, granting Spain sovereignty over all the land and sea located one hundred leagues west of the Azores and Cape Verde "not possessed by any Christian prince." Spain's claim to the lands called the Indies was immediately contested by Portugal. Moved by the need to restrict Spanish maritime activity in the South Atlantic, protect their African interests, and secure their route to the Orient, the Portuguese pushed the imaginary boundary 270 leagues west. This agreement was ratified on June 7, 1494, in the Treaty of Tordesillas, which established the final dividing line at 370 leagues west of the Azores.[15]

By 1504 there was a growing awareness that the new route to the Spice Islands Columbus had encountered led to a land that was neither Cathay (China) nor Cipango (Japan). The increasing expeditions that set out subsequently reshaped the map of the "discoveries," making it clear that what had been found was in fact another continent. Taking advantage of local knowledge, diplomacy, and force, in 1513, Vasco Núñez de Balboa marched through the forests of the Isthmus of Darien (later renamed the Isthmus of Panama) to "discover" the South Sea (the Pacific Ocean).[16] In 1519, the same year Cortés arrived in Mexico, Ferdinand Magellan's onerous circumnavigational voyage revealed the extension of the continent as well as the true western route to the East. This landmass was initially seen as a barrier, hindering Europe's direct access to Asia. Furthermore, Magellan's voyage exposed the immensity of the Pacific Ocean and the difficulties of reaching the East through a western route. When the Portuguese set foot on the Molucca Islands in 1513, their victory over Spain in the quest to reach the East was assured. However, Portugal's triumph was short-lived. In 1519, Hernán Cortés began his expedition along the Yucatán Peninsula. Three years later, the defeat of Tenochtitlán yielded an unexpected and amazing treasure, followed by the riches obtained in the conquest of the Tawantinsuyu of South America. Hence, when Charles I of Spain became emperor of Germany, his empire "where the sun never set" made him the envy of the other European monarchs.

Despite Spain's legal claim over the new territories, as soon as the sea route to the New World was defined and word got out about the riches to be found there, other European nations quickly ventured toward the new continent, challenging Spain's claim. In trying to ensure and expand their control, the Spanish established settlements such as Santo Domingo (1504), San Germán (1508), and San Juan de Puerto Rico and Havana (1511), to provide a base for their first expeditions and offer their vessels protection from storms and any possible attacks. In 1517 the Spanish shifted their interest westward, exploring the coasts of the Yucatán, Tabasco, and Mexico, leading to Hernán Cortés's expedition to the land of Moctezuma and the establishment of New Spain as the center of the Spanish colonization effort on the mainland. The expeditions to the southern part of the continent continued, although they were much less rewarding in comparison to the riches obtained in Mexico, until Francisco Pizarro's capture of Cuzco in 1533.

Considering the vast extension of the new territories, it was impossible for Spain to maintain tight control over its possessions. In the Caribbean, the Spanish settled primarily in the Greater Antilles, in the islands of Hispaniola, Cuba, Jamaica, and Puerto Rico, leaving open the Lesser Antilles, a large group of extremely small islands southeast of Puerto Rico and north of the Venezuelan coast. The Caribbean Sea became the center focus of the pirates, for these small islands scattered across the waters offered ideal hiding places from other vessels and refuge from the winds. The French were the first to take advantage of this situation, settling on and organizing their attacks from several islands.[17] San Cristóbal was the first they occupied, and shortly afterward they took over Tortuga, which would become a central base from which some of the most violent piratical attacks would be launched during the seventeenth century.

Unlike the colonial ventures of the French, English, and Portuguese at this early stage, the Spanish sought to Christianize, that is, "civilize" the native people they encountered. Spain therefore kept a close watch on immigrants. The Spanish Crown enacted numerous rules and regulations to guarantee order and justice and secure its economic benefits throughout the New World. Colonial administration was centralized in Spain, specifically Seville, from where the Royal and Supreme Council of the Indies enacted all legislation, and the Casa de Contratación controlled all commercial activities related to the Indies.[18] The colonies were given little political and economic freedom. They were prohibited from trading with foreign nationals, and manufacturing was kept to a minimum. Consequently, industry was never stimulated except to fulfill the specific needs of the Iberian Peninsula. The colonies were to provide metals and raw materials that would be exchanged for finished Spanish products. In this way, Spain made sure the colonies did not compete with its own manufactured goods and secured a market for its own products. Spain, however, could not fulfill its end of the colonial pact. Because it did not produce enough manufactured goods to satisfy the needs of its enormous colonial empire, Spain undermined its own monopoly and opened the door to contraband with English, French, and Dutch traders.[19]

As indicated earlier, Spain's sovereignty over the New World was not universally accepted. The French, no less Catholic at the time than the Spanish and Portuguese, rejected it; "The sun shines for me as for others," claimed King Francis I. They would be joined by the English and other northern Europeans in their disapproval. England and France sent their own explorers to the New World as soon as they learned about the new lands. In fact, King Henry VII of England sent John Cabot across the Atlantic to undertake a voyage of discovery as early as 1496. Most of these initial trips were made along the northeastern coast of America in the hope of finding a short route to Cathay and of gaining further knowledge of the lands. However, this area did not prove to be as rich and attractive as the territory Spain was exploring. The Portuguese, who took possession of the area that would become Brazil in 1500, were also initially disappointed with their findings.

The first organized attacks on Spanish vessels crossing the Atlantic were carried out under the French flag. As a Catholic monarch, Francis I deeply resented the Vatican's favoritism toward Charles I of Spain, whom Francis considered his most serious rival.[20] His celebrated protest of Adam's will made explicit that he would not accept the partitioning of the world between Spain and Portugal: "I should very much like to see the clause in Adam's will that excludes me from a share of the world."[21] The two monarchs would go to war a number of times during their reigns. Francis I took advantage of this rivalry to launch several expeditions against Spanish territories. During the first war between France and Spain over Italy (1521–1526), a Florentine navigator from Dieppe, Giovanni da Verrazano (better known among the Spanish as Juan Florentín or Juan Florín), was sent by France to the northwest passage of the new continent. Although he did not make it to the western Atlantic coast in his first trip (1522), between the Azores and Spain, Verrazano captured two of three caravels carrying some of the fabled Aztec treasures Hernán Cortés sent to the Crown.[22] This first assault was significant in opening the door to piracy as an alternative and profitable means of undermining Spain's possessions. It also announced an important change in European warfare, as the Indies became the new theater for political and economic conflicts.

Throughout most of the century, France was intermittently at war with Spain. During the peaceful intervals, French aggressions in the Caribbean decreased, although they did not disappear completely. In fact, the French not only multiplied their assaults on Spanish vessels but also began raiding colonial settlements. In 1537 they pillaged Chagres on the Isthmus of Panama; invaded Honduras; raided Puerto Rico, Hispaniola, and Santiago de Cuba; and attacked nine vessels carrying treasures from Peru.

By 1540, as the Spanish Crown began capitalizing on its extraordinary conquests, piratical aggressions proved to be a thriving business for the French and were openly encouraged by the government until 1559, when the peace Treaty of Câteau-Cambrésis put an end to the war. Even then, the piratical attacks decreased only temporarily. Among the well-known French pirates raiding the Spanish colonies were Jean Ango of Dieppe; Jean François de la Roque (sieur de Roberval), known by the Spanish as Roberto Baal or Baal, who attacked Cartagena de Indias, Santiago de Cuba, and La Habana; and the Calvinists François le Clerc (better known as Jambe-de-bois or Pié de Palo), the one-legged pirate who harassed Puerto Rico and Hispaniola, and Jacques de Sores, who practically destroyed La Habana in 1555.[23]

The Spanish Crown did not simply stand by watching how the French disrupted their commerce. To protect their territories, the Spanish built fortresses near their ports and walls to surround their cities; they established a coast guard service and protested continuously to the European courts. In 1503 the first organ of colonial administration, the Casa de Contratación de las Indias, was established by royal decree in Seville. Its function was to promote and regulate trade and navigation to the New World; sailings to the Indies had to obtain clearance from Seville, and all fleets, without exception, had to return there.[24] Furthermore, as a means of protection, after 1526, Spanish merchant vessels were instructed to sail together in order to guard their cargo. They would have to go in fleets armed according to rules set by the Casa. In 1537 a royal armada was dispatched to the West Indies to protect the transportation of gold and silver to Spain. It was the first of the great treasure fleets, which would become permanent and mandatory in 1561.[25] Each year, two fleets were organized in Spain. One, known as los Galeones (the galleons), sailed in the Spring to Cartagena in Nueva Granada, and

Nombre de Dios (later Porto Bello) on the Isthmus of Panama. The other, La Flota (the fleet), was destined in August for San Juan de Ulúa (Vera Cruz) in New Spain. The galleons were formed by five to eight war vessels carrying from forty to fifty guns and were accompanied by several smaller and faster boats called *pataches,* in addition to a fleet of merchant vessels varying in size.[26] The trip across the Atlantic took about two months. The ships wintered in the Indies and gathered at La Habana the following March in order to sail back for Europe together. Once in Spain, all the merchandise was registered at the Casa, where tax was collected cn every article, including royal bullion.

The monopoly imposed by Seville barred all commerce between the Orient and the Spanish colonies, except for the port of Acapulco in New Spain. Each year two galleons, known as the Manila Galleons, sailed between Manila and Acapulco. Chinese silk and porcelain, Persian and Chinese carpets, cotton from India, jewelry, uncut gems and spices, in addition to gold, were brought in from the Orient. Although these galleons were a pirate's dream, they were harder to find in the Pacific, and pirates dared not attack the heavily fortified port of Acapulco. Only four galleons were ever captured, the first by Tomas Cavendish in 1587. Trade between Europe and South America via Buenos Aires was also barred; everything to South America had to be supplied by way of the Isthmus of Panama and then travel down the Pacific. Similarly, all the goods and treasures coming from Panama and the Pacific coast had to be transported by land to Nombre de Dios (Porto Bello), from which they were shipped to Spain. This congregation of treasures transformed certain ports into an amazing gold mine for pirates. While the treasures were transferred to the galleons in the harbor, merchants carried on their trade. This was the beginning of the famous fairs at Porto Bello, where merchants from all over the continent came to the marketplace and spent sixty days trading. Despite heavy defenses, the fair became a target for pirates and was raided numerous times.

During the first half of the sixteenth century, the English Crown sent one expedition against the Spanish in the Caribbean. In 1527 John Rut was "commanded" by Henry VIII to find a way to gain access to the riches controlled by the Spanish.[27] Unlike John Cabot's expedition, a discovery voyage in which he planted the English flag on the shore of Nova Scotia, Rut's expedition was strictly an English enterprise with a "hidden purpose": to pierce Spain's supremacy in the Indies. On his way down from Newfoundland, Rut stopped in Santo Domingo, hoping to trade goods with the Spanish. While official negotiations were under way a shot was fired that changed the course of action. Fearing an attack from the Spanish, the English left abruptly but apparently returned to raid the town of clothes, chickens, and other provenders. Rut's would be the last English sail to be seen in the Caribbean for some years. At the time, England was Spain's ally against the French. After the creation of the Church of England and the dissolution of the monasteries (1539), Henry VIII tried to avoid conflicts with Spain. Consequently, he directed English commercial activities towards Portuguese territories, where the trade between Guinea and Brazil had by then proved to be fruitful. By midcentury, relations with Spain began to deteriorate. When England invaded France in 1544, the Peace of Crépy-en-Laonnois, signed that same year between France and Spain, left Henry VIII segregated from the rest of Europe. The treaty conceded trading rights to the French in exchange for Francis I's promise to leave the Spanish in control of whatever kingdoms and estates Charles V then possessed.[28] It also allowed Spanish and Flemish carriers to transport French goods while claiming protection under neutral flag. At war with France, England declared French goods lawful prizes and asserted they could be seized wherever found. Licensed by their king, the English began attacking French and Spanish vessels. The Hawkins family, having established a marine business in Plymouth and having become extremely powerful in England, was heavily involved in confiscation and contraband activities.[29]

As the Spanish population in the West Indies grew, so did commerce, creating new markets that demanded more goods, particularly slaves for the profitable sugar plantations and mines. The Spanish had been the first to bring slaves from Africa to the Antilles under strict contracts and licenses, *asientos*, which were neither allotted to everyone nor cheap. John Hawkins was one of the first to get involved in the slave trade and undertook three transatlantic expeditions, funded by London, for this purpose. In his first trip (1562), in exchange for the slaves he brought from Sierra Leone and sold at a much cheaper price than the Spanish, Hawkins received hides, ginger, sugar, and pearls.[30]

The success of Hawkins's trip received a great deal of attention from Queen Elizabeth, who decided to encourage this type of activity. During the preceding years, many Englishmen had fled religious persecutions in their country under the Catholic reigns of King Edward VI (1547–1553) and Queen Mary (1553–1558). A considerable number of them settled temporarily with the French in the West Indies. When the English began attacking the Spanish colonies, the settlers provided them with crucial information concerning the commercial activities and raids in the Indies. During her reign (1558–1603), Queen Elizabeth welcomed back her subjects and encouraged their raids on the colonies, which she partially funded, although she did not hesitate to disown these privateers when necessary to maintain good relations with Spain.[31]

In October 1564, Hawkins returned to the Spanish colonies as a naval officer of the queen and as a merchant adventurer. During this trip, he encountered a number of unexpected difficulties, both in obtaining slaves along the coast of Africa and in selling them at a price he considered adequate. There were a few minor confrontations between the Spanish and English in Río Hacha, on the Colombian coast, but Hawkins was able to convince local authorities that his only interest was to trade goods. Bad weather and lack of knowledge of the sea currents deterred him from staying longer in the Caribbean. After finally selling his wares at only a small profit, Hawkins sailed home northward along the coast, stopping in Florida, where he helped a Huguenot colony of French Protestants in dire straits because they had run out of provisions.

By Hawkins's third trip (1567), Spain had formally protested his presence in its territories and sent rigorous instructions to the islands and the mainland to be on the lookout for him and to prevent him from trading. Although he sailed with a formidable fleet, he encountered new resistance from Spanish officials. Hawkins stopped at Río Hacha, at Cubagua on the island of Margarita, at Curaçao, and at Borburata, in the province of Venezuela. Having completed his trade and heading back to England, Hawkins had to turn westward to avoid tempestuous weather. He reached the harbor of San Juan de Ulúa, off the Gulf of Mexico, where he sought admission for the repair of his fleet. Concurrently, Spanish ships had arrived, loaded with silver and gold, and were awaiting the convoy that would escort them to Seville.

Afraid of being attacked by the Spanish protecting their fleet, Hawkins made arrangements with the Spanish authorities to keep peace. Although viceroy Martín Enríquez agreed, neither the English nor the

Spanish trusted each other, and a confrontation did take place. The English claimed that the Spanish went back on their word and attacked. The Spanish, on the other hand, justified their change of position by claiming that the English had taken over a fortress of San Juan de Ulúa and were a threat.[32] In any case, the confrontation was brutal, and Hawkins had to fight a battle in which he was greatly outnumbered. The *Judith,* commanded by Francis Drake, was able to get home safely. Hawkins followed in the *Minion,* and after an arduous trip, he made it back to England in 1569 with only half of his men, vowing revenge against the Spanish.

This devastating and humiliating defeat, which revealed to the English the amazing riches the Spanish had, marked the beginning of a new phase in the history of foreign incursions into Spanish America. Until then, most of the voyages by the French and English had been trading ventures, although they were often accompanied by the use of force. That would change. Convinced that the source of Spain's economic strength was its colonial empire, the English and French were determined to destroy Spain's monopoly over the colonies. The English were able to take the lead in these ventures for several reasons. The decline of the Antwerp cloth trade, which had been England's commercial stronghold together with the availability of a mobile capital resulting from the disposal of church and royal lands, tempted merchants and bankers to place their gains into new enterprises and seek new markets.[33] They would turn to the Spanish colonies.

Spain's reaction was to further tighten its security and intensify maritime defense in the colonies. Admiral Pedro Menéndez de Avilés took the royal orders seriously. The Huguenot colony Hawkins had assisted during his first trip was strategically located where the Spain-bound fleets needed to pass. The original intention of the colony, founded by Réné de Laudonnière, was to organize a large-scale attack on Spanish America. The peace Treaty of Câteau-Cambrésis put an end to the plans, though not to the founding of the colony. In 1565 Menéndez de Avilés slaughtered the Huguenot colony. This was an important coup for the Spanish, for the colony seriously threatened Spain's imperial communications. This defeat, in addition to Hawkins's overthrow, engendered an intense hatred of the Spanish in both the French and English while providing a rationalization for the numerous and violent attacks both countries would go on to make on Spanish territories.[34]

Of the pirates raiding the Spanish colonies during this period, Sir Francis Drake was by far the most famous. A member of the Hawkins expedition, after the disaster of San Juan de Ulúa, Drake was particularly adept at presenting his destructive attacks in the Caribbean as a patriotic revenge for what the Spanish had done to the English. During 1570 and 1571, he made a number of secret excursions to the Caribbean, befriending Spanish-hating maroons (escaped black slaves) and obtaining information on the best way to attack the silver fleets leaving Peru. By then, the queen of England, excommunicated by the pope in 1570, fervently encouraged any plundering against Spain and offered her support through secret funding.

It was Drake's raid of 1572 to 1573 that brought him fame. Despite his extremely modest force of only two ships, the *Pasha* and the *Swan*, Drake took the renowned emporium of Nombre de Dios with its "golden harvest" by surprise. Together with his right-hand man, John Oxenham, Drake managed to break into the king's treasure house, where the gold and jewels were stored. The town awoke in terror that night when "divided in two parties, with clatter of drums and blare of trumpets, brandishing their blazing fire-pikes and uttering horrible yells, they [Drake and his men] rushed by two different ways to the marketplace."[35] Although they had to abandon fifteen tons of silver and untold quantities of gold, gems, jewelry, porcelain, and other treasures, Drake's men were able to make off with "goodly booty." However, the Peruvian treasure that Drake coveted had not yet arrived. So Drake took refuge in the Gulf of San Blas, where he left some of his men, and went on to raid Cartagena, Santa Marta, and Curaçao. A few months later, on January 5, 1573, the fleet, intended to escort the silver treasure from Peru, reached Nombre de Dios. This was the moment Drake had been waiting for. Aided by maroons, the Frenchman Guillaume le Testu, and his faithful captain, John Oxenham, Drake captured a stunning booty of two hundred mules, each carrying approximately three hundred pounds of silver and gold. Drake sailed back to England with the monumental sum of 150,000 pesos worth of gold and silver.

A few years later, he embarked on his epic circumnavigation (1577–1580). Having set sail in five ships, Drake completed his trip three years later with only one, the *Golden Hind*—previously named the *Pelican*. He was the first Englishman to cross the Strait of Magellan and the Pacific.[36] During this trip, he sacked the coasts of Chile and Peru, capturing a number of treasures and assaulting many of the populations along the coast. He also nailed a brass plate to a tree in San Francisco Bay, claiming that area for the queen. Drake's legendary assaults would be portrayed by the English as well as by Spanish epic poets and chroniclers. His extraordinary exploits would be evoked in the nineteenth century by Spanish American novelists as well. Soledad Acosta de Samper focuses on Drake's devastating attack on Cartagena, and Vicente Fidel López depicts Drake's daring seizure of the Spanish treasure on the *Caçafuego,* off the Pacific coast.

In 1586 Drake returned to the Caribbean. He first occupied the city of Santo Domingo, from which he obtained a generous ransom, and then Cartagena, which had become famous for its gold, silver, and pearls. Meanwhile, other English privateers such as John Oxenham, Francis Knollys, George Clifford, and the earl of Cumberland were also raiding Spanish settlements or assaulting their ships. Some, like Sir Walter Raleigh and Sir Richard Grenville, were much more active in the waters further north, although this did not curtail their attacks on Spanish ships. In the case of Walter Raleigh, his main interest in the Spanish Main was to find the famous heaven of El Dorado.[37]

The 1580s proved to be a difficult decade for the Spanish Crown as relations between Spain and England deteriorated. The increasing looting of the Indies by the English and their intense shipbuilding and mercantile activity alarmed the Spanish. England was bursting with energy onto the seas. War was inevitable. The Armada, the Spanish fleet sent to attack the English, suffered a crushing defeat in 1588, in a harsh battle in which Francis Drake and John Hawkins played a crucial role. Although the defeat was a serious blow, it did not signify the extinction of Spanish sea power. By 1592, four years after the defeat, Philip II had forty galleons under construction and was determined to demonstrate Spain's strength once again.[38] A few years later, the Spanish were successful at driving both Drake and Hawkins away while causing them heavy losses as they attempted to assault Panama. Unlike on his other raids, Drake was surprised to find Nombre de Dios barren; Porto Bello had become the new base for ships and cargoes. The English ended up lost in the jungle, combating rains, snakes, and insects and suffering from dysentery. Then, under the direction of Don Pedro Tello de Guzmán, the Spanish intercepted John Hawkins's attack on San Juan de Puerto Rico;

Hawkins was killed during the battle. A few months later, in January 1596, Francis Drake fell victim to malaria and died north of Porto Bello — still devastated over the defeat of Panama. This was Spain's extraordinary victory, but the piratical attacks continued for many more years.

The Age of the Buccaneers

The seventeenth century marked a new era in the history of piracy of the West Indies. From lawless intruders stealing whatever they could get their hands on and trying to thwart Spanish power, the French and English gradually became settlers and colonizers to secure their presence in the Caribbean. The Dutch began their incursions in the West Indies only at the end of the century, once they declared their independence from the Spanish in 1581, although they would remain at war until the Twelve Years' Truce of 1609. Previously, Dutch traders had ventured to the Indies exchanging slaves and manufactured European goods for hides, tobacco, and sugar. In the mid-1580s, Dutch smugglers began operating on the Brazilian coast, selling cloth and slaves. When the Spanish imposed a general embargo on Dutch traders in the Iberian Peninsula in 1598, the Dutch States formed an alliance with England and France against Spain and carried the war to the Spanish colonies.

The Dutch quickly established a number of trading posts along the east and west coasts of South America. They expanded their merchant fleets and organized new trading companies. In 1621 the Dutch West India Company, a government agency working with private corporations and dedicated to piracy and conquest, was formed. Soon the Dutch were robbing ships off the coasts of Chile and Peru, as well as off the coast of Brazil and in the Caribbean islands. These raiders were known among the Spanish as Pechelingues or Flexelingas (from the name of their island port of Vlissingen, or Flushing).[39] The Dutch were so persistent and audacious in their pursuit of Spanish ships that the name "Hollander" became synonymous with "corsair" and "pirate."[40]

One of the earliest and most famous Dutch pirates was Piet Heyn, known to the Spanish as Pata de Palo, who was sent to Spanish America and Brazil by the Dutch West India Company. He was to take over the town of São Salvador on the Brazilian coast. Since the acquisition of Portugal in 1580, the Spanish Crown controlled and defended former Portuguese plantations in Brazil as well as their forts, factories, and slave barracoons in West and East Africa. Despite Spanish resistance, Heyn displayed great audacity in attacking the strongly fortified city, which was surrounded by a fleet of fifteen Spanish vessels. The high point in Piet Heyn's naval campaigns was his capture of the entire Silver Fleet on September 8, 1628, off Matanzas Bay in Cuba. The booty included forty-six tons of silver, huge amounts of gold, as well as pearls, spices, indigo, hides, sugar, and logwood. The total amount was valued at fifteen million guilders, enough to pay the cost of the entire Dutch army for eight months. Heyn quickly gained great fame among his compatriots, and his achievement constitutes one of the glories of the Netherlands' history. Unlike the English and French at that stage, the Dutch were mainly interested in obstructing Spanish commerce. Although well-known and feared throughout the Spanish colonies, Heyn did not attack civilian populations; nor did he ransack towns and cities. Instead, he preferred to capture Spanish vessels at sea.[41] Among the Dutch pirates who plundered the Pacific coast were Simon de Cordes and Olivier van Noort, the latter being the first Dutch captain to sail around the world in 1601.

From 1609 to 1619, the French, English, and Dutch established a number of settlements in Guyana, between the mouths of the Orinoco and the Amazon rivers. By 1625, St. Christopher (today St. Kitts)—one of the first islands in the West Indies to be populated—had both English and French settlers. This process continued throughout numerous other small islands such as Barbados, Nevis, Barbuda, Antigua, Montserrat, Guadeloupe, and Martinique. However small and insignificant these islands might have been, the Spanish did not look the other way. In 1629, under Admiral Fadrique de Toledo, the Spanish decided to retaliate and invaded the islands of Nevis and St. Kitts to rid them of foreign "trespassers," but the islands were soon repopulated.

At the beginning of the sixteenth century, Hispaniola had been one of the most important Spanish strongholds in the Caribbean. However, after the conquests of Mexico and Peru, many Spaniards left the island, seeking their fortunes elsewhere. Furthermore, the Spanish never occupied the northwestern shore of the island. It was in this uncultivated part of the island that scattered groups of hunters, both French and English, lived, killing wild cattle and curing the flesh, which they traded with foreign vessels passing by. According to C. H. Haring, how these men came to the island is unknown.[42] Perhaps they were deserters or chance marooners, or perhaps even political and religious refugees. Whatever the case, these were the first "buccaneers," the seventeenth-century pirates famous for their ravages in the West Indies and the South Seas.

Most of the information available about the lifestyle and customs of the buccaneers is provided in *The Buccaneers of America*, written by Alexandre Olivier Exquemelin.[43] The book was an immediate best-seller. Originally published in Amsterdam in 1678, under the title *De Americæneche Zee Roovers*, it was quickly translated into French, German, Spanish, and English and was republished numerous times throughout Europe. Far from portraying a dazzling life of adventures and treasure finding, this firsthand account of life among the buccaneers describes the hardships of these disreputable looters under the brutal command of Francis L'Ollonais and Henry Morgan.

The origin of the name "buccaneer" is given in Exquemelin's narrative. In it he explains that the term comes from the process of curing wild cattle meat under a slow-burning flame to give the meat an excellent flavor. The cattle hunters learned this process from the Carib Indians, who called the spit on which the strips of meat were smoked "boucan." With time, the dried meat came to be known as "viande boucannée," and the hunters became "boucaniers" or, as pronounced by the English, "buccaneers."[44] When these hunters began committing acts of piracy, the word "buccaneer" was used to identify them; consequently, "buccaneer" came to signify, at least in English, the same as "corsair" or "freebooter." The French, however, refrained from using this term, preferring "flibustier" instead. The origin of the term "flibustier" is not as clear, although according to James Burney, it preceded "buccaneer." Haring, who also provides an explanation of the term "buccaneer," claims "flibustier" was the sailor's way of pronouncing the English word "freebooter." Francisco Mota defines a "freebooter" as a persecuted buccaneer, thus placing the emergence of the term "buccaneer" first, as did Sierra O'Reilly. Another version asserts that the word "flibustier" derives from "flyboat," or *fluyts*, a type of vessel that the French in Hispaniola bought from the Dutch. But Burney claims that this theory is quite unlikely.[45]

The Spanish tried to rid their territories of the cattle hunters and raided the northwestern section of the island. Those captured were executed on the spot. Their cattle were slain to eliminate any possible supply of beef to the survivors. Many individuals were able to take refuge in a small, rocky island to the northwest of Hispaniola, called Tortuga because of its turtle shape. The island proved to be ideal. It offered its inhabitants great protection and was inaccessible on the north side. Arrival of all vessels from the south side could thus be easily controlled. Because the island had little to offer in terms of food, however, the buccaneers took to the sea and began capturing Spanish ships. As more and more people arrived, the island became something like a pirate base, controlled alternately by the French and the English.[46]

The Spanish did not give up chasing the foreigners out of their territory. They continued to attack the buccaneers in Tortuga, though without much success. Ultimately, their raids forced the interlopers to search for a place that would not be subjected to such periodic attacks. This turned out to be the island of Jamaica. From the earliest known records, Jamaica was considered one of the most beautiful islands of the Caribbean. Legend has it that a group of men were so stunned by the island's beauty that they deserted their English captain and enlisted in the Spanish ranks. In 1655 Oliver Cromwell, lord protector of the English Commonwealth (1653–1658), sent an expedition with the object of gaining strength among the Spanish possessions and the instructions to occupy Hispaniola. Unable to comply with the orders because of Spanish resistance, the English anchored in Jamaica.

One of the principal promoters of Cromwell's scheme was Thomas Gage, an Englishman sent to Spanish America by the Dominican order he had joined. He spent many years as a priest in various places, especially Mexico. In 1641 he returned to England, announced his conversion to Protestantism, and became a minister. His book *A New Survey of the West Indies,* published in 1648, was invaluable for the English.[47] It not only was extremely entertaining but also showed how valuable the Spanish American territories would be to England and how easily they might be seized. Another important figure in encouraging Cromwell's plan was Colonel Thomas Modyford, a Puritan soldier who became duke of Albermale. First governor of Barbados, Modyford would go on to become governor of Jamaica. He was convinced that transforming

Trinidad and the Orinoco into English bases would allow the English to take control of many more Spanish possessions.

In the beginning, Jamaica was only a temporary base for the English, but they would soon discover its strategic importance. To gain control over the island quickly, the English sent a very unselect group of individuals.[48] Thanks to their looting and plunder, Port Royal soon became one of the richest cities in the Caribbean; it was also considered the "wickedest."[49] When Charles II was proclaimed king of England in 1660, hostilities with Spain ceased, and England gave explicit instructions forbidding assaults against the Spanish. Nevertheless, Sir Charles Lyttleton, deputy governor of Jamaica, was adamant about maintaining privateers on the island and disregarded the Crown's mandate.[50]

By 1665, Jamaica had become a unique haven for pirates, who were usually uncontrollable and often dangerous. One of the most famous and unruly English buccaneers based in Jamaica was Sir Henry Morgan. Captured by the Spanish during his youth, Morgan harbored a fierce hatred of the Spanish and was determined to do them as much harm as possible. He and his men not only sacked and burned Panama—which had become a rich colonial center of commerce—and the coast of Costa Rica but also plundered Campeche, Cuba, Grenada, and the cities of Cartagena, Porto Bello, and Maracaibo, among others. His tactics were ruthless: he looted churches, raped women, and tortured prisoners in search of the valuables hidden among the population. Exquemelin's account of Morgan's activities provides a detailed illustration of the pirates' tactics, from their violent modes of celebration to their methods of torture. For example, during the attack on Panama, trying to obtain more information, the pirates tortured a slave in the following manner:

> Not being able to extort any other confession out of him, they first put him upon the rack, wherewith they inhumanly disjointed his arms. After this, they twisted a cord about his forehead, which they wrung so hard, that his eyes appeared as big as eggs, and were ready to fall out of his skull. But neither with these torments could they obtain any positive answer to their demands. Whereupon they soon after hung him up by the testicles, giving him infinite blows and stripes while he was under that intolerable pain and posture of body. Afterwards they cut off his nose and ears, and singed his face with burning straw, till he could

speak nor lament his misery no longer. Then losing all hopes of hearing any confession from his mouth, they commanded a negro to run him through with a lance, which put an end to his life and a period to their cruel and inhuman tortures.[51]

Lyttleton's successor as governor of Jamaica, Sir Thomas Modyford, was originally expected to halt the activities of the buccaneers, but he became one of Morgan's strongest supporters and commissioned him to engage in a number of piratical ventures. Modyford's goal was to transform Jamaica into an international market for the entire Caribbean area, and to this end, he planned to use, in a controlled fashion, the buccaneers. But the buccaneers allowed no one to determine what their actions should be, so Modyford had to loosen his restrictions on them and opted simply to give them specific commissions. However, in 1667, Sir William Godolphin, the English envoy to the court of Madrid, began to negotiate a peace treaty with Spain, which was finally signed in 1670. According to the treaty, Spain officially recognized English holdings in the Caribbean, and both nations agreed to prohibit pillaging against the other and punish those who disobeyed. Governor Modyford ignored the treaty and sent Morgan "to doe and performe all matter of Exploys which may tend to the Preservation and Quiett of Jamayca."[52] Morgan went on to destroy Panama. The contradictory views toward piracy are evident in the response England and Spain had to these events. To placate Spain's anger, Modyford and Morgan were called back to England. Modyford was held prisoner in the Tower of London for two years before returning to Jamaica with Morgan, who had been tried but not convicted given his fervent popularity. Morgan had become a popular hero. Like Francis Drake, Morgan was even knighted in 1674, before returning to Jamaica as lieutenant governor. International diplomacy condemned these attacks, but England was in fact pleased with its territorial occupation and conquests in the Spanish colonies and did not shy away from recognizing its subjects' achievements. When Morgan returned, he found himself in the position of having to suppress the buccaneers of his island. According to some historians, despite a personal reticence, he did. Philip Gosse states that Morgan "seems to have taken his new duties loyally," and Peter Gerhard agrees, adding that Morgan "did much to suppress piracy."[53] Neither, however, offers information to sustain his assertion. It is more likely that Morgan complied with his new role "with indifferent efficiency," as Mendel Peterson concludes.

Morgan's retirement as a buccaneer in the late 1670s opened the possibility for the French, now securely established at the western end of Hispaniola and on the island of Tortuga, to take over. The French continued the acts of cruelty and violence previously perpetrated by the English. Among these pirates were Pierre Le Grand, Alexandre Bras de Fer, Michel Le Basque, and Pierre de Franquesnay. But it was undoubtedly Jean-David Nau, called L'Ollonais, or el Olonés in Spanish, who would inherit Henry Morgan's notoriety. Hence although the Spanish were able to harness one of their assailants by means of a peace treaty, they still had to deal with the Dutch and French forces.

Protected by the governor of Tortuga, Monsieur de la Place, L'Ollonais devastated the populations of Santo Domingo, Cuba, and Maracaibo and looted the coasts of Honduras, Nicaragua, and the Yucatán. Like Morgan, L'Ollonais was well known for his cruelty and barbarism. The following description by Exquemelin not only illustrates the pirate's inhumane actions throughout the Caribbean but also places L'Ollonais among the uncivilized "other," for his conduct is reminiscent of the cannibalism of which the Spanish accused the Indians:[54]

> It was the custom of L'Ollonais that, having tormented any persons and they not confessing, he would instantly cut them in pieces with his anger, and pull out their tongues; desiring to do the same, if possible, to every Spaniard in the world. (102–3)

Failing to obtain the information he was seeking,

> L'Ollonais grew outrageously passionate; insomuch that he drew his cutlass, and with it cut open the breast of one of those poor Spaniards, and, pulling out his heart with his sacrilegious hands, began to bite and gnaw it with his teeth like a ravenous wolf, saying to the rest: *I will serve you all alike if you show me not another way.* (103)

These signs of savagery highlight the pirates' barbarism as their distinctive quality, portraying their world as a dangerous realm of heretics and untamed beasts.

By the late 1670s, as booty became more difficult to obtain, buccaneers began attacking vessels of all flags indiscriminately. Consequently, more

"The Cruelty of Lolonois," in *The History of the Buccaneers of America from their first original day to this time, written in several languages and now collected into one volume,* by Alexandre Olivier Exquemelin (London: Printed for the Newborough, 1699). *Courtesy of the Mount Holyoke College Archives and Special Collections.*

nations viewed these men as outlaws and robbers and began to hunt them down. When war broke out between France and England, the buccaneers were forced to enlist in the service of their respective kings as privateers or auxiliary troops. Former companions-in-arms thus found themselves fighting each other as their nation's enemies. This change eventually led to the end of the buccaneers as such. During the War of the Grand Alliance, the Dutch, English, and Spanish united against Louis XIV. The Treaty of Ryswick ended this war in 1697, but war broke out again over the succession to the Spanish throne in 1701, as King Charles II of Spain did not have a direct heir. The Peace of Utrecht, signed in 1713, not only ended the battle for succession in Spain but also brought piracy to a halt.[55]

A significant factor to the elimination of piracy was the increasing importance the slave trade had come to play in the European economy. Slavery was essential to the preservation of the sugar plantations, which, by the mid–seventeenth century, had become an extremely important enterprise. The development of the sugar industry had been gradual but steady. Given that most of the Indians on the islands had been killed, African slaves were brought in for labor. In 1663 the Company of Royal Adventurers of England stated to King Charles II that "the 'very being' of the plantations depended on the supply of Negroes."[56] On this point, Europe was unanimous. Hence European interests shifted toward organizing their trading companies to secure their place in the new market.

The effect that almost three centuries of piracy left behind was felt in a variety of ways, from economic distress to the fear hovering over the daily life of the civilian population. Despite Spain's efforts, little could be done to keep away covetous foreigners in search of a fast and easy prize. Whether they were corsairs, pirates, or buccaneers, they all felt that they had a right to the immense riches the New World had to offer. Although piracy ended during the mid-1700s, the assaults in the Caribbean continued throughout the eighteenth century, in tandem with a vigorous illegal slave trade; in fact, a different form of piracy would even surface with a certain magnitude during the emancipation movements at the beginning of the nineteenth century.[57]

Looking back at the history of Spanish America, it is clear that piracy acted as a powerful and constant force on political and economic events from the beginning of colonization to the formation of independent nations. In the end, the pirates' destructive methods, in many cases backed by their home governments, gave way to a different form of colonization, one that contrasted sharply with the Spanish colonial enterprise. Ultimately piracy paved the way for a new form of imperialism that would rise in the eighteenth century and flourish, under England, during the nineteenth. Piracy not only changed the map of the New World but also announced the economic, political, and cultural forces that would be prevalent in the struggle for nation building during the nineteenth century.

CHAPTER TWO

The Sea Monsters of
the Colonial Era

Llora de compasión el pecho tierno
y el ánima compuesta y alumbrada,
de ver tan sin cathólico govierno
esta çiega nación desventurada,
guiados al profundo del infierno
por una bestia falsa desalmada:
aquel gran charlatán y mostro ficro
que fué Martín Luder o mal Lutero
—Juan de Castellanos, "Discurso de el Capitán Francisco Draque"

The publication of the first part of *La Araucana* by Alonso de Ercilla (1569) marks the beginning of an important genre in the history of Spanish American colonial literature: epic poetry.[1] Throughout the sixteenth and seventeenth centuries, lengthy poems focusing on the historical events and geography of the New World were an extremely popular genre. Faced with a completely unfamiliar nature bursting with a distinctive flora and fauna, colonial authors found themselves living in what Europeans imagined as "epic times." These poets, often soldiers participating in the events narrated, reconstructed the discovery, conquest, and colonization of the land, intertwining their personal memories and amazement as they entered the realm of what they found to be a land of dreams and, at times, nightmares. This sense of discovery present in the first poems, chronicles, and *relaciones,* as well as in other texts, gives a distinct flavor to the literary production of the colonial period.[2]

Among these texts, it is common to find references concerning pirate attacks. Battles with pirates offered an ideal opportunity for chroniclers and poets to glorify the actions of Spaniards in defending their territories and their faith. In addition, they enabled authors to construct an elaborate system of difference through which those opposing the cultural and religious values endorsed by Spain were positioned as "others."

Of the numerous pirates who attacked Spain's American domains, Francis Drake is undoubtedly the most well known. The first to write about Drake was Juan de Castellanos, a Spanish priest and chronicler who came to the Indies around 1534. The exact date Castellanos arrived in the New World is unknown, but in 1536 he was among the men accompanying Jiménez de Quesada in the conquest of the Nuevo Reino de Granada, a traumatic expedition in which more than 85 percent of the soldiers died. Born in 1522, in Alanís, Sevilla, Castellanos led an adventurous life, participating in a number of expeditions in the continent. In 1554 he was ordained in Cartagena, where he settled for a number of years, until 1562, when he became parish priest of Tunja until his death in 1607.[3]

Castellanos's voluminous poem, entitled *Elegías de varones ilustres de Indias,* is the result of a long and carefully documented, though unsystematic, endeavor.[4] Around 1544 Castellanos started to write his chronicle in prose; beginning in 1577, he spent the following ten years rewriting it in verse. There are four major parts to this versified chronicle. The first, published in Madrid in 1589, deals with the earliest Spanish expeditions to the New World, from Christopher Columbus to Pedro de Ursúa and Lope de Aguirre. The second part focuses on the history of the province of Venezuela and the governors of Santa Marta, and the third contains the history of Cartagena, Popayán, and Antioquia, in addition to the renowned "Discurso de el Capitán Francisco Draque." Finally, the fourth part of the *Elegías,* entitled "Historia del Nuevo Reino de Granada," presents the founding of Bogotá, Vélez, Tunja, and Guane, as well as the governments of Jerónimo Lebrón, Pedro de Ursúa, and Andrés Díaz de Venero y Leiva, first president of the Audiencia del Nuevo Reino.

The "Discurso de el Capitán Francisco Draque" consists of a poem of 715 stanzas written in octaves and a letter in tercets, which collectively reconstruct Drake's numerous ventures against the Spanish. Around 1591, the poem was censored by Pedro Sarmiento de Gamboa and thereafter was no longer included in editions of the work. The only testimony of the poem's existence was the mark of torn pages and a few crossed-out verses in a collection of documents gathered in the eighteenth century, along with a scribble signed by the censor instructing that the verses be deleted.[5] The poem was finally discovered in 1886 and reinstated in the third part of the *Elegías*, where it had originally been included.

Although Castellanos's main focus in his "Discurso" is to reconstruct Drake's attack on Cartagena de Indias in 1586, the author goes back to the first English excursions along the Spanish Main and includes Drake's circumnavigation (1579) and seizure of Santo Domingo on his way to Cartagena. Claiming to offer a "truthful and fair" account of the events, the author begins his heroic poem with a general description of colonial society at the time of Drake's attack on Cartagena. Castellanos is thus able to underline the problems that gave pirates easy access to Spanish treasures and exposed the civilian population to serious and, in the opinion of the author, unnecessary dangers. Castellanos accuses the colonials of being overconfident, falling asleep and "snoring" instead of being alert and cautious, certain that no one would dare defy their authority, especially the authority of the Spanish Inquisition. Merchants, *letrados*, and notary publics, he explains, were fun-loving individuals and thus inept fighters. Their lust is a recurrent theme throughout the poem and reflects Castellanos's moral critique: "Prevention is missing, counsel is missing / protection is nowhere to be found. / Comfort and adornments are often spurs to the enemy" (33). The poet blames especially the governors and higher authorities for failing to take the necessary precautions to protect the population. Spanish colonials are thus represented leaving the door open to the pirates' raids:

nosotros, no con cercas ni con muros,
sino de todo desaperçibidos,
pocos que sepan militar oficio
por carescer del uso y exerçiçio. (32)

[not with fences nor with walls
but with everything unprepared
few of us knowing the military trade
for lack of use and excercise.]

The world of the epic is a complicated one of questions in which the ways of God are not completely understood, though they are accepted.[6] The epic tries to make sense of perplexities; it is a poetic form that seeks to explain an order determined by fate. In this context, Francis Drake functions as a classic example of God's capriciousness, for he brings fear, uncertainty, and danger to the established world order. Drake is identified with England, a "perfidious nation, blindly malignant, wretched enemy of the divine honor" (88). Hence, from the beginning of Castellanos's account, Drake is portrayed as different and dangerous. He is the "other," the ultimate enemy. Drake stands out among all the other pirates of his time, for his success is predicated on his tactic of surprising the enemy, penetrating where no other vessel had dared enter before:

> quando Francisco Draque, luterano,
> entró por dó cosarios no venían,
> ni jamás supo robadora mano
> sobresaltar a los que allí vivían;
> y ansí fueron en gran summa los robos
> por estar sin sospecha destos lobos. (25)

> [when Francis Drake, a Lutheran,
> entered where corsairs had not dared
> nor pilfering hands were known to rob
> to assault those dwelling there
> great was the plundering
> for none imagined such wolves lay in wait.]

In describing Drake and his actions in the Spanish colonies, the discourse of amazement takes preeminence.[7] The enemy produces not only fear but wonder. Consequently, the negative connotation to be expected in the presentation of such a dangerous enemy is, momentarily, displaced as Castellanos brings Drake onstage. Here we are presented with an extremely articulate individual openly defying Spain's claim to her territories:

> Pues que tenéis tan buen entendimiento
> hacedme de esta duda satisfecho:
> ¿Adán mandó por algún testamento
> a solos Hespañoles al provecho?

la cláusula mostrad y de momento
haré renunciación a mi derecho,
porque si lo contrario desto fuese,
avría de llevar más, quien más pudiese. (42)

[Since you have such great understanding
clarify for me this doubt:
Did Adam order through any testament
that Spaniards be the only ones to profit?
Show me where 'tis written
and I at once will resign my right,
but if it be the contrary,
let he who can, take the most.]

Drake's defiance undermines the authority of the papal dominations. It is a poetic synthesis of Francis I's protest regarding "Adam's will," and the English challenge to Spain's claims according to the doctrine of effective occupation.[8] Drake is extremely knowledgeable and clever. He gets the Indians to side with him by promising they will not be forced to go to church or receive beatings. He knows when to hold back from attacking a vessel, and he even knows when to be courteous, or to let go of the prize he has captured to save himself. In fact, because of his successful tactics, Drake was known as the *astuto luterano*, the astute Lutheran, throughout the Indies.

Astuto is undoubtedly the most recurrent adjective used by Castellanos and other colonial writers to describe Drake. In Spanish it refers to someone "sagacious for realizing what is most profitable. . . . Able to obtain what he wants with deceptions and schemes."[9] Drake is shrewd, unscrupulous, and artful in deceiving his opponents. He is capable of anything in order to rob the Spanish. Although Castellanos does not hide his amazement at Drake's daring and cleverness, he condemns him for being an ambitious, bloodthirsty, and dangerous Lutheran. The discourse of amazement is thereby controlled and contained by the imposition of a second discourse, that of morality.[10] By constantly reiterating the moral opposition between Spanish Catholics and English Protestants, Castellanos clearly delineates the division between good and evil, religious and heretical. Through the discourse of morality, he is able to expose not only the dangers and uncertainties present in this new world but also his own critique of the colonial system without undermining the official religious and political values of the time. Morality becomes the shaping force that defines and secures the uncertain order of the world and ultimately distinguishes the "other." Hence, despite the simplicity of these two discourses, their interaction and confrontation suggests a world much more complex and intriguing than at first seems apparent.

Drake is positioned as immoral for his cruelty. A brutal man who pillages cathedrals, churches, and private homes, he confiscates everything, from the treasured relics of saints to people's bedcovers. After his attack, the innocent are left bereft, desperate and in tears, as they watch their churches and homes ransacked and burned by the monstrous heretic. The intensity of Castellanos's account is heightened by his personal pain as he remembers the events:

> ¡O fiera crueldad, furor insano,
> nefando crimen, infernal motivo!
> La pluma se me cae de la mano
> con un frío temblor, quando escrivo. (91)

> [Oh, beastly cruelty, insane furor
> infamous crime, infernal motive!
> As I write, my pen falls from my hand
> with an ice cold tremor.]

According to Castellanos, it is the Spaniards' responsibility to be faithful to their religious beliefs and to document for the world Drake's selfishness and hypocrisy, for his only goal is "to enjoy what this land holds" (42). No matter how astute Drake might be, he is above all a heretic without morals and faith and will stop at nothing to satisfy his greedy desire. Juan de Castellanos reminds the Spanish that it is their obligation to prepare themselves for these piratical attacks, protect their people, and uphold the true teachings of the Church.

By portraying truly religious Spaniards as morally superior, Castellanos concludes that if the pirates are able to disrupt the population, it is because of mistakes by the Spanish authorities. Castellanos's overt critique of the colonial authorities is perhaps the reason—or at least one of them—that Pedro Sarmiento de Gamboa, acting in the Consejo Real y Supremo de Indias, censored the "Discurso de el Capitán Francisco

Draque"; after all, Sarmiento de Gamboa had been in charge of chasing Drake after his attack on Lima and Callao, and as others before him, he too had underestimated the pirate's potential and let him get away.

The interaction between discourses is also emphatically articulated in Martín del Barco Centenera's vast poem *La Argentina,* published in Lisboa in 1602. Born in Lograsán, Extremadura, in 1544, del Barco Centenera arrived in Asunción del Paraguay in 1572, where he became archdeacon three years later; he also held a number of ecclesiastical positions (archdeacon, clergyman, vicar) in the cities of Tucumán, Charcas, Lima, Cochabamba, and Oruro until he was dismissed for his unethical conduct. He returned to Spain in 1595.[11]

Divided into twenty-eight cantos, the first part of the poem presents the history and geography of Argentina. It then moves on to recount a number of important events throughout the River Plate, Paraguay, and Brazil. In this poem, Francis Drake is openly admired for his courage and dexterity. He is presented as a noble gentleman, "spirited and courageous," "friendly and generous." Claiming to narrate only the truth, even if that means recognizing the amazing exploits of the enemy, del Barco Centenera describes Drake's boldness in crossing the Strait of Magellan, a feat that the author regards as a triumph. He goes on to recount Drake's subsequent attacks along the coasts of Chile and Peru, where he took one of his most famous prizes.

> Su hambre, tan canina y tan rabiosa,
> De plata bien hartó aqueste adversario.
> Que es cosa de decir muy monstruosa,
> El número de plata, y temerario
> Negocio nunca visto ni leido,
> Que a cosario jamás ha sucedido. (248)

> [His hunger, so canine and ravenous,
> This adversary filled with silver.
> A sight quite monstrous
> The amount of silver, and frightening
> profit never seen nor heard before
> That ever a corsair did achieve.]

Del Barco Centenera's account is based on the reports of individuals who lived through Drake's attacks. It is perhaps this distance and the effusive emotions the author brings forth from the reports of people's experience that allow him to depict Drake's actions with a disturbing tone of wonder. Showing much less apprehension than Castellanos, del Barco Centenera does not refrain from expressing his amazement at Drake's achievements; nor does he hold the Spanish accountable for the pirate's conquests. Instead, the poet reconstructs the extreme anguish and despair the Spanish subjects felt, which in turn highlight the pirate's greatness. Nevertheless, in underlining the fear Drake brought on the inhabitants of the Indies, del Barco Centenera also gives way to the discourse of morality, for Drake's arrival opened the door to future tormentors: "The sudden fear / caused insanity among all. / . . . / Everyone was in such fright / worrying about evil future sights" (247). More than anything else, it is the panic that Drake's presence produces among civilians that takes center stage, not his cruel actions. In fact, in this epic, Drake does not actually commit any individual acts of cruelty. This is perhaps why, in his reconstruction of Drake's attacks on the Spanish Main, the nineteenth-century Argentine author Vicente Fidel López will cite this text to legitimize his heroic and audacious portrayal of the British pirate.

Having no cruel acts to charge Drake with, del Barco Centenera articulates the discourse of morality by focusing on Drake's guilt, despite his "noble" qualities, that lies in his lack of "true" faith: "But what's most important and most necessary / He lacks: the love of Jesus Christ" (245). Thus, notwithstanding his "nobility" and courage (and the author's admiration), Drake belongs to the "others." Building on the clear and explicit understanding of the differences between Protestants and Catholics, del Barco Centenera does not need to explain the consequences of Drake's lack of faith: being a Lutheran places him among the immoral. Morality is here defined exclusively by one's religion. Right and wrong are determined by the law of the Church. By the mere fact of being Protestant, Drake is placed among the heretics and dangerous "others" harassing the colonies. In this way, del Barco Centenera's portrayal of Drake stands out for its effusive display of emotions rather than its itemized reconstruction of wrongful acts.

The important role religion plays in the reconstruction of these events, as well as in the recounting of most episodes concerning the exploration, conquest, and colonization of the New World, cannot be sufficiently underscored. The missionary commitment entrusted to Spain ensured the Church a decisive imprint on Spanish colonial organization.[12] Explorers, conquerors, and governors were instructed to Christianize and "civilize" the natives of the territories they occupied. This interweaving of Spain's military actions with spiritual conversion engendered a unique social symbiosis of judicial and political significance. The Crown and Church depended on each other for their existence; as Fernando de los Ríos noted, "the will to power and the will to *imperium* . . . reached through Spain its apex [sic]"[13]

To ensure religious unity from the beginning, the Inquisition— founded in Spain in 1478—sent its representatives to oversee the moral conduct of the Crown's subjects and make sure that no other faith was professed. The first tribunal of the Holy Office of the Inquisition was established in Mexico in 1571, although there existed ecclesiastical judges who had enforced the faith and morals of the Church from the early years of the Mexican conquest.[14] The function of the Inquisition was to prevent contact with heretics and other individuals believing in false doctrines who might have arrived in the Indies. With the outbreak of religious wars among European nations, foreigners caught assaulting Spanish territories were defined no longer by their nationality but by their religious beliefs. In a similar fashion, those committing such attacks used their religious convictions to justify their actions against the Spanish. In this way, the piratical assaults became resignified as religious battles. Those caught were either judged by the Inquisition in Spanish America or sent to Spain, where they were dealt with accordingly.[15]

In the colonial poems written in the sixteenth and seventeenth centuries, religion is the key element defining the limits of what is acceptable or unacceptable. It established a distinct hierarchy and provided a context within which to make sense of the pirates' actions. Juan de Miramontes y Zuázola is another epic poet who locates Drake within these parameters. His *Armas antárticas,* which includes a reference to the English pirate's ventures in the New World, was written circa 1608 to 1614 and published for the first time in 1921 by Jacinto Jijón y Caamaño. Very little is known about Miramontes y Zuázola. In 1576 he participated in Captain Diego de Frías's campaign against the English pirate John Oxenham, one of Drake's lieutenants. Years later he is said to have marched to Peru with general Miguel Angel Filipón, and in 1604 he was declared *gentilhombre* in the *Compañía de lanzas y arcabuces* of the viceroy

D. Luis de Velasco. After 1614, there is no information about his life, and he is presumed to have died shortly thereafter.[16]

The twenty cantos (1,698 stanzas) glorifying Spanish accomplishments in South America begin with Pizarro's conquest of Peru and the founding of Lima. The author then displaces his account to England, where Drake is presented explaining to Queen Elizabeth his plans to attack Panama and repeat Magellan's amazing trip around the world. Drake's only request is to be given a "valiant and expert companion," John Oxenham, to accompany him on the journey. After reaching Spanish territories, Drake and Oxenham part ways. Drake goes on to replicate Magellan's route and to attack the Pacific coast much more successfully than his lieutenant. Oxenham stays behind in the Caribbean, befriending the maroons, the fugitive black slaves, and preparing his assault on Panama. The Spanish, however, are able to defend their possessions and chase away Oxenham and his men. Oxenham is ultimately taken prisoner by Spanish forces.

Reconstructing the pirates' assaults on the Spanish territories throughout eight cantos, Miramontes y Zuázola shifts the focus back and forth from Drake to Oxenham while proceeding in chronological sequence. The author seems amazed by Drake's ventures, for he opens the account by describing him as "audacious, valiant, considerate, cautious, ingenious, sagacious, astute, eloquent, prudent, dexterous, daring, strong, fortunate" (45). The poet goes on to describe Drake's struggle across the Strait of Magellan, where, faced with a brutal tempest, the English pirate "gave proof of his valiant spirit," while his men, overcome by fear, prayed to Christ, promising, if saved, to worship in "Roman Catholic altars" (98). Of the five ships, only Drake's succeeds in crossing the Strait unharmed. Continuing his trip along the coasts of Chile and Peru, he takes by surprise a number of Spanish vessels full of gold, sending a wave of fear throughout the population.

What amazes the author most seems to be the way Drake takes advantage of every circumstance to pull off his attacks successfully. Rather than burning the Spanish ships or sending them to the bottom of the ocean once they have been emptied, Drake sets them adrift so that the sailors, fearing an immediate wreck, will concentrate on regaining control of their ship rather than chase after him. As a result, "Drake obtained fame and profit: / fame of not committing harm and profit from his venture" (143). Drake, however, would go on to inflict great damage not only on Spain's vessels but also on civilians. He is well remembered for his devastating attack on Cartagena a few years later, although this event is not included in this poet's depiction.

Toward the end of the poem, Drake's image as daring mariner gives way to that of a selfish traitor who abandons his companions and compatriots in need. Again, the discourse of amazement is displaced by that of morality. Personifying the model of Protestant individualism, Drake chooses to save himself and his loot above all else. He decides to abandon Oxenham, who—as previously agreed and despite being pursued by Spanish troops—has been faithfully waiting for him. Having set Drake apart for his strategic brilliance and audacity, Miramontes y Zuázola simply reformulates those outstanding qualities to portray Drake as corrupt, for what sets him apart is also what places him as a dangerous adversary. His audacity becomes carelessness, and his ambition greed as he disregards the well-being of his own men. In this redefinition, Oxenham, momentarily, appears as a victim; otherwise he is portrayed as a cruel and vengeful pirate. He befriends the maroons of Ballano to guide him through the rivers to reach the South Sea and gets them to build him a fortress to seek refuge between attacks. Miramontes y Zuázola presents him as a violent, impetuous rogue, driven by greed, ransacking houses, seizing jewels, clothes, gold; a treacherous corsair "with indignant arm and sacrilegious hand" brutally destroying homes and churches. Although Oxenham was successful in reaching the South Sea and captured considerable booty near Ecuador and the Pearl Islands, he was never as fortunate as Drake. In the end, Oxenham is attacked by the Spanish, who had been informed of his whereabouts, and is eventually caught and punished for his crimes.

Drake, however, appears as a more complex character. Despite his unruly actions, for example, Miramontes y Zuázola highlights a certain gentlemanliness that distinguishes Drake from Oxenham. Drake fights with a purpose; he is astute, but he has principles and is not moved by sheer brutality or an unfounded hunger for violence. Oxenham, on the other hand, has no qualms in forging an alliance with the maroons, the ultimate enemy, and revels in his savagery. As a daring individual who presented one of the most serious challenges to the Spanish Crown, Drake undoubtedly had to have some exceptional quality. The reference

to Drake's "refinement"—which, of course, does not extend to his men—
clearly places him above the social strata to which pirates, the appall-
ing ill-bred rogues, by definition belonged. It is only when the religious
discourse is momentarily suspended that chroniclers can portray their
amazement at Drake's extraordinary achievements, which are, in this
case, simultaneously secured under an illusory and temporary class distinction.[17] Hence Drake's greatness is exposed but carefully contained
to underscore the Spanish triumph and justify their superiority, which
is defined in terms of religious convictions.

Miramontes y Zuázola presents the Spanish, opposing the ruthless
pirates, as faithful Catholics determined to fulfill their duties and defend their territories against the English, in spite of their fear of pirates.
Among those willing to fight against the heretics, the poet names Juan
de Apalo, Miguel Angel, Pedro de Córdova, and Rodrigo Campuzano,
and their courageous general, Pedro de Arana. Evoking images of Roman gods and Greek heroes (characteristic of the epic), the author describes each soldier's readiness to engage in battle:

> Y tú, mi general Pedro de Arana,
> venerable, sagaz, prudente viejo,
> que imitas en edad nevada y cana,
> a Marte en brío, a Néstor en consejo,
> en yegua velocísima, lozana,
> que parece una tigre en el pellejo,
> armado sales a ordenar el campo
> como en esta ocasión, Maestre de Campo. (138)

> [And you, my general Pedro de Arana,
> venerable, wise, and prudent old man,
> who, snowy and white in age, imitates
> Mars in strength, Nestor in counsel,
> on swift and vigorous mare
> resembling a tiger's hide
> you go forth armed to command the field
> as on this occasion, Master of the Field.]

As Miramontes y Zuázola describes the armed encounter between the
English and the Spanish, he is overwhelmed by emotion. Although the

Spanish are unable to catch Drake, they do succeed in tracking Oxenham down, capturing him, and confiscating his loot. Thus the Spanish are not only depicted as having good intentions; in this case, they are also victorious as befits their zealous and "noble souls." Miramontes y Zuázola carefully emphasizes the courage of the Spanish, "so deft and agile," as well as the energy and determination with which they confront the English pirates:

¡Oh hidalgos, españoles arriscados,
tan nobles como de ánimos feroces,
cuánto os ablanda el afligido y triste
que a vuestro invicto brazo no resiste! (169)

[Oh noble, daring Spaniards,
of such virtuous and ferocious spirits
weakened by frailty and sadness
but unable to resist your invincible arm!]

The poem clearly suggests that the Spanish are able to defeat the English because the Spanish are profoundly religious and believe in their just cause. The English, on the other hand, have no morals and will make pacts and promises with anyone. The system of oppositions is patterned as a constant process of assertion and denial. The Spanish *are* good and morally superior because they *are not* like the violent heretics. The Spanish must ultimately overcome the English because the Spanish *are* Catholic and *not* Protestant. The Spanish are faithful; the English selfish: they betray their own men. The Spanish are dutiful subjects, whereas the English lack any sense of patriotism. For Miramontes y Zuázola, the primary force separating the Spanish from the English is greed. This is why Oxenham and the maroons decide to work together:

¡Monstruosa bestia, hidrópica, sedienta,
torpe, viciosa, hinchada, detestable,
que cuanto más el pasto se te aumenta,
tanto despiertas la hambre insaciable!
¿Quién sino tú, codicia fraudulenta,
pudo trabar en liga inseparable
dos diferentes géneros de gentes,
remotamente en todo diferentes? (86)

[Monstrous beast, voracious, thirsty
clumsy, vicious, swollen, hateful
the more grass you are given
the more your endless hunger grows
Who else, but you, fraudulent greed
could tie inseparably together
two people
in every way so different?]

The avarice of the English and their lack of morality is apparent in their disregard for all distinctions with the "other," as they commit the most unconscionable act of any civilized race: a pact with the maroons, the rebellious "savages." This behavior underscores their true nature: unrestrained by laws and responsibilities, governed only by greed, the English have no project, no sense of purpose, no "real" understanding of difference. They have become traitors to their own race. This positioning allows the author to locate the English among the "other" while dislodging them from their priviledged Europeanness. Despite their exceptional physical strength, the English are weak, for they can be corrupted, co-opted by that "other." Their bond with the maroons makes the English dangerous: it reflects their detachment from true civilization. They are menacing because they destroy all barriers of civilization, not because they are morally superior. Consequently, they must be erased from this spatial setting; it is only through the system of oppositions that the process of erasure can achieve its neutralizing effect.

According to the Spanish, the English are by definition corrupt. Their country has refused obedience to the Holy Father. England has thus become "hateful to the world and to God" (44). Their attacks on the Spanish colonies have only one objective: to satisfy English greed. For the Catholics, the Protestants exemplify individualism (in opposition to communal solidarity) and moral disintegration; consequently, they deserve to be punished, eliminated. The most terrifying aspect of Drake's attacks is that his success is almost inexplicable according to the religious beliefs of the Spaniards. How could a heretic cause so much damage to the Spanish empire and its subjects and get away with it? Bewildered by this outcome, Miramontes y Zuázola cries out:

¡Incomprensible Dios! ¿Este pirata
no borró de su frente aquella marca

que del pecado original rescata
al que navega en la romana barca?
Pues ¿cómo tan gran suma de oro y plata,
permites que al católico monarca
hoy robe? Justas son, Señor, tus obras,
con que maravilloso nombre cobras! (146)

[Incomprehensible God! Did this pirate
not erase from his brow the mark
that rescues from original sin
he who sails upon the Roman ship?
Why allow such sums of gold and silver
to be taken from the Catholic Crown today?
Your work, Lord, is indeed just
with which you claim marvelous fame!]

The ironic tone of the last two verses reflects the impossibility of com-
prehending why these English heretics should be able to deprive the just
and law-abiding Spaniards of their possessions. This incomprehension
is at the center of most colonial reconstructions of Drake's assaults. The
Spanish claimed that if they followed the teachings of the Church, they
would be able to overcome any adversary. Drake's astonishing success,
however, shook their belief. Because he was English and Protestant, his
successful plunders openly defied Spain's military and religious hegemony. He was, moreover, a heretic whom the Spanish seemed incapable
of punishing. If Drake's military achievements were indeed successful,
they had to be morally condemned. Thus, the need for the Spanish to
reaffirm their moral and religious differences with the English through
a system of oppositions. Religion enabled the Spanish to establish that
distinct order, which located the English in the position of the "other."

By explaining and making meaningful the surrounding "reality," religion ensured a way of seeing and understanding the world that allowed
the individual to make sense even of the most inexplicable events.
Chaos, on the other hand—a tumult of undecipherable events—renders
that "reality" obscure, hindering all forms of interpretation and inter-
pretability.[18] The lack of order leaves the individual with unanswered
questions in an extremely unsettling "reality," which must somehow be
overcome.

One could say that these epic poets found themselves lost in the process of interpretation when it came to explaining Drake's success, for he was the first pirate to defy the Spanish empire in such an astounding way. Drake, however, is merely the embodiment of a force bringing chaos to the well-framed world dictated by the Church in the Spanish colonies. These poems are not only about Drake (or any other pirates, for that matter) and his devastating attacks, or about England's relationship with Spain; they are also about Catholicism battling against Protestantism, precisely at the time when—as a result of the Counter-Reformation—this battle had taken center stage among European states. In this sense, these poems can be read as coetaneous reenactments of this religious struggle, a struggle in which the cosmic order that Catholicism had established had to be reconfirmed. This provides the rationale for situating all pirates among the heretics. Embedded within these epic poems is a need to make sense, to comprehend, what happened to a world so brutally shattered by the intervention of Spain's enemies.

Throughout these chronicles, the arrival and departure of pirates stand as important moments in the construction of the Hispanic American colonial identity. The recording of these events not only helps recall and order the past (time is measured before and after the pirates' arrival), but more importantly, their proximity instills among the community a sense of wholeness. Religious and political authorities, as well as the general population, come together in preparing to confront the enemy. These are moments of collective awareness. Every individual will remember the pirates' arrival and its effect on his or her community. Whether it is because of the damage inflicted on the community or simply because of the fear the pirates' presence generated, it is unlikely that anyone would forget a piratical attack. Hence, these attacks can be seen as moments of historical awakenings. They mark specific instances when society as a whole unites to define itself against the enemy. These are the founding moments of a national consciousness.

Silvestre de Balboa Troya y Quesada's poem *Espejo de paciencia*, written in Cuba in 1608, offers a unique example of this type of awakening.[19] Balboa was born in the Canary Islands (isla de Gran Canaria) and held the position of notary in the Cabildo of Puerto Príncipe. His poem, also written in octaves and tercets, was discovered in 1838 by José Antonio Echeverría, who found it in the archives of the Sociedad Patriótica de la Habana in the *Historia de la isla y catedral de Cuba*. The poem describes the attack that Gilberto Girón, a French pirate, made on the island four

years earlier. Dedicated to the bishop of Cuba, Juan de las Cabezas Altamirano, the poem reconstructs the pirates' assault on the town of Yara,
and the kidnapping of the bishop and his eventual rescue, organized by
the town of Bayamo, under the direction of Gregorio Ramos, who fear-
lessly confronted the pirates and killed the French corsair.

Throughout the poem, the courage and determination of the islanders
is underscored, beginning with the heroic composure of the bishop
when he is kidnapped. This equanimity explains the poem's title. As Balboa clarifies in his introduction: "The patience with which this saintly
bishop endured his imprisonment moved me to write about it. This is
why I gave it the title it bears, obliged by his exemplary life, good deeds
and pure blood" (9). The simplicity of a language peppered with local
expressions, and the vivid description of the island's vegetation and
fauna, reveal the author's interest in highlighting the "Cuban" particu-
larity (cubanidad) already evident in this seventeenth-century colonial
society.[70] It is perhaps this need to underline a sense of communal unity
that leads the author to couple the Spanish whites with the "nationally"
heterogeneous blacks and aboriginal Indians, presenting them all as criollos. Gilberto Girón is, in fact, killed not by Ramos or any well-known
Spaniard but by a black slave suitably named Salvador, who in turn becomes a hero just like the rest of the Spaniards fighting the pirates.

What further unites the population of the island is their religiosity
in contrast to the arrogance, cruelty, and sacrilegious attitude of the
French pirates. Girón's actions are compared to those of a dangerous
wolf attacking a flock of innocent sheep (24). When the criollos confront
the pirates, Ramos reminds his men that they must give an exemplary
punishment to the pirates for mistreating their bishop and defying the
teachings of Christ and the Catholic Church. The islanders' triumph is a
triumph of religion, presented as a singular statement of "Cuban" unity,
because they do not look to Spain for help but are ready to take on their
own defense.

Inscribing Identities through Ambiguity:
Narrative Hybrids

In addition to epic poems dealing with the piratical attacks on the colonies, there are other texts—chronicles and narrative hybrids—that place

these attacks at the center of their accounts or, at the very least, include a number of references to them. The narrative hybrids are particularly interesting because of the ways their authors thread fiction and history together, creating a narrative form marked by a discursive "ambiguity."[21] Traditionally, literary history has classified Spanish American colonial texts according to a rigid format that reduced this ambiguity and, in turn, dismissed the existence in the Americas of certain genres during this period, such as the novel and the literary essay.[22] Recently, however, the traditional ways these different narrative forms have been categorized have been called into question.[23] Whether one can define certain hybrids as novels is still under discussion and is not pertinent to this analysis. As Walter Mignolo emphasizes, what is imperative is to avoid classifying these texts according to traditional notions of contemporary genres. Rather than forcing the texts to fit into any specific category, it is more appropriate simply to recognize their hybridity and underline their relation with other discursive forms characteristic of the time.[24]

Whatever their narrative strategy, the authors of these discursive hybrids claim that their accounts are "truthful," thereby appropriating for themselves one of the distinguishing traits of colonial historiographic discourse. *El Carnero,* for example, by the Santafereño Juan Rodríguez Freyle, illustrates this clearly.[25] Born in Santa Fe de Bogotá in 1566, Rodríguez Freyle, as a son of "the first conquerors and colonizers of the kingdom," feels very much a part of the history of his city. He studied there until 1585, when he left for Spain, where he joined the court in the employ of Alonso Pérez de Salazar. On his return to America, six years later, he took part in the pacification of the Pijaos and then began working as a farmer. He soon realized that this form of employment offered little recognition among his peers compared to that of a conquistador or colonizer. With this in mind, he set out to write *El Carnero* as a way of achieving respect among the colonials of his society.

Written between 1636 and 1638, this text, which has been classified in part as a picaresque novel,[26] reconstructs colonial life in the Nuevo Reino de Granada from the beginning of the conquest. Instead of focusing on the great events already recorded by other chroniclers (namely, Pedro Simón and Juan de Castellanos), Rodríguez Freyle prefers to fill in the gaps of the untold story of the Nuevo Reino—events he has "seen and heard." These moralizing *cuadros,* or sketches focusing on colonial life, intertwined with other well-known events, are the elements that separate his text from more traditional chronicles. However, in spite of the *cuadros*, the author claims that his *relación* is, albeit rough in style (*tosco*), "succinct and truthful, without the rhetorical embellishment that stories demand, nor does it have any poetical reasonings. Only the naked truth will be found in it" (6). Rodríguez Freyle's narrative presents the events concerning Nueva Granada in a more personal perspective and a less ornate style, though his main purpose is to record for posterity ("guardar memoria") those events and accentuate their moral significance. The reference to "el Corso" Drake in this text is minor and coincides with the author's stay in Spain. The portrait once again reflects Drake's astuteness in knowing how to vary his behavior depending on circumstances. Having found himself caught on a sandbar in San Lúcar de Barrameda, Spain, Drake quickly informs the authorities he has no interest in attacking the Spanish coast and would simply like some provisions for his men. The duke of Medina complies with his request, and Drake sails off after politely thanking the duke for his friendship. Drake's intelligence lies in knowing when to engage in a battle and when to rely on his eloquence to avoid it (308–9).

An earlier and more complex example of a narrative hybrid dealing with pirates is the *Peregrinación de Bartolomé Lorenzo*, written by the Jesuit chronicler José de Acosta in 1586.[27] A historian and naturalist, José de Acosta was born in Medina del Campo in 1540 and arrived at Hispaniola in 1572. A few months later, he left for Peru, where he carefully studied the climate, flora, and fauna as well as the customs of the indigenous civilizations. On his return to Spain, he published his well-known *Historia natural y moral de las Indias* in 1590. Concurrently, while conducting research, Acosta wrote the *Peregrinación* and sent it to his superiors in Rome.

Acosta's narrative recounts the biography of a Portuguese man, Bartolomé Lorenzo, and his journey from Hispaniola to Lima via Jamaica and Panama. Dedicated to Father Claudio Acquaviva, head of the Jesuit order in Peru, Acosta constructs his biography following the model of hagiographic discourse and offers his text as a testimony to the power and protection that true Catholic conviction bestows on its believers.[28] Bartolomé Lorenzo's life is exemplary. His adventurous journey through the Indies is transformed into a pilgrimage. Following the hagiographic model, Bartolomé Lorenzo flees from society. Learning to survive with the bare necessities, he begins a quest for perfection that takes him on a spiritual pilgrimage that guides him to the Jesuit order.[29] Reasserting the truthfulness of his report, Acosta states in his dedication: "Knowing the truth and simplicity of this Brother, I have no doubts, nor can anyone have doubts about the veracity of what I tell here" (30). By simply knowing Bartolomé, a simple and amicable person who is, moreover, a member of the Jesuit mission—as was Acosta himself—there can be no doubt as to the reliability of the account. The authority of the discourse relies no longer on the author's being the actual eyewitness of the events, but in his being able to assert the authenticity of his informant's account.[30] Acosta does this by becoming a scribe who "faithfully" relates what he has been told. The emphasis in this text is placed not on a great historical event but rather on a personal tale that nonetheless illustrates God's greatness.

Having been forced to leave his home to avoid a suspicious run-in with the authorities (though we are told Bartolomé "had no fault"), the young man is sent to the Indies by his father. In Cape Verde, where the ship stops to pick up a cargo of slaves, Bartolomé falls ill. Surprisingly, after two days on the edge of death, Bartolomé is cured and able to continue his trip. This illness, by taking possession of his body, is transformed into a rite of purification. It is a form of cleansing his soul before entering the New World and beginning a new life. More importantly, while preparing him for his future experiences, this purification erases all vestiges of doubtful conduct that may have been attributed to his previous life.

Once in the Indies, Bartolomé finds himself having to move from one island to another, forced out either by the arrival of pirates or by a hostile nature—earthquakes, fires, and a horrifyingly unusual vegetation. These difficulties will lead him on a mystical journey and attest to his exemplary life. The first encounter with adversity is in Hispaniola, just as he disembarks on the island. Bartolomé and the other crew members aboard the vessel are captured by French pirates. These "luteranos piratas" reproach the Portuguese for being "Papists" and beat them. As they are about to be killed, another French vessel appears, this time bringing pirates who are Catholic and consequently behave in a more humane fashion. In spite of the Lutherans' wish, the Portuguese are set free by the Catholic pirates. This differentiation between pirates based on their religious beliefs is at the heart of Acosta's worldview. The religious opposition between Catholics and Protestants has a strong moral connotation. No matter how ill-directed their lives may be, Catholics are inclined to save individuals whereas Protestants seem to take pleasure in killing. Hence, even pirates can be redeemable if they are Catholic.

Religion is the determining line between good and evil in this text, yet the *Peregrinación,* as other hybrid texts, does not articulate the confrontation of discourses (amazement and morality) in the same way as the epics. The central figure of the hybrid texts is no longer a dangerous enemy but rather a young individual who undergoes a series of adventures or a traumatic experience that leads to some form of awakening, either religious or personal. Furthermore, there is no particular pirate to be amazed at; instead there are numerous pirates, often without names, only nationalities or religions. Thus, the astonishment is not at any specific accomplishment a pirate might achieve. What takes preeminence is the fear provoked by their encounter and the courage, or astuteness, of the hero as he escapes from the pirates' treacherous hands—boldness and audacity now characterize the Spanish. The pirates become one of many antagonistic forces (diseases, hostile inhabitants, inhospitable vegetation and weather) the Spanish encounter in the New World. Placing the pirates within a general category of evil underscores the religious or personal endeavor of the hero to overcome adversity. In this way, elements of the opposing discourses are intertwined and reconfigured as these hybrid narratives begin to explore the religious and personal development of their young hero.

In the *Peregrinación,* the religious development is evident from the beginning. Bartolomé's life on the island is never easy. He falls ill a number of times and is constantly losing his way and running into danger. Yet he is always saved and able to find his way back by invoking God. Delivering him from all kinds of evil, God is his constant savior: "Lorenzo raised his eyes to his Creator and, trusting his mercy, prayed to be freed from danger" (41). In another instance, Lorenzo is facing a dangerous animal and, "turning to Our Lord, said in his heart: 'Dear Lord, if I am to be eaten by this beast, let it be Your will, who am I to resist Your orders?'" (52).

When Bartolomé is not fleeing from French pirates, he is struggling through enormous marshes, "rocky boulders," or swarms of vicious mosquitoes "that mercilessly bite until making the person ill." In the *Peregrinación,* nature is untamed, often described as resembling Dante's *selva selvaggia,* while offering at the same time fantastic fruits and vegetables.[31] Bartolomé is able to survive because he learns to deal with the island's vegetation and accepts it, even if that means living at times in a cave with only a bit of corn to eat, or sleeping under a tree in the wilderness. This teaches him to face adversity with stoicism and transforms his adventures into a spiritual pilgrimage.[32]

The religious allegory in Acosta's narrative ends with a twist. Stressing the differences between religious orders, the monolithic image of the Church breaks down. After his great ordeal wandering through the islands, fleeing from pirates, and living in solitude in the most inhospitable places, Bartolomé Lorenzo is invited to serve with the Augustinian order. He declines the offer. Yet, once in Lima, after undergoing penance and abstinence, Bartolomé feels that he must change his way of life:

> Siempre le parecía que aquel modo de vivir que tenía de presente no era el que le convenía para servir a Nuestro Señor con el agradecimiento que debía a las grandes misericordias que de su poderosa mano había recibido, y los grandes trabajos y peligros de que le había librado. (65)

> [He always thought his current way of life was not best suited to serve our Lord. Neither was it suited to give thanks for the great compassion he had received from his hand nor for the great trials and tribulations from which he had been delivered.]

Having made the decision to change his way of life, Bartolomé arrives at a Jesuit mission. He is impressed with the members' conduct and the way everyone is treated, regardless of their origins. He decides to stay and join their order.

> El no sabía qué religión era la Compañía de Jesús, ni tenía noticia de ella; pero miró mucho a aquellos Padres, y pareciéndole bien y; especialmente notó su mucha caridad en no negarse a nadie, por bajas que fuesen las personas, y que con todos trataban de su salvación. Y también le agradó mucho que a sus solas en la posada guardaban grande recogimiento, y el ver que traían hábito común de clérigos le tiró la inclinación, porque siempre se le había hecho de mal ponerse capilla. (66)

[He did not know what religion the Jesuits belonged to, nor did he know much about them; but he especially watched those fathers and he was satisfied; and he especially found them very charitable, giving of themselves to everyone, however lowborn they might be, and trying to save everyone. He also liked that they spent time alone in their cells, and that they wore a common friar's habit. This particularly inclined him to join the order, since he had always hated wearing a hood.]

By presenting Bartolomé's decision as the result of his pure and sincere feelings, rather than of any prejudiced indoctrination, Acosta's narrative not only sheds light on the power of his religious faith but also constitutes a staunch defense of the Jesuit order. The rationale behind this ending becomes comprehensible if one looks at the religious and political circumstances at the time Acosta wrote the *Peregrinación*.

From the moment the Spanish arrived in the New World, the Church secured Spain's dominance by imposing its presence and culture, particularly through friars. Dressed in patched homespun, these men set out on their missionary work, crossing vast territories to convert Indians to the Christian faith and to offer spiritual guidance to the colonizers. The first Franciscans reached Santo Domingo before 1500; the Dominicans arrived in 1510; other orders soon followed. Owing to their success, these missionaries became so indispensable that in 1521 Pope Adrian VI awarded the Franciscans extraordinary powers as parish priests in the Indies, allowing them to perform as secular clergy.[33] To further encourage the friars' relocation, the Crown—empowered by the *patronato* of the Indies—provided for them until their orders were able to establish a community of their own and helped with certain provisions such as wine, candles, and oil, in addition to funding the construction of their monasteries.[34]

As more missionaries arrived, they began spreading out among the population, teaching and preaching the Catholic faith, uprooting the old gods, constructing schools and missions, and baptizing thousands of Indians. The missionaries' influence quickly extended to the educational and social activities of colonial society, and they became an extremely powerful group. It was then that many friars lost their humility and monastic simplicity and relaxed their discipline in the luxury of their monasteries.

During the colonial period, it was common to find biographies and hagiographies written by the members of different orders geared toward establishing their history as well as to highlighting their importance. This explains Father Acosta's dedication to Claudio Acquaviva, the general of the Jesuit order, who was responsible for organizing several missionary projects and increasing the number of members significantly.[35] Written forty-six years after the official foundation of the Society of Jesus, the *Peregrinación de Bartolomé de Lorenzo* is clearly a text intended to be used for publicizing the order and promoting the moral precepts that distinguished the Jesuits.

Another colonial hybrid dealing with pirates that is presented as a life story is *Infortunios de Alonso Ramírez,* by the celebrated author Carlos Sigüenza y Góngora.[36] Born in Mexico City, Sigüenza y Góngora (1645–1700) was a Jesuit who later abandoned the order. Excelling in a number of areas, he was a well-known mathematician who taught at the University of Mexico, historian, poet, antiquarian, and chronicler of the court of the viceroy. He was royal cosmographer to the king and was often consulted for engineering and scientific problems. In addition to his scientific research, he also studied indigenous languages and pre-Columbian societies, though his work in this field has been lost. A friend of Sor Juana Inés de la Cruz, he was considered one of the most illustrious men of colonial Mexico.

Infortunios is a fictionalized autobiography told by a young boy from Puerto Rico, Alonso Ramírez, who describes his adventures in Mexico, his captivity among English and Dutch pirates in the Philippines, and his eventual freedom and safe return. The interplay of different textual levels makes *Infortunios* a particularly interesting narrative. Having completed his account, Alonso explains to the readers that he was instructed by the viceroy Gaspar de Sandoval, Cerda, Silva y Mendoza, Conde de Galve, to visit Sigüenza y Góngora, cosmographer and mathematics professor, who is in fact the person responsible for transcribing his story. Alonso's oral account is thus transformed into a *relación.* Hence it is only at the end, when the first-person narrator steps out of the text to bring in the scribe, that readers discover the play between the telling and the writing of *Infortunios.*[37]

The telling of the story itself is also twofold. In Sigüenza y Góngora's dedication to the viceroy, he presents his *relación* with the intention of helping Alonso and states that "the doors of Your Majesty's palace are never closed to the needy." The purpose of the narrative becomes explicit: to obtain recognition for Alonso's sufferings. But it is also a text that does the same for Sigüenza y Góngora, whose titles at that point were, as he states, "worth very little." According to Alonso, he is ordered to tell his story to Sigüenza y Góngora either because of the affection the viceroy had for him or perhaps because Sigüenza y Góngora was sick and Alonso would distract him with the tale of his misfortunes:

> Mandóme (ó por el afecto con que lo mira o quizá porque estando enfermo divertiese sus males con la noticia que yo le daría de los muchos míos) fuese á visitar á Don Sigüenza y Góngora, cosmógrafo y catedrático de matemáticas del Rey. . . . Compadecido de mis trabajos, no solo formó esta Relación en que se contienen, sino que me consiguió con la intercesión y súplicas que en mi presencia hizo al Excmo. Sr. Virrey, Decreto para que D. Sebastián de Guzmán y Córdoba, factor veedor y proveedor de las cajas reales me socorriese, como se hizo. (130–31)

> [[Mendoza] sent me to visit Don Sigüenza y Góngora, royal cosmographer and professor of mathematics (either because he appreciated him or perhaps because Sigüenza y Góngora was ill and Mendoza thought I would entertain him with the tale of my many misfortunes). . . . Taken by my travails, he wrote this *relación,* which tells everything. Furthermore, he obtained through mediation and pleading to his excellency Mr. Viceroy, a decree so that Sebastián de Guzmán y Córdoba, tax collector and provider of the royal treasury, would help me, as he did.]

Sigüenza y Góngora was successful in his quest, for Alonso informs us that he did receive help. Thus the future and the past of the narrative are contained within the text. The time of the telling and that of the writing fold into each other, as one mirrors the other.

Sigüenza y Góngora was well acquainted with Acosta's *Peregrinación;* he possessed the well-known collection of the "Biblioteca de hombres ilustres" that included Acosta's text. Furthermore, despite the chronological differences, there are important similarities between Acosta's and Sigüenza y Góngora's texts. Besides relating someone else's story, the two authors conceive their texts with a specific, although different purpose: Acosta aims to praise the Jesuit order; Sigüenza y Góngora seeks to obtain recognition for Alonso as well as for himself, even though Alonso makes clear that his own purpose is to entertain audiences and seek compassion from them.[38] So the doubling of discourses is justified as a means of obtaining legitimacy for one's actions or sufferings. Finally, although *Infortunios* is defined as a *relación,* in his dedication, Sigüenza y Góngora declares it a pitiful pilgrimage, "una peregrinación lastimosa."

Alonso's adventures begin at the age of thirteen when, fleeing from poverty, he abandons his homeland in search of a better life. This beginning and his roaming from job to job without much luck is one of the characteristics connecting *Infortunios* to the picaresque novel.[39] With each failure, Alonso quickly loses his innocence, but only when he sets sail on a galleon heading for the Philippines and his adventures become more dangerous does he really understand what survival is all about and the importance of having a spiritual guide.

The pirates involved in Alonso's circular voyage—from Mexico, to the Philippines, to India, and finally back to Mexico—are relatively unknown: Captains Donkin and Bel, and quartermaster Dick are the only ones mentioned. Although their central activity is contraband, we see them brutally pillaging towns and committing outrageous acts. In one instance, the young narrator remembers how the pirates returned from a raid with a human arm, which they kept munching on, praising their delicious meat (58). The pirates' cannibalistic attribute reinforces their position as the dangerous "others" while evoking one of the main reasons the Spanish used in justifying the need to conquer the "uncivilized" indigenous populations. Cannibalism confirmed savagery. The relation between piracy, heresy, and barbarism is stressed once again.

Having lived with them for some time, Alonso learns to deal with the pirates. In his own way, he discovers how to manipulate them, pretending at times to be courageous and, at other times, to be a coward. Fearing to be left among "the barbarism of the black Moors," Alonso pleads with one group of pirates to let him continue aboard. However, because he does not want to become one of them, he cleverly takes advantage of their stereotyped vision of the Spanish to keep himself at a distance:

> Les respondí con afectada humildad el que más me acomodaba á servirlos á ellos que á pelear con otros, por ser grande el temor que les tenía a las balas, tratándome de español cobarde y gallina, y por eso indigno de

estar en su compañía, que me honrara y valiera mucho, no me instaron más. (70)

[I told them with affected humbleness that I much preferred serving them to fighting against the others, as I was very much afraid of the bullets, a cowardly Spanish and a chicken, and unworthy to be among their company, which I truly honored and valued. They did not insist.]

Although religion is still the structuring force, Sigüenza y Góngora's narrative moves away from fixity and absolutes. In fact, his writing is emblematic of the struggle of forces that characterizes the baroque of the Indies.[40] Hence, *Infortunios* can also be read as a quest for identity, a Creole identity, caught between the imperial values of Spain and the abyss of appropriating one's own space. By articulating the relativity of events through perception, the narrative calls into question the categorical imperatives society has imposed. Good and bad actions have become relativized. Not only is the point of view of the narrator alluded to in the text, but the reader's perception is also explicitly addressed. Although Alonso has no qualms in using any type of trick to protect himself, he is concerned about what the readers might think. Thus he defends his unorthodox behavior by bringing in the readers and forcing them to share the particular circumstances of his situation: "Put yourselves in my place to understand how great was my fear and the distress I was in" (75). Alonso needs his audience/readers to share his outlook, to understand his point of view, so that his actions may be accepted.

Ultimately, Alonso's actions will be legitimized by opposition to those of the pirates. They have no moral values. Cruel heretics, they are moved by greed; interested in obtaining a good loot, they will even attack innocent civilians. We see them drunk, beating their prisoners, pillaging towns, and killing traitors. They seem determined to inflict harm on all the Spaniards they encounter. Yet Alonso recognizes that some pirates can be human, because they eventually let him go free and give him a boat to fend for himself.[41] Alonso's success is amazing. From the young and innocent boy who first sets out, he has matured and become the captain of his own boat, respected for his knowledge of the waters he sails and his consideration toward others. As Alonso makes it back home on his own and takes control of his life, he begins exteriorizing his religiosity, praying to God and the Virgen of Guadalupe, without whom "my freedom would have been impossible" (77).

In the end, Alonso has his audience believe that it is the Spaniards' spirituality that places them above the heretical pirates, that his religious devotion saved him. This underlying message—that true Catholics can overcome all—transforms Alonso's adventures into a *relación* that the well-known author Sigüenza y Góngora considers worthy of being transcribed.[42]

The presence of pirates in these colonial texts illustrates the cruelty and violence that heretics were known to commit and also exemplifies the dangers facing all those who do not embrace the Catholic faith. Furthermore, these texts prove that the only individuals capable of surviving an encounter or confrontation with pirates are those who have firm religious convictions. This explains why when faced with pirates, those individuals who perhaps did not seem to have such strong religious convictions quickly begin to assert their Catholic faith. Thus for the Spanish, piracy does not only represent heresy; it also exemplifies the need to be a true Catholic to survive in colonial Spanish America.

This last point is illustrated in an extremely complex and baroque colonial text entitled *El desierto prodigioso y prodigio del desierto,* by a clergyman from Nueva Granada, Pedro de Solís y Valenzuela.[43] Solís y Valenzuela (1624–1711) was born in Santa Fe de Bogotá, where he studied in the San Bartolomé Seminary. Among his responsibilities as a priest, he had to collect payments for the Church, a task that embroiled him in a number of lawsuits, since many people were either late or poor and could not pay. He was also a member of the Inquisition tribunals. In addition to *El desierto* and a few texts that have been lost, his literary works include *Epítome breve de la vida y muerte del ilustríssimo doctor Bernardino de Almansa* (1646), *Panegírico sagrado, en alabanza del serafín de las soledades, San Bruno* (1646), and *La Fénix cartuxana: Vida del gloriossísimo Patriarca San Bruno* (1647).

El desierto is a world full of labyrinths, doubles, and disguises in which structural elements pertaining to the pastoral novel, hagiographies, meditations, poems, bucolic narratives, and fantastic tales, among other genres, are mixed together. It is also in part the life story of the hermit Arsenio as told to a group of passersby.[44] Among the many experiences he recounts is a short but frightening encounter with Dutch pirates.

In this episode, the narrator is traveling on a Spanish vessel with his cousin Don Vicente and his friend Ascanio when their ship is overtaken by Dutch pirates. Although the Spanish are outnumbered, they put up a good fight, causing the Dutch heavy losses. But the toll for the Spanish is also considerable: many die. Arsenio is wounded, and his cousin Vicente is killed. As soon as the Dutch take control of the ship, they throw all the dead overboard, "stripping them with the most impious cruelty" (206), and begin killing those who are left alive. Inexplicably, instead of killing Arsenio, who was severely wounded, the pirates show pity and cure him. They also spare the life of his friend Ascanio. Despite their pain and fear, Arsenio and Ascanio do not die. The need to make sense of this remarkable act that saved their lives forces Ascanio to turn to religion, for only a true miracle could explain the pirates' decision. It is then that Arsenio repents from all his past mistakes and finds solace in God: "These tribulations have this virtue: they make man turn to God. In the midst of so many difficulties, this was my only port of consolation" (207). Arsenio has another mystifying moment when the pirates have pity and free him and Ascanio, abandoning them along the coast.

Throughout these colonial texts, whether epic poems, chronicles, or other narrative forms, it is religion that draws the most distinct dividing line between good and evil and determines the place of the "other." The purpose of these texts is not just to tell a story of captivity or relate the pirates' assaults on Spanish territories. The narrators want to persuade, *persuadir*, their readers of the superiority and importance of the Catholic faith and shed light on the dangers represented by all those "others," heretics and foreigners, assailing the Spanish empire. Religion is what truly transforms the enemy into a foreigner. Religion transcends national divisions, as Acosta's *Peregrinación* shows, distinguishing the French Catholic pirates, who prove to be noble individuals, from their cruel and despotic Lutheran compatriots.

The importance assigned to religion in these texts echoes the tenacity with which the Catholic faith was propagated throughout Spanish territories during the colonial period. Furthermore, as most of these texts were written by religious men, it is not surprising to find religion at the center of their reconstruction. Consequently, even those authors who voiced their amazement at the cleverness exerted by certain pirates —namely, Francis Drake—never ceased to consider him a dangerous heretic. Thus, the discourse of amazement is systematically overshadowed by that of morality. Pirates are barbaric and commit ungodly crimes because they are Lutherans, Protestant heretics. As such, they must be expelled from Spanish America. The pirates' crimes, in essence, played right into Spanish doctrine. They exemplified the danger that if uncontested, these "others" would bring to the Spanish empire and its subjects. The only way to confront this foreign menace was through the power of the Church. Yet it is important to underscore the awe Spanish colonials often felt when reconstructing the pirates' attacks, for it is the tension between the sinfulness of their actions and their extraordinary achievements that will give way to the multifaceted portrayal of the pirate after independence.

The nineteenth-century texts reconstructing the piratical attacks that took place during the colonial period also situate religion at the center of their narratives. The place and role of the Church in these works, however, is seriously questioned by many of these later authors. These narratives also use the piratical attacks to "persuade" and exemplify the role played by Spain during the colonial period; but unlike writings of the sixteenth to eighteenth centuries, there will be no consensus as to what that role was or how it should be interpreted. Writers will have the freedom to construct their own traitors and heroes. As nineteenth-century writers in Spanish America looked back on their past, they sought to understand and define their identity through the lingering fragments of the crumbled empire. Because these writers could no longer look at Spain to impose a homogenous world order, their interpretations of that past would multiply, each struggling to impose its voice over the other.

CHAPTER THREE

Defining National Identities through Piracy

Come liberi volano i venti
Per le immense pianure dei mari,
Così corron gli arditi corsari
Pugna e preda sull'onde a cercar.
Patria e regno n'è il fiotto spumante,
Nostro scettro la rossa bandiera:
Noi sappiamo con anima altera
I perigli, la morte affrontar.
—Giuseppe Verdi, *Il Corsaro*

In contrast with the portrayal of the pirate presented during the colonial period in Spanish America—a dangerous heretic who plundered the seas, envious of Spain's riches in the New World—the nineteenth century offered a much more complex and diverse image. Whereas colonial writers depicted the pirate for the most part as a dangerous national enemy, nineteenth-century authors reconstructing their colonial past provided conflicting images of the pirate that ranged from evil and unscrupulous to chivalrous and heroic. These contrasting images present in the literary production of postindependence echo the impassioned debate that marked the process of nation building throughout most of the century in Spanish America.

Independence in Spanish America owed more to the political collapse of the Spanish monarchy and the Napoleonic invasions than to national sentiment throughout the continent. The new republics that emerged were distinctly shaped by the arbitrary limits Spain had imposed on its newly acquired colonies. The Crown erased all pre-Columbian boundaries and replaced them with divisions that facilitated its economic, political, religious, and cultural control over its colonies; these large units were the viceroyalties out of which the independent nations would later be carved.[1] They depended completely on the Crown, which appointed all officials: from the viceroys representing the king, to the archbishops and bishops representing the Church, to the judges of the Royal Court who legislated throughout the continent. Throughout most of the colonial era, the Crown did not permit *criollos* to occupy the highest posts; those positions were reserved for *peninsulares.* Hence independence in Spanish America meant more than anything freedom of choice and expression for the *criollos,* and a staunch rejection of Spain's centralism. Lacking experience in self-rule, the independent nations also had to face the enormous differences that distinguished them: vast distances, geographic confines (jungles, cordilleras, deserts), diverse populations, and disparate economies. It was only after independence was attained that the new Spanish American countries began defining their national project. Only then did Spanish Americans look within their boundaries and begin to establish their own separate identity, a slow and at times violent process that would end with the consolidation of the state in the latter part of the century.

Political emancipation in Spanish America ended Spain's trade monopoly and unlocked direct commercial ties with the industrial powers of northern Europe. England was able to establish trade with the new republics before the rest of continental Europe. Her support became essential for the fragile new governments, and this in turn allowed England quickly to dominate the Spanish American market.[2] British and later continental European commercial penetration not only had important economic consequences in the new republics but had social and political ones as well. As the importation of industrial goods increased, consumption patterns changed significantly. Fashion, furniture, and other features identified with modernization altered everyday life. In some countries, the new value system inevitably led to the displacement of a number of traditional institutions, among which the Catholic Church was the most important. Having played a crucial role during the colonial period, the Church was not inclined to accept the numerous restrictions the new republics tried to impose on its power, or to allow the

Protestant ethics of individualism and private enterprise to displace its own. The Church's rejection of "heretical" values and the strong loyalty toward religious traditions among the population had serious political consequences. The problem in Spanish America soon became deciding to what extent the precepts and values of European countries (primarily England and subsequently France) that were identified as the emblem of "progress" could be transplanted to the Americas. This was the critical debate that divided most nations. Within the governing elites there was no consensus. Were Spanish Americans to be governed by a monarchy or a republic? Was slavery to be abolished? Was there to be one unified and centralized government, or were the provinces to be allowed a certain autonomy? What should the role of the Roman Catholic Church be in the new society, and what would relations with the Vatican be? What should the role of education be? These questions highlighted the imperative need to consolidate a representative form of government and establish a specific political program.

Although the issues in question were articulated differently in each country, the debate, which was sustained between clericalists and liberals, centralists (*unitarios*) and federalists, *radicales* and conservatives, dominated much of the nineteenth century and affected all the former colonies.[3] In general terms, two main ideological positions encompassed all others: the *conservadores* (conservatives) and the *liberales* (liberals). For the latter, becoming part of the free and modern world meant rejecting everything associated with Spain, which was seen as representing dependency and backwardness. The *conservadores*, on the other hand, felt that the cultural heritage Spain had left behind could not be denied and was in fact an essential part of their identity. Fearing the Europeanization propelled by the liberal elite, many conservative intellectuals spoke strongly against Protestant ethics and claimed that loyalty to their religious tradition was not incompatible with progress.[4] These tensions ignited a period of severe turmoil, governed by what Leopoldo Zea termed a "philosophy of disruption" during which everything was subject to debate: from the formal organization of the political institutions to the use of the Spanish language itself.[5]

The literary production during postindependence responded to this need of creating a sense of national identity and recovering Spanish America's cultural heritage. Political projects embedded within the texts were often the force articulating the fictional plots. In this sense, literature acquired a "guiding" undertone as it reflected the plottings of different political projects battling each other.[6] At a time when national identities were being delineated and national projects were emerging in Spanish America, piracy—as an act of appropriation, usurpation, robbery—ceased to be viewed exclusively as an ignoble act performed by foreigners; it also became a form of heroism. This shift in the fictional portrayal of the pirate reflects the absence of a hegemonic discourse capable of defining the nations' identity and of controlling the official imaginings that help secure a collective national consciousness. Thus the pirate becomes a "social signifier," an icon embodying both enemies and heroes battling the wars of national identity.[7]

No longer identified exclusively with the English, French, or Dutch, pirates were also portrayed as Spaniards and even as Americans.[8] Cruelty, once pirates' distinguishing trait, ceased to be their unique feature. In many instances, in fact, their cruelty was even justified. In addition to their traditional image of wretched thieves, pirates were also cast as good, honest human beings who were either victims of an unjust colonial system or defiant advocates of true independence and freedom. Once Spain had ceased to hold control over the American continent, the identity of the pirate was determined no longer by Spain, but rather by the new Spanish American countries. Depending on the author's ideological position and the political project endorsed, piracy was portrayed as a liberating force or a dangerous foreign menace. Consequently, the numerous identities assigned to the pirates who besieged the colonies can be read as a reflection of the way Spanish Americans looked at themselves during the nineteenth century and how the reconstruction of their colonial past was used to consolidate a specific national identity.

Extending the Boundaries to England: Vicente Fidel López

The impact of these political confrontations varied enormously throughout the continent. The southern cone, particularly Argentina's *generación del '37*, is perhaps one of the best expressions of the liberal ideology. Domingo Faustino Sarmiento, Juan Bautista Alberdi, José Mármol, and

Esteban Echeverría are a few of these important figures who sought to appropriate European models in the name of "progress."[9] In his well-known work *Facundo: Civilization and Barbarism,* Sarmiento set forth the basic ideology of the elite.[10] The opposition he established between civilization and barbarism subsumed the conflict between culture and ignorance, freedom and despotism, and became for Argentine liberals the normative difference that divided the world.[11] Recounting the life and death of the caudillo Facundo Quiroga, Sarmiento exposes "the evil from which the Argentine Republic suffers": the vast unpopulated land, surrounded by dangerous savages who "fall like packs of hyenas" on plantations and dispersed settlements, uprooting any civilizing project (2). Dominant culture, during postindependence, was deeply rooted in the landscape, hence the confrontations were often articulated between "the emblem of civilization," the city, molded after Europe, and the barbaric, uncontrollable wilderness. Intertwining biography, history, fiction, and a clear political agenda, Sarmiento sets out to civilize his country's demographic and discursive emptiness. Writing was a means of overcoming the internal fragmentation of Argentina, a way of ordering the American "barbarism" that governed the surrounding wilderness. As Julio Ramos has underlined, for Sarmiento, writing was one of the most important civilizing forces.[12]

Argentina needed to be inhabited and industrialized, and according to liberal politicians and statesmen, the only viable model was Northern Europe. It is precisely for this reason that the spatial configurations of this generation became so powerful and infused their writings. The image of progress was embodied in the city. From within the walls and protection of the urban space, Argentine liberals felt empowered to moralize the country that they imagined, and they used literature to begin outlining the national grid they were convinced would overcome the barbarism reigning over their surrounding pampas. Europe represented civilization, and if Argentina and Spanish America were ever to become part of the free and modern world, they would have to be reshaped in accordance with the principles of progress exemplified by Northern Europe.

To eradicate the native barbarism undermining modernization, Sarmiento strongly encouraged immigration (preferably English and French) and underlined the importance of attracting foreign investors.

Order and stability had to be guaranteed to ensure those activities that in turn would bring wealth and greatness to the Argentine nation. Despite Sarmiento's convictions that Spanish America had to be reshaped following foreign models, he also recognized the difficulties of simply transferring the European model to America. Thus he advocated the importance of first understanding (listening to) that "other" part of America to know how to ensure order and modernization. *Facundo* is the illustration of the dangers of that "other," uncivilized Argentina.

Vicente Fidel López, a prominent historian and member of the *generación del '37*, clearly endorses the liberal dogma in his historical novel *La novia del hereje o la Inquisición de Lima (The Heretic's Sweetheart, or the Inquisition of Lima)*.[13] As the son of Vicente López y Planes, author of the Argentine national anthem, López belonged to one of the most well-known families closely identified with the birth and history of Argentina as an independent republic. Like Sarmiento, López also led an extremely public life, always involved in the debates concerning his country, whether literary or political. His essays are varied, ranging from philology, classicism, and romanticism to history and economy. In addition to editing a number of newspapers and writing several comprehensive histories of Chile and Argentina, his works include legislative speeches, translations, constitutional projects, and teaching manuals.[14]

In the prologue to his novel, López stated that his main objective was to retrieve the spirit of the family and the customs of the past. He considered it a truly "American" project, for he sought the understanding of a society of which he, as an American, was part. His novel focuses on the confrontations between the Spanish colonies and England, specifically on the attack Sir Francis Drake made on Lima in 1578. The novel is a love story in the best of romantic tradition. María, born in Lima of Spanish parents, is the beautiful heroine who falls in love with the "virtuous" British hero, Robert Henderson, Drake's right-hand man. They meet for the first time on the high seas, when Drake and his crew ransack the *San Juan de Orton* (better known as the *Caçafuego* or *Cagafuego*), a Spanish vessel transporting riches to Spain. Felipe Pérez y Gonzalvo, María's proud and heartless father, is in charge of the Spanish ship. Accompanying him are his wife and daughter; *la zamba* Juana, María's servant; and Antonio Romea, the man Don Felipe has chosen as his daughter's husband. While the gold is transferred to the English vessel,

Caca Fogo.

Caca Plata.

"The Capture of the *Cacafuego*," in *Sechte Theil, Kurtze, Warhafftige Relation und Beschreibund der Wunderbarsten Vier Schiffarten so jemals verricht worden als nemlich: Ferdinandi Magellani Portugalesers mit Sebastiano de Cano. Francisci Draconis Engeländers. Tomae Candisch Engeländers. Olivarij von Noort, Niderländers . . . durch Levinum Hulsium,* by Levinus Hulsius (Noribergae: Impensis Collectoris, 1603). *Courtesy of the Beinecke Rare Book and Manuscript Library, Yale University.*

the Spaniards are held hostages; it is then that María and Henderson fall in love. Although pirates, Drake and his men treat their prisoners with respect and deference. Having confiscated the gold, Drake allows the crew to depart for Lima unharmed. On their return, Antonio Romea, enraged at what has happened between his fiancée and the British pirate, denounces María for having fallen in love with a "heretic" and maliciously sets out to destroy María's father's wealth and social status. María is imprisoned until Henderson is able to rescue her and carry her off to England, where, in spite of Romea's revengeful ploys, they will live happily ever after.

The representation of an English pirate as a gentleman who saves the *criolla* heroine does not correspond to the traditional colonial perception of piracy. Although López claims to write an American project, he substitutes the American heroes one would have expected to encounter with British pirates. This displacement of heroes, and consequently of nations the heroes represent, is reinforced by the final dialogue between Mateo, a servant, and his former master, whom Mateo meets by chance in London. Mateo complains about his inability to adapt and feel at home in an English-speaking country. "What wouldn't I give up to live with my lord, his wife and children, in a land where Spanish is spoken like I am now speaking with my lordship?" he laments (702). Moved, Don Manuel invites his former servant to accompany him back to Spain and work for him. At first Mateo is overjoyed, but he soon becomes somber. Realizing that the Inquisition is still present and strong in Spain, he declines the offer, stating, "Ah! pues entonces, no, amito! Prefiero quedarme entre estos *bozales*!" [Oh no, my lord! Then I prefer to remain within these *muzzles*] (419). The play of meanings in the word *bozales* is interesting. On the one hand, *bozal* is a muzzle, but it also refers to newly enslaved blacks (freshwater slaves). Hence, when Mateo claims that he prefers to stay among these *bozales,* he is not only referring to the fact that he cannot speak the language and therefore feels gagged, but also expressing his situation as a mulatto, which is that of a black and slave in a foreign "free" country, where he is nonetheless still bound.

Despite his yearning, Mateo, a mere servant, is capable of recognizing the importance of living in a "civilized" country, one that López has stressed has no Inquisition, the emblem of Spanish power (in Protestant countries). Mateo thus turns down Don Manuel's offer, preferring to stay in England. By rejecting the Spanish language and religion,

López implicitly erases Spain from the future American project the novel endorses; a manifest expression of the Argentine liberal dogma. Along with the exclusion of Spain, however, an essential part of Spanish American identity and cultural heritage has been obliterated.

The need to define one's identity by establishing specific alliances with others reflects the subject's own instability and the lack of a hegemonic discourse in which that subject may be inserted. The alliance with the "other" offers an established order capable of dissipating internal conflicts and tensions. As a result of the civil wars flooding Spanish America during postindependence and the inability to resolve the political tensions from within, a longing for stability was compelling. Thus, economic and political order was sought from outside with the hope of providing the necessary stability to ensure economic prosperity and secure the well-being of the population.

In his novel, López advocates the English model as he shifts the setting entirely from Spanish America to England, where the final scenes take place. We discover not only that María has been able to form a home in England, but more importantly that it is a democratic one, where politeness, respect, and love rule, clashing noticeably with the oppressive authority that had governed her Spanish home. As the narrator goes on to argue, the English home is the ideal in more ways than one:

> En una de esas bellas casas de campo que los ingleses llaman *country-mansion,* y a las que sólo ellos saben dar ese aire de grandeza, ese brillo del orden, ese aspecto risueño, rico y tranquilo a la vez, que une de un modo particular lo más exquisito del arte con lo más vivo de la naturaleza, se levantaba un hermoso caserío rodeado de rejas, de alamedas más allá de las rejas, y de prados más allá de las alamedas; todo respiraba allí el orden, la riqueza y la cultura. (410)

> [Within a beautiful set of houses surrounded by gates with tree-lined boulevards, and fields beyond the boulevards, lay a country house that the English call *country-mansion.* Only the English know how to bestow that air of greatness, that glitter of order, both rich and calm, pleasantly blending the most exquisite art with nature's vibrancy. Everything exuded order, richness, and culture.]

The parallelism established between the home and the nation is present throughout the novel, but only in the English home can a sense of well-being and prosperity be found. This "happy" ending, which takes place outside the geographic boundaries of Spanish America, reflects the need for the continent to reshape itself following the English model. Order, wealth, and culture were the hallmarks of progress represented by England. Without order, a key element in nineteenth-century modernity, only barbarism and chaos can be found, as Sarmiento incessantly repeated. Wealth is merely the direct result of a well-administered household/nation. Hence, if Spanish America is to become a modern continent, it inevitably has to transform itself into England's image. This process, as López emphasizes, has to begin in the home. These liberal convictions are at the core of López's patriotic act: the mapping of a national identity that can come into being only outside its own territory. An act that, far from reconstructing the colonial past, advocates the recolonization of Spanish America's future.

The scene between Mateo and Don Manuel reveals one of the central issues that marked the debate of nation building in Spanish America: the importance of establishing boundaries and alliances. In trying to forge a national identity, the need to set limits becomes a determining factor, whether these limits are based on language, geographic territory, or a political enterprise.[15] The difficulty Spanish American countries faced was the coexistence of two distinct and opposing models, which ultimately fragmented the nations and obliterated the possibility of looking within the national boundaries to focus on each country's distinctiveness.

In his insightful and now often cited book *Imagined Communities: Reflections on the Origin and Spread of Nationalism*, Benedict Anderson discusses the idea of the nation as an *imagined* political community. The nation is imagined because "the members of even the smallest nation will never know most of their fellow-members, meet them, or even hear of them, yet in the minds of each lives the image of their communion" (7). This definition takes into account the emotional aspect of nation building, for a nation will exist only when its members can feel, "imagine," themselves united. Creating a sense of community is crucial: it is precisely this element that will bond together the different members while giving them a common identity that in turn will define their nation. In other words, communities will be distinguished "not by their falsity/genuineness, but by the style in which they are imagined" (6).

According to Anderson, one of the necessary conditions for creating the basis of the imagined national community is the consolidation of vernacular languages through print culture (notably the novel and the newspaper). But rather than drawing inward and reflecting on the unique elements that determined their political community separate from others, writers in Spanish America used print culture to define their country's identity by relating to, and aligning themselves with, the outside world (mainly Spain or England). In *La novia del hereje*, López constructed his imaginary community by associating it with England in the same way other authors regarded Spain as the founding nation and model for America's identity. Hence, throughout the process of nation building, one of the most important elements in Spanish America remained unresolved: setting limits.

The difficulty Spanish American nations had in establishing their own boundaries during this period is not surprising given the process of formation of the new republics. Boundaries are the specific features that unite the members of a community and allow them to define their own identity; they are crucial in developing a national consciousness.[16] As each community promotes a particular organization of the world in accordance to its national ideal, the place of the foreigner, the one who does not belong, is delimited. But with alliances constantly shifting during the second half of the century, the place of the other is also constantly redefined. In fact, at times it was precisely the foreigner who was sought to impart a particular identity to the country, as Sarmiento and Alberdi strongly advocated. Thus, even those born in Spanish America could become foreigners in their own country.

Throughout the process of national consolidation, the horizon in which the national subject is inserted and recognized as a member of a specific sociological landscape must be fixed. Nineteenth-century historical novelists who reconstruct the colony focusing on a specific piratical event place the national identity of the pirate at the center of the conflict. These authors use existing national models (the English and the Spanish) to discuss their own future national project and fix the limits of their nation. There is no longer a single undisputed adversary as there had been during Spain's colonial domination. In the nineteenth century, it is the author's contemporary imaginings of his or her nation that will determine what nations or political projects are considered allies or beneficial and how far their national boundaries should extend.

In *La novia del hereje*, the pirates are initially presented as dangerous foreign trespassers capable of inordinately cruel actions. But unlike their sixteenth- and seventeenth-century counterparts, being a foreigner will in fact make the pirates worthy individuals. López initially presents the English as heretics only to reveal the stupidity of such a portrayal, endorsed by the Spanish. His purpose is to expose those individuals who accept Spain's long held claim that pirates are "sons of the devil" and "heretics" as ignorant and separate them from those individuals who do not. In so doing, López separates right from wrong, truth from fallacy, and projects his own construction of piracy and enemies.

María articulates the Spanish view according to López as she tells her servant what she imagines an encounter with these ferocious "heretics" might be like:

> ¡yo me moriría si tuviese que verlos! ¿De qué andarán vestidos, eh? ¡Qué cosa tan horrible serán! y dicen que no hablan; que son como los animales, que sólo entre ellos se entienden, y que se comen a la gente. (45)

> [I would die if I had to see them! How might they be dressed, huh? What a terrible sight! I have heard they don't speak; that they're like animals, they only understand themselves and eat people.]

Being monstrous cannibals and lacking language—the first sign of civilization—places pirates among the dangerous "others" of the unknown. This construction of the pirate as a dangerous and uncivilized foreigner corresponds to how the spatial and cultural boundaries imposed by Spain during the colonial period were set up: America versus Europe (Spain being aligned in this instance with America and separate from the rest of Europe); the familiar versus the strange.[17] The topos of the barbaric "other," the savage, once identified with America, has momentarily been inverted and is now directed toward England. Having no travel account of her own to corroborate her vision of piracy, María speaks without knowledge, and her description is ridiculed by a true witness, a sailor, who interrupts the women's conversation aboard the ship:

> ¡Los herejes son hombres como yo, señoritas! los hay hermosos como un roble, y sus mujeres son lindas como las estrellas. . . . Esas cosas que allá en la tierra cuentan los frailes, son pamplinas buenas para ellos y para

embaucar la gente que no sabe lo que es mar. ¡Si dijéramos los moros!
¡eso ya sería otra cosa! ¡estos sí que son retratos del diablo en lo negro y
en lo feo! (45)

[Heretics are men like me, my ladies! Some are handsome and strong
and their women are as beautiful as stars. . . . Those stories the friars tell
back on land are so foolish, only good for them and to deceive people
who don't know what the sea is. Now, if we spoke about the Moors!
That would be a different story! They really are the portrait of the devil
himself in their blackness and ugliness.]

The enemy has been redefined. The Moors, as black devils, are the un-
questionable adversaries, whereas the English, despite their origin and
religious beliefs, are brave sailors and true gentlemen. Furthermore, as
López proceeds to show, Englishmen are neither black nor ugly. It is
interesting to note that the sailor is the one who corrects María. Having
traveled around the world and seen and fought against these "feared"
individuals, the sailor becomes the authority. He actually knows, or can
at least claim to know, what the Moors are like; he has a direct experience. Consequently, he is the only one who can refute the fallacious
Spanish allegations. In this context, the sailor does not merely voice
López's liberal convictions. He also reproduces the belief of many liberals that by traveling to England and France, one would be exposed to
"true culture."

What is also evident in López's argument is the contradiction embedded within the definition of the imagined community. On the one
hand, the sailor discards and ridicules the portrait of the "heretic" traditionally endorsed by Spain; on the other, he simultaneously reinforces
part of that colonial legacy in reconfirming the Moors as "other." In trying to establish specific boundaries, the differential structuring of the
colonial past is essential. The terms are simply redefined, though not
completely. Furthermore, the sailor's assertion reflects his own ignorance as well as the profound racism embedded in the liberal doctrine —
particularly in Argentina. Those looking at Northern Europe as a pro-
grammatic model substituted religious differences for a more "visible"
marker. Hence, the racialized body stands as the signifier of the enemy.
In uniting blackness with cultural difference, it becomes clear that the
project endorsed by Argentine liberals is centered on the illusion of a

democratic, all-encompassing whiteness. The problem is that whiteness cannot be a unifying characteristic when Spanish America's identity is marked by its hybridity, *mestizaje.*

López defines "civilization" and "culture" when the Spaniards confront the British pirates. Expecting a black and ugly man, María is stunned when she sees Henderson. He is young, fair skinned, and extremely handsome. The surprise is such that her servant Juana exclaims, "Oh my God! He is a Christian like us!" (64). Furthermore, not only do the English look like Christians, but they also treat their prisoners with respect and civility, qualities that, according to the Spanish, were clearly not attributed to the English, much less to pirates.

By confronting what colonial society had positioned as the "wild" and the "civilized" in this scene, López demonstrates that the English have been unjustly condemned as heretics. In fact, the novel redefines the spatial limits of the law and of the nation as it positions the corrupt Spaniards as the real enemies. Romea, for example, the Spanish suitor and a former seminarian, denounces his own fiancée to the authorities, forcing her to be imprisoned. He is interested in María only because of her wealth and her physical beauty. Unlike his English rival, Romea does not genuinely love or care about María; she is just a commodity. Henderson, on the other hand, despite being a "heretic," keeps his word and risks his life to save her. Like most Spaniards portrayed in the novel, Romea is a rapacious individual who is seemingly in Lima only to make a profit. As his friend confesses, "After all, why have we come to America? Just like you, I have come to make a fortune and enjoy it in my own way when I return to Spain" (30). This assertion furthermore alludes to the resentment most *criollos* felt toward the *peninsulares* who came to America to govern in the name of Spain, or else to make a fortune for themselves, but never looked at America as a place to actually establish a home of their own.

The intricate subplots and characters in the novel are aimed at highlighting the selfishness of Spaniards who governed their colonies despotically. In addition to being Lima's grand inquisitor, Father Andrés is the viceroy's confessor. A ruthless man who supports Romea in his perverse schemes, Andrés uses his religious and political power for his own benefit. And of course there is María's father, Don Felipe, a rich Spaniard who decides his daughter's marriage to secure specific benefits within the Church and does not hesitate to cut a deal with Drake to keep his gold on the ship. There is not a single worthy Spaniard in the novel.

This portrayal allows López to contrast the Spanish characters with the positive attributes of the British pirates and to situate the latter as the real heroes of the novel. The contrast is so sharp that Drake and his crew become emblems of political and religious freedom merely by being English and Protestant. They are the ones who defy Spain's authority and its powerful institution: the Inquisition. They represent, as Miguel Cané perceptively remarked in his review of the novel, the "civilizing race" that will bring forth order, wealth, and culture, crucial to Spanish America's modernization:

> El objeto que se propone este trabajo literario es de suma importancia como justificación de la independencia americana del gobierno español, y como prueba del progreso que hace el país en el aumento, hoy sin las trabas, de su población, introduciendo en ella una raza civilizadora, ejercitada en la vida positiva e industriosa y comerciante.[18]

> [The goal of this literary work is of utmost importance. It is a justification of American independence from the Spanish government and a confirmation of the progress the country is presently achieving without obstacles, increasing its population by introducing a civilizing race, experienced in a positive, industrious and commercial way of life.]

For Cané, as well as for López and other liberals, the conflict in Spanish America was between two races: a "civilizing" one and a despotic one; in other words, England and Spain, the future versus the past, order versus chaos, development versus backwardness. In this context, American's independence was the first step toward progress.

Of all the things López rejects, the foremost is Spain's colonization. This is evident in the first few chapters when the narrator describes America as a pure and innocent continent. Destruction begins with the arrival of the Spaniards. They are the ones who condemned and devoured the land with their despotism. We are told that there cannot be any redeemable Spaniard in America because from the very beginning, Spain's guiding principle was "to conquer, pillage and oppress." This was the maxim that subsequently sponsored an army of fanatic priests who, according to the narrator, "took into their hands the Christian cross and, as if it were a banner of blood, made it into the symbol of war and conquest" (24).

In *La novia del hereje*, López portrays how Spain destroyed what had once been "her most treasured prize," the American continent. In doing so, he carefully inverts the precepts the Spanish had used to build England into a tyrannical foreign power of dangerous heretics and situates Spain in that very same place. Thus the image of the pirate as enemy and outlaw is redefined. Not only is the pirate positioned within the societal order of "civilization"; through his transgression and defiance of the Spanish law, he has in fact established a new order and himself become the emblem of "civilization."[19]

Defending the Spanish Heritage: Soledad Acosta de Samper

In contrast with López's national imagining and critical portrayal of Spanish forces in America, the Colombian author Soledad Acosta de Samper presents a strong vindication of the Spaniards and the need to retrieve the Spanish heritage in her historical novel *Los piratas de Cartagena*.[20] Acosta de Samper reconstructs a series of attacks both British and French pirates made on the city of Cartagena during the colonial period. Her novel is divided into five different chapters or sketches (*cuadros*), each focusing on a specific historical incident; together they span two centuries, from 1544 to 1738.

The opening story, "La venganza de un piloto (1544)," recounts the first time Cartagena was attacked by pirates. Its main interest is that it provides a general introduction about pirates and what defined them as such. In her second *cuadro,* entitled "El almirante corsario Francisco Drake, 1586," Acosta de Samper recounts Drake's brutal attack on Cartagena.[21] The story begins with a brief description of Cartagena. The cathedral, one of the richest in South America at the time, the elegant buildings, and the presence of wealthy and "cultured" Spanish families reflect refinement and pride in the Spanish heritage. Unlike the portrayal of Spanish Catholics in *La novia del hereje*, Acosta de Samper presents them as virtuous and forgiving Christians who faithfully comply with their pious duties. This makes the contrast with the bloodthirsty and violent foreign heretics even stronger. Drake not only attacks Cartagena

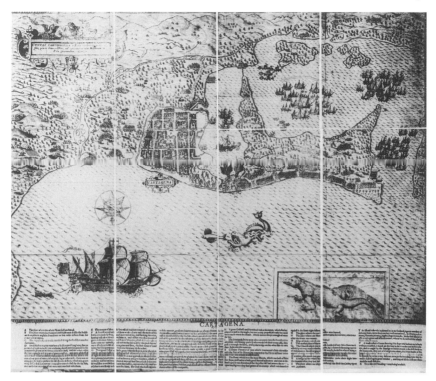

"Drake Captures Cartagena," in *A Summarie and True Discourse of Sir Frances Drakes West Indian Voyage, wherein were taken the Townes of Sainct Iago, Sancto Domingo, Cartagena and Sainct Augustine* (London: Richard Field, 1589). *Courtesy of the Beinecke Rare Book and Manuscript Library, Yale University.*

on Ash Wednesday, a sacred day for Catholics marking the first day of Lent. He proceeds to ransack the churches and burn them down while viciously assaulting the population. A religious confrontation is at the center of Acosta de Samper's narrative. Presented as cruel, violent, and brutal thieves, the English are the perfect heretics. Their only interest in the continent is plunder. Unlike the Spanish, they have no commitment to the Americans, nor do they wish to build a future there. In fact, had it not been for the Spanish, who responsibly defended their colonies, the English would have devastated the continent. This portrayal of the English, which contrasts sharply with the image of "civilized" individuals articulated in López's historical novel, illustrates Acosta de Samper's defense of Spain's colonization and legacy, and the danger of endorsing a Protestant ethos.

Religion is constantly invoked as an ordering principle in the national constructions of nineteenth-century Spanish America, not only because it stems from the colonial order, but more importantly because religion provides a cosmic guarantee that allows individuals to comprehend the world and also gives "a precision to their feeling, a definition to their emotions."[22] By shaping reality as it did throughout the Spanish conquest and colonization, religion orders and explains even the most unintelligible aspects of life.

In the postindependence era, the debate over the separation of Church and state was the cause of serious controversy throughout the continent, causing at times violent confrontations and periods of political instability. In Colombia—as in numerous Spanish American countries—the liberal movement to reform the Church was particularly strong between the period of 1850 and 1880. Although the liberals had already come to power in Colombia before 1850, the division between the Church and the state was finally established in the constitution of 1863, symbolizing an important victory for their principles.[23] A decree issued two years prior had authorized the government to expropriate Church property and auction it off. The clergy protested fiercely and refused to disclose information concerning the Church's property holdings. In retaliation the government enacted new laws that further eroded the Church's position. In 1884, frustrated with the results of liberal reforms and troubled by the rising economic debt, Rafael Núñez, a former president who had once been a doctrinaire liberal, formed an alliance with the conservatives and was reelected president.[24] Núñez's second presidency marked the beginning of a conservative hegemony in Colombia, which would last roughly until 1930. His administration initiated the period known as the Regeneration. He is credited with enacting the 1886 constitution, which was reformed only in the 1990s, and with the revival of Hispanic traditions, including the strengthening of the Church's position in Colombian society.

Although Soledad Acosta de Samper was educated in a Protestant household and her mother and grandmother were Protestants, she became Catholic and actively supported Núñez's policies. A strong advocate of her Spanish heritage, she zealously participated in the national reorganization of her country, becoming one of the most prolific and respected Colombian writers of the nineteenth century. In addition, her marriage to one of the foremost literary and political figures, José María de Samper, gave her access to the elite literary circle formed by her husband and other well-known figures such as José María Vergara y Vergara, Rafael Pombo, and José Eusebio Caro. After the consolidation of the republic (1821), these writers focused on documenting the geography, customs, and traditions of their country; they felt it was their task to prepare Colombians for the future.[25] Colombia's pronounced regionalism marked its political formation as well as its literary production, creating deep antagonisms and misunderstandings. Yet the literary *costumbrista* style was shared by writers throughout the country, enabling regional authors to document and project their own cultural identity. Nevertheless, the literary production during most of the nineteenth century remained in the hands of the elite.[26]

Until recently, women were not recognized for their role, whether political or literary, during those formative years in Colombia, yet they published a great deal.[27] Josefa Acevedo de Gómez, Agripina Samper de Ancízar, Agripina Montes del Valle, and Eva Verbel y Marea are just a few. Among them, Soledad Acosta de Samper was particularly active in her literary endeavor: she founded and edited *La Revista Americana*, the newspaper *El Comercio*, and *La Mujer*, a periodical published solely by women. In addition, she wrote numerous novels, short stories, essays, plays, *cuadros de costumbres*, biographies of illustrious men, articles, and histories. Her work reflects a fervid commitment toward women and the consolidation of a Spanish tradition and identity for Colombia.[28]

Dedicated to president Núñez "as a public testament of the great and sincere friendship I profess to the regenerator of my country," *Los piratas de Cartagena* (defined by the author as "cuadros histórico-novelescos"— a series of historical and fictional *cuadros*) illustrates Acosta de Samper's ideological commitments (18). In her introduction, she explains that the purpose of the novel is to uncover Spain's glory and heroism in its fight against the British and French pirates, who, envious of Spain's power and fortune, assaulted the American colonies. Hence, in this text, Spain is presented as the emblem of "goodness" and the model of the "civilized." Not only are the Spaniards good Catholics willing to give up their lives to save their colonies, but their fight—as it is presented in the novel—is also just. Rather than showing her contempt toward the "other" as López did, Acosta de Samper recognizes the strength of the English but presents them as morally wrong. When describing Drake's attack, the narrator exclaims, "Even though the English seemed to be many, the valor of the Spanish was proverbial, and if God protected them, there was no doubt they would repel the English"—which they did (49). What distinguishes the Spanish from the others is that God is on their side. Consequently, the defense of their colonies and riches is presented almost as a religious obligation. In this way, Spain, justice, and God are united under the symbol of the cross that will prevail above all evil: in *Los piratas de Cartagena,* this means all foreigners (English, French, Dutch, as well as North Americans). Furthermore, the strength of the English, which is their number, is only an illusion. On the other hand, the Spanish are courageous and good Catholics; therefore God will protect them, and they will be victorious. This layout is crucial. It is what allows Acosta de Samper to intelligently structure each *cuadro* in such a way that Spain is always the triumphant force, regardless of the battle's actual outcome.

In the case of Drake's attack, an event in which numerous Carta-genians were brutally tortured while their city was left in complete shambles, Acosta de Samper does not end her narrative with the defeat of the Spaniards. Instead, she includes an epilogue that takes the reader ten years forward. This final section presents one of the soldiers, Hernán Mejía Mirabal, who had courageously fought against Drake in Carta-gena, telling his wife about his second encounter with Drake, this time in Panama. In relating the events, he exclaims triumphantly that unlike the previous incident with Drake, this time the Spanish forces were able to defeat the wretched pirate:

> El peligro fue conjurado sin mayor dificultad, porque logramos rechazar y derrotar a los ingleses, los cuales (es decir, los que quedaron vivos, que fueron pocos) se volvieron a sus bajeles mohínos y cabizbajos. Encontra-ron al Drake enfermo de fiebres, las cuales aumentaron con la ira que le dio el mal éxito de la expedición; y como dirigiese los buques hacia Portobelo, murió de improviso, a la vista de la ciudad y a la entrada de la bahía. (68)

[The danger was prevented without major difficulties because we were able to repel and defeat the English. The few who remained alive returned to their ships sulking and downhearted. They found Drake ill with fevers that increased with the wrath he felt when the expedition failed. While leading his fleet to Porto Bello, he suddenly died, in sight of the city and at the bay's entrance.]

Although the Spanish did not actually kill Drake, his death is viewed as a Spanish triumph. Further enhancing their victory is the fact that the English forces lost at the mouth of the Magdalena River the vessels carrying the little gold they had been able to secure. Hence, those who finally succeeded in returning to England arrived empty-handed and humiliated. The narrator focuses on these two events to belittle, in an ironic tone, the English, who have been stripped of glory and riches.

Los piratas regresaron a Inglaterra a dar cuenta a la reina de las muertes de Hawkins y de Drake, e Isabel les insultó con palabras muy poco comedidas, según la costumbre de la hija de Enrique VIII. (68)

[The pirates returned to England to report Hawkins and Drake's deaths to the Queen, and Elizabeth insulted them with very improper words, as was the habit of Henry VIII's daughter.]

That the author refers to Queen Elizabeth as the daughter of Henry VIII (1491–1547), the king of England (1509–1547) who broke with the papacy and established the Church of England, and portrays her as unrefined and vulgar reinforces the image of Protestants as ill-bred heretics who clearly deserve to be branded as "uncivilized."

Acosta de Samper's ending is diametrically opposed to the one presented in López's novel. Where the Americans had to recast their culture and language to ensure a "happy" ending, here happiness is guaranteed as long as the Americans are able to fend off all foreigners, in this case, the English. The key issue in nation building is the future and the implementation of a political project that can ensure a "happy" ending. Both narratives place this future development and well-being within the parameters of specific alliances across the Atlantic. In addition, both texts present the opposition between the English and Spanish in terms of their cultural differences, differences that ultimately respond to two different ethos: the Protestant and the Catholic.

For Acosta de Samper, religion is essential because it outlines the

path of moral rectitude and distinguishes between the wild and dangerous and the redeemable. In her third *cuadro,* "Los filibusteros y Sancho
Jimeno (1697)," she reconstructs the heroic actions of Sancho Jimeno battling against the French buccaneers. The same attack is also re-created
by Carlos Sáenz Echeverría in his "historical legend" *Los piratas,* also
dedicated to President Núñez.[29] Unlike Acosta de Samper, who extends
her story to the Treaty of Ryswick in 1697, Sáenz Echeverría only focuses
on the violent attack and the brilliant defense led by Sancho Jimeno, who
is presented as one of the most illustrious figures in Cartagena's history:

> Inerme Cartagena, vió sus templos
> por enemigas huestes profanados
> pero en las hora de dolor y prueba
> jamás sus nobles hijos se humillaron;
> y en el inmenso libro de sus glorias
> y en la primera página, estampado
> con la luz inmortal de los recuerdos
> brilla el ilustre nombre de DON SANCHO! (41–42)

> [Cartagena saw its temples
> desecrated by enemy forces
> but during the hours of pain and trial,
> never did her noble sons give in;
> and in her immense book of glories
> and in the very first page, stamped
> with the immortal light of memories
> shines the illustrious name of DON SANCHO!]

In Acosta de Samper's portrayal, Sancho Jimeno displays such heroism in defending the Boca Chica fortress that his enemies are amazed.
When the French pirates Sieur de Pointis and Jean Baptiste Ducassé take
over the fortress, Sancho Jimeno refuses to surrender. He is determined
to die fighting. Pointis, who heads the attackers, realizes that in spite
of their great artillery and troops, taking over Cartagena is not going
to be as easy as they had originally expected: the Spanish were putting
up a good fight. Again the implication is that no matter how many
pirates or how well organized they might be, the Spanish always excel in
their fight because they truly believe in their cause; their fight, in other
words, is a just one. As the battle continues, Acosta de Samper under-

lines the differences between the French captains by focusing on their personal conduct. When the French finally occupy Cartagena, Pointis gives his word to respect the population and their sacred places, but the "real" pirates quickly begin ransacking the churches and brutalizing the Cartagenians. Outraged, Pointis and his men abandon Cartagena while Ducassé and his pirates stay behind, raping the women and plundering the city. When they finally depart, Cartagena is devastated. Again, Acosta de Samper refuses to end her story here, prolonging it to 1697, when France and Spain sign the Treaty of Ryswick and the holy sepulchre, stolen during the attack, is returned to the cathedral of Cartagena. Justice once again sides with Spain.

Although Acosta de Samper's implicit intention is to defend the Spanish presence in Colombia, she does not support them indiscriminately. Recognizing that all too often the higher Spanish authorities, such as the governors (in the case of Sancho Jimeno), looked onto the colonies for their economic interests and did not fulfill their mandate to protect the well-being of their subjects, Acosta de Samper focuses on the less prestigious yet evidently more committed local authorities. Sancho Jimeno and Sánchez Mirabal are both dedicated soldiers willing to defend their territory with their lives. They are the true embodiment of the Spanish legacy in American soil. Acosta de Samper reconstructs political events while giving them a concrete and local significance. Hence, she does not advocate the defense of all Spanish actions in America but rather insists on the need to recognize and reappropriate the positive elements with which the Spanish legacy endowed the American continent.

In the same way that she does not defend all the Spanish, Acosta de Samper does not criticize all foreigners. She carefully distinguishes between Pointis, a French "sailor of notable reputation," and Ducassé, a pirate and former slave trader. What further sets them apart is that Pointis keeps his word not to ransack Cartagena; he also decides to spare Sancho Jimeno's life and honor his determination and valor, despite being his enemy, something Ducassé would not conceive of doing. Although religion is not the distinguishing trait in this case, morality is. The ability to keep one's word and to show respect for a brave soldier, even if he is an enemy, is a clear class marker of refinement and having a moral code. Acosta de Samper consistently aligns morality with religion. She makes distinctions among pirates not only to appear objective but also to prove that despite the fact that some Protestants, as Christians, may have certain moral and decent traits, they are ultimately perverse and uncivilized because they are fighting for a booty and care nothing about the population. For Acosta de Samper there is no intermediate position: either one belongs to the civilized or one does not.

Religion not only identifies the enemy and justifies the battle but also is a spiritual force capable of eliminating the enemy. Acosta de Samper illustrates the Church's spiritual power in her fourth *cuadro*, "El obispo Piedrahita y el filibustero Morgan en Santa Marta," in which both English and French pirates attack Santa Marta, a neighboring city of Cartagena, under the command of the well-known buccaneer Henry Morgan. Searching for gold, the pirates burst into the church, demanding that the bishop in charge hand over all the relics. Furious with the few riches they obtain, the pirates take the bishop hostage and present him to their commander after the assault. Rather than commending his men for their actions, Morgan locks them up and apologizes to the bishop, promising to free him as soon as possible. Once they are alone, Morgan requests his benediction, shamefully confessing that though he is a pirate, his mother was Irish Catholic and so he cannot be at peace with himself until he is blessed. Amazed yet delighted, the bishop complies with his request. He also insists that Morgan refrain from considering himself a heretic, for if he chooses, he may cease to be one: "It is never too late to return to the right path" (139). Two years later, in Panama, the bishop receives a letter from Morgan explaining that "after reflecting maturely on the words you spoke before leaving, I decided to abandon the military career forever" (141). Morgan explains that he is now happily married and living in Jamaica. The bishop, proud of his deed, exclaims:

> Bendito sea Dios! . . . a lo menos se logró sacar esta alma del camino de una irremediable perdición. ¿Habrá esperanzas de salvarla? ¡Sólo Dios podrá saberlo en su misericordia infinita! (142)

> [Blessed be God! . . . at least we were able to save this soul from irredeemable loss. Might there be hope to save it? Only God knows in his infinite compassion!]

It is quite surprising to find this English pirate, famous for his plunders in the Caribbean as well as his ruthlessness and violence, portrayed as an individual showing repentance. It is a masterful emplotment of the historical events. Acosta de Samper uses the capture of the bishop of Piedrahita and Morgan's secret need to be blessed by a Catholic clergy member to justify Morgan's future decision to settle in Jamaica and presents it as the direct result of the bishop's words, almost as if it were a religious conversion. The narrator focuses on Morgan's sorrow and "shame," barely mentioning his well-known vicious acts. In this way, his piratical attacks become simply "military actions" that are ultimately downplayed, allowing the Spanish to claim credit for his change of conduct—a change that has strong religious connotations, for he is abandoning a "military" career for a more spiritual life, one that includes a family. Thus his transformation is not only a political victory (he is no longer a menace to the Spanish) but also a religious triumph of Catholicism over Protestantism.

Acosta de Samper presents the role of religion in much the same way as colonial Spain did: a unifying force that distinguishes between those individuals who belong in America and those who do not, those who are "civilized" and those who are corrupt. The link between religion and national consciousness can be very strong, as religion has the power to create a sense of communion, of brotherhood, uniting people who perhaps have little else in common.[30] By imposing a law of its own, religion is capable of overcoming political differences. Acosta de Samper illustrates this effect in her representation of Henry Morgan. The English buccaneer is able to rectify his life and become part of the civilized world, not because he renounces being English, but because he accepts the higher authority of Catholic law. The connotation, however, is obviously political; in Acosta de Samper's narrative, Catholicism is identified exclusively with Spain.

As *Los piratas de Cartagena* ends and the English are expelled from Spanish America, the narrator explains how her *cuadros* should be read:

> Preferimos no discutir aquellos hechos dolorosísimos de la epopeya de nuestra independencia en la cual los descendientes de los mismos que combatieron juntos para rechazar el extranjero, se hacían entre sí tan ruda guerra. . . . Corramos un velo sobre aquellos acontecimientos; y por ahora no recordemos sino que las glorias de España fueron también las nuestras durante tres siglos en América, así como las habían celebrado nuestros mayores desde la época de Numancia hasta la de Zaragoza, bajo una misma bandera. (216)

[We prefer not to discuss those terribly painful events of the epopee of our independence in which the descendants of those who fought together to repel the foreigners fought a brutal war against each other. . . . Let's pull a veil over those events, and for now, let us simply remember that Spain's glories for three centuries in America were also ours, as our ancestors celebrated the glories from the time of Numancia until that of Zaragoza, under one flag.]

Spain's grandeur is to be considered part of the American tradition and should be used to build America. This is how the past should be understood: as a time of magnificence when Spain and America were united under one flag, and all other nations were enemies. And it is under the same flag that a religious and linguistic hegemony is secured, separating the world between those countries protected by God and the godless, those governed by law and the lawless. These were the values Spain called on to raise the walls that would enclose the space separating "us" from the "others," the "others" who consequently could only be represented as barbarous "heretics."[31]

The two texts endorse a different characterization of what constitutes "civilization" by opposing the civilized to the wild and immoral. In Acosta de Samper's text, the Spanish are the emblem of civilization because they oppose the violent, heretical pirates. In López's, the English embody civilization because they oppose corrupt and immoral Spaniards. The inability to present a positive self-definition reflects a moment of crisis in which cultural categories have not yet been redefined.[32] Thus, the need to identify oneself by what one is not. This process of self-definition by negation shifts the focus away from "civilization" per se and places the definition of the enemy, the foreigner, at the center of the discussion. Given that neither national identity, language, nor religion can be the determining trait of the American hero, the enemy becomes the decisive component in defining the American nations. He represents what civilization is not, he is outside the law, his presence is a menace; and yet he is essential to secure one's identity, for he marks the line between "us" and the "other." This lack of absolutes is what enables López to conceive the foreigner as the hero because he is precisely the one who exposes the corrupt internal enemy that must be conquered.

The division established between Spain and the other Northern European countries is evident in both *La novia del hereje* and *Los piratas de Cartagena*. The difference is that López claims that the spatial and cultural division defined by Spain is a mistake and should be reversed, whereas Acosta de Samper advocates its permanence if America is to consolidate its true identity. These are just two fictional models of self-determination. Yet certain questions still remain unanswered: Could America cease to look at itself and its past through Spain or England? Could Spanish America project itself independently? If so, what did this entail? Where would its focus be placed?

A Shifting Identity:
Eligio Ancona and Justo Sierra O'Reilly

It is apparent that during the nineteenth century retrieving the past and transforming it into a national tradition was an essential part of defining Spanish America and shaping the future nations. The two discordant representations of the pirate analyzed thus far reflect the contradictory national projects that coexisted in Spanish America. As outsiders, pirates came to personify a number of different features that were perceived as both positive and negative. For López, pirates were good foreigners that Americans should try to emulate, whereas Acosta de Samper saw them as evil outsiders, interested in crippling Spain's power and ultimately destroying America. But where the figure of the pirate embodies the complexity of the process of nation building in Spanish America is when the American is cast as a pirate. In these instances, the pirates come from within the nation; they are individuals who have been shut out from their own countries, forced to become outsiders. They are neither completely evil nor good: rejected from their original community, they must set sail in search of another identity that they do not desire; they are innocent foreigners or lost Americans. These disparate images or positionings of the foreigner reflect the difficulties writers had envisioning their own national identity during the nineteenth century and how intimately nation building is linked to political, economic, and cultural alliances with the outside world.

The intricacy of national consolidation in Spanish America is further manifest by the fact that throughout the continent, nations claimed a shared identity as Americans while at the same time Mexicans, Argentines, Colombians, and even Cubans who were still not politically independent debated what distinguished "lo mexicano," "lo argentino," "lo colombiano," "lo cubano." Defining a national identity is not exclusive to countries that have secured political independence. The cases of Puerto Rico and particularly of Cuba illustrate that nationhood is not conditioned by the existence of a nation-state. Although Cuba remained a Spanish colony until 1898, from the beginning of the century, the discussion about how to define a Cuban identity separate from Spain was a central issue in the literary, cultural, and even political spheres in Cuba, especially during the 1830s and early 1840s.[33] However, once the state is consolidated and a hegemonic discourse is articulated, specific spatial and cultural boundaries are defined, even though these boundaries are never permanently fixed, and the nation begins to take shape. The imposition of an "official" discourse plays a key role in controlling the constant shifts to which national identities are subject, yet it does not impede the emergence of other destabilizing nationalist discourses. The complex relationship between Yucatán and Mexico, for example, reveals how even within relatively established political boundaries, a uniform concept of nation was not ensured.

During the nineteenth century, the state of Yucatán occupied the whole peninsula and was only one of the several states that formed independent Mexico. Geographically, it was separated from the rest of the republic by an extremely dense and barely accessible jungle. In addition, as of 1814, the Yucatecs had secured the rights to issue their own commercial regulations to export and import products directly to and from Europe and other American ports.[34] In 1835, when a new centralist constitution was devised under the orders of Antonio López de Santa Anna, the Yucatecs rebelled and declared their independence from Mexico for thirteen years (from 1835 to 1848). When Mexico went to war with the United States, Yucatán remained neutral, reaffirming its separateness. A few years later, in 1847, as the exploitation of the Mayan people and their lands increased, a bloody racial war, known as the Caste War, broke out between the indigenous Mayan population and the Spanish-speaking whites and mestizos of Yucatán. It was the major Indian rebellion in nineteenth-century Spanish America. Defending their land and freedom, the Indians fought against the Yucatán elite, who, seeking to expand their sugar and henequen plantations, claimed to be battling for "the holy cause of order, humanity and civilization."[35] The landowners appealed to the United States to put down the insurgents and subsequently requested to be annexed so that they could maintain control over the indigenous population. Only after the United States rejected their offer (1848) did the peninsula return to the Mexican Federal Union.[36]

In discussing the future of his nation, the Yucatec historian Eligio Ancona (1836–1893), one of Mexico's most prominent scholars, looks back on the past to highlight the heroic actions attributed to the men and women of his native state. Like many literary figures, Ancona played an active role in the political affairs of his country, as governor of Yucatán and deputy to the national congress. He was also judge of the Supreme Court of Mexico, and as a journalist, he wrote in *La Píldora* and *Yucatán* defending the liberal cause.[37] Ancona's interest in history is evident throughout his work. He is the author of five historical novels and an extensive history of the Yucatán entitled *Historia de Yucatán*.[38] In his historical novel *El filibustero* (1864), Ancona vindicates the courage and determination of his fellow countrymen to fight the corruption of the colonial government and the pirates that infested the coasts of his country.[39] Although Ancona does not attack the Spanish conquest per se, he makes a point of criticizing the individuals who committed abuses and allowed corruption to rule America, namely, the *encomenderos*, governors, and friars.[40]

Although the action in *El filibustero* is set during the early eighteenth century in the city of Valladolid, Leonel's odyssey has a distinct parallelism with the history of the Yucatán during the nineteenth century: it is a quest to come into being, a fight for self-determination, an armed battle against corrupt authorities. Leonel is a kindhearted eighteen year old who falls in love with Berenguela, the daughter of his adoptive family, the Villagómezes. Not knowing who his real parents are—in other words, ignorant of his true origin, class, and heritage—Leonel fears that he will never be accepted by the aristocratic society in which he lives. He will always remain an outcast and never be able to marry Berenguela. His fears come true when Berenguela's parents, concerned about their daughter's relationship with Leonel, try to put some distance between them and decide to marry off their daughter. Determined to marry Berenguela, Leonel sets out to build an identity of his own. He intends to make a name for himself that is based on his own merits, not on borrowed ones.

Holding on to past structures inhibits the possibility of projecting a new and independent identity. Leonel realizes that he can never appropriate and make his own a name or position that has been bestowed on him by others because ultimately they will always see him as different, a foreigner. No matter how hard he tries, he cannot become a Villagómez. Rather than focusing on the past, Ancona advocates through Leonel's resolution a form of self-determination that breaks away from the prevailing foreign models that have locked the options for the future. Trying to become something or someone one is not will ultimately lead to failure, for it entails the erasure of the inner being. A national project, in other words, cannot be molded according to a foreign nation's project. Ancona believes that to be successful, Yucatecs must look within their own parameters and build from within. They must imagine their own future. This imagining would seem to reject all foreign alliances.

Throughout the novel, nationalities and lineage are constantly underscored. Gonzalo Villagómez, the *encomendero,* can proudly trace his ancestors back to the Pelayos and Alfonsos of Spain; his wife is said to be a descendant of a conquistador. Heritage conveys identity; it also places tradition as the structuring force determining the cultural boundaries of those who belong to the community and those who must be excluded from it. Hence, those lacking proper ancestors are nobodies: "And who was Leonel? An orphan, a nobody, a poor devil with no name" (4).

The novel is divided in two distinct parts: Leonel's coming of age, and his battle for self-determination. The first part recounts Leonel and Berenguela's childhood and mutual love. As they get older, Leonel's tutor, Friar Hernando, and Doña Blanca, Berenguela's mother, constantly try to separate the two children. The reason behind this is not that Leonel's origin is unknown. Rather, it is because it is all too known, though it has been kept secret from everyone. Leonel is the son of Friar Hernando and Doña Blanca. In other words, Leonel has not only been conceived in sin but is also Berenguela's half brother. Friar Hernando convinces Leonel to confine himself to a convent and study. Leonel accepts on the condition that Berenguela wait five years for him. After that, if he has been unable to make a name for himself, he will renounce all hope of marrying her. But when Leonel finds out that the Villagómez family has arranged Berenguela's marriage a few days later, he becomes furious. Friar Hernando hounds Leonel through Valladolid, creating all sorts of obstacles, including getting him imprisoned under false accusation to keep him away from Berenguela. Leonel manages to escape and goes into hiding. Persecuted by the local authorities, having nowhere else to go, rejected by the people he loves, and unable to find a place for himself in society, Leonel thinks about committing suicide. Debating what to do on a deserted beach, Leonel experiences a sudden awakening:

> El globo del sol mostró su faz rojiza allá en lontananza entre las aguas y el cielo, y el mar pareció convertirse un momento en un lago de fuego. Leonel dió un grito de admiración. *Dios se le acababa de mostrar en todo su esplendor.* (160; emphasis added)

> [The globe of the sun showed its red face afar between the waters and the sky, and the sea seemed to become, in an instant, a lake of fire. Leonel shouted in admiration. *God had just shown himself in all his splendor.*]

That the first part of *El filibustero* ends with a religious awakening that will lead Leonel into piracy is key to understanding the ideological significance piracy has been assigned. Cornered against his will, with nowhere else to go and no means of legal protection, Leonel must fend for himself the only way he can. Piracy in this novel is resignified. It becomes a way of securing an identity, a way that enables Leonel to take his life into his own hands. It is a legitimate act that, as the narrator implies, is even accepted by God. Piracy is presented as a means of self-recognition, a way to erase the stifling foreign markings that have been unjustly imposed. The parallelism between Leonel's quest and the Yucatecs' battle against Mexico is evident to the extent that the fight for independence would allow the Yucatecs to take charge of their own political and economic affairs.

The second half of the novel takes place three years later and presents Leonel having succeeded at making a name for himself. He has become Barbillas, a "famous pirate" of the Gulf of Mexico.[41] In Ancona's text, however, the only enemies that appear are corrupt Spaniards, particularly Spanish governors and high religious authorities. The English are also portrayed as villains. They roam along the coasts of the Spanish colonies with the sole intention of harming local commerce and preventing Spain from sending aid to her colonies. Hence, both foreign models are portrayed as negative forces for the well-being of the Yucatecs. The only trustworthy and hardworking individuals in this novel are the Yucatecs themselves. They are the ones who must defend their own interests, in the same way Leonel must fend for himself, alone.

In the introduction to his novel, Ancona includes the pirates among the perilous "evils" of the Yucatán Peninsula. Together with religious and political authorities, they are guilty of making the Yucatán "one of the most unhappy countries in Spanish America." Ancona claims that their devastating actions still remain in everyone's memory. That is why he chooses to focus his novel on the temples they desecrated, the people they tortured, and the riches they confiscated. Curiously, the portrayal of Leonel as a pirate is far from that of a wretched thief. He is never shown exerting violence arbitrarily or raiding any ships for the sheer pleasure of it. He is, in fact, presented as a noble man who, in spite of being unfairly condemned because of his origin, refuses to take revenge on society and chooses to fight to expurgate the corruption in his land. He becomes a sort of national hero who can fight for his people and culture only through piracy.

Leonel is first and foremost a Yucatec; in spite of becoming a pirate and changing names, he remains faithful to Yucatán. When his men take over a vessel carrying the future governor of the province, Don Fernando Meneses Bravo de Saravia, Leonel makes a point of informing the governor of the corruption existing in Yucatán. He cites names, dates, and actions to prove the guilt of the men he accuses. Amazed at Barbilla's interest and knowledge of the events in the colonial province, in addition to his impeccable Spanish, Don Fernando wonders if he is not an old Castilian. Offended at being taken for a Spaniard, Barbillas proudly cries out, "I am a Yucatec." He immediately proceeds to explain the difference between the Spanish pronunciation and the American: "An old Castilian does not confuse the pronunciation of the c and z with that of the s, nor the v with that of the b, nor the y with that of the ll" (195).

Linguistic differences are explicit forms of establishing an identity; they are distinct boundaries. Ancona makes a point of underlining the significance of linguistic differences; they are a crucial factor in enhancing the political projects that separate Spain from America as well as those separating Spain from the Yucatán. Leonel insists on distinguishing between his Spanish and that of Spain and considers English a "horrible dialect." As a pirate, he has learned to speak different languages, yet he can only feel at home speaking his own Spanish. It is only among Yucatecs that he will be completely understood. In this way, Leonel claims his identity as a Yucatec and rejects not only other "foreign" languages and nations but also Spain's, which is traditionally considered the founding nation.

Ancona's novel offers an alternative to the model of nation building presented by both López and Acosta de Samper. Instead of focusing on the alliances with other nations, *El filibustero* argues for the Yucatecs to take charge of their own affairs. Leonel's personal struggle for self-determination is carefully intertwined with his countrymen's fight for independence. In spite of whatever good intentions they may have had, the Spanish governing the colonies have proved to be immoral and greedy, just like Leonel's parents. The English have acted in the same fashion. Hence it becomes evident that if the Yucatecs are to progress, they must believe in themselves and take control of their country. As Leonel gains confidence in himself, his pride in being a Yucatec also grows, prompting him to become a zealous defender of his country's interest.

Ancona's reconfiguration of the pirate illustrates the violence embedded within the Spanish American independence movements. Illustrating how detrimental the governing laws of the Spanish are to the well-being of the Yucatecs, being a pirate, an outlaw, places Leonel in the right. Because the legal authorities oppress the Yucatecs, creating a corrupt and sinful society, the only way out is fighting the law. Hence the lawlessness identified with piracy is in fact a reaffirmation of the positive elements that it can represent. What must be underlined, however, is that not all pirates are seen as positive forces. There are foreign pirates, like the English, and there are "national" pirates, who have been unjustly cast as outlaws. It is the latter kind of piracy that is presented as a liberating force. Rather than idealizing any of the foreign models commonly sought during the nineteenth century to project the nation, Ancona advocates introspection so that the building of the nation responds, in this case, to the internal needs of the Yucatecs.

In contrast with *Los piratas de Cartagena* and *La novia del hereje,* the ending of *El filibustero* is heartbreaking. As Leonel breaks into the convent where Berenguela has been secluded, he is confronted once again by Friar Hernando. Realizing that nothing will stop Leonel, Friar Hernando reveals the secret of their relationship. Leonel is shocked but rejects his father: "My father would never have sacrificed me for his own interest, my father would never have preferred two strangers over me, my father would never have sold me to human justice, my father would never have covered me with infamy" (373). Friar Hernando is unable to admit his own faults and the harm he has caused Leonel. When he refuses to let his son search for Berenguela, Leonel kills him. This parricide has an initial liberating effect for Leonel. Leonel is now free to embark on his own project; he can no longer be swerved from fulfilling his dream with Berenguela. But when he is finally reunited with Berenguela, she too dies. Only then is he devastated. Planning suicide, he requests to be buried with Berenguela and leaves part of his fortune to the couple that helped him find his beloved, with instructions that the rest of his money be distributed among the poor.

In the epilogue, the narrator implies that Leonel's actions were not in vain, for with the money received, the couple created a home where "farmers, proletarians, orphans, the elderly and in general, all those in need, found a secure remedy to their adversities" (414). The idea of projecting a home for "proletarians" is strikingly anachronistic within a colonial reconstruction. It is significant inasmuch as it reflects a specific nation image that is projected: one in which workers have a prominent place and are not simply dismissed by the creole elite. This unique home/nation exists for all those who have been silenced in the novel, who have been excluded from the political project of the nation. In this sense, the epilogue articulates the relation between the implicit and the explicit embedded within the text; it names its own absence, making the invisible visible.[42] In the midst of that home lies Berenguela and Leonel's tomb, surrounded by flowers. The novel's tragic ending implicitly suggests the unlikelihood of Yucatán's independence surviving, just as Leonel is unable to survive his own quest. Nevertheless, in spite of his parricide and the disastrous outcome of his final reunion with Berenguela, because their deaths were somehow able to bestow happiness on others (the true Yucatecs), the novel's ending could be read as a sign of hope in the Yucatán's future.

Another Yucatec author committed to defending his country's independence is Justo Sierra O'Reilly (1814–1861), Mexico's first historical novelist. A fervent liberal, doctored in theology and law, Sierra O'Reilly held a number of public offices such as minister of commerce and district judge in Campeche. He was also elected deputy to the National Congress in 1852 and 1857. He served as secretary to Colonel Sebastián López Llergo in the campaign against the Centralists, and his name appears on the decree declaring the independence of Yucatán. He was also elected president of the Academia de Ciencias y Literatura of Mérida.[43]

Sierra O'Reilly's literary work is closely linked to the legends and history of his native Yucatán. Although he is considered the "literary father of the peninsula," his work has been greatly overlooked.[44] His novel *El filibustero* was originally part of a history of piracy along the Yucatán coast. But Sierra O'Reilly did not complete his project and instead restricted his short historical narrative to the life of Diego "the mulatto," one of the most feared pirates of the seventeenth century, who occupied and devastated the city of Campeche. Although Diego is a pirate who works for the English or Dutch forces (it is unclear in the novel), he is not a foreigner. He is an American. But as the son of a Spanish (?) father and a black mother, he is a *mulato*, not a *criollo*. This difference is extremely important, for it is what causes him to be rejected by society, to be exiled.[45] Because lineage is what assigns each individual a specific identity and role within society, Diego's impure, or "bastard," heritage makes him an outcast and forces him into piracy. It is a position for which he strongly resents and blames his father:

> Vos me habéis dado el ser en el crimen: nací en el crimen: arrancasteis la vida de mi madre, sin mas motivo que por ser de distinto color al vuestro; he allí un nuevo crimen. Vos me instruisteis y educasteis en el crimen. Vos me habéis inclinado al robo, al asesinato y a la piratería.[46]

> [You have given me life through crime: I was born because of a crime: you ruined my mother's life for no other reason than for being of a different color than yours; that is another crime. You brought me up and educated me in crime. You have pushed me to rob, to kill, and to piracy.]

In both Yucatec novels, the father is guilty of the son's unhappiness; he is the cause of the son's unfair treatment, in the same way that Spain was held accountable for treating its colonies as children and therefore forcing them to fight against their "fatherland" to become truly independent. The founding fathers—political, religious, as well as genealogical—must be extirpated so that the future sons/nations may come into being.[47] The act of independence, of individualization, is a violent one.

During one of his attacks on Campeche, Diego falls in love with Conchita, the daughter of a well-known *encomendero* who was killed a year before in another of the pirate's attacks. Diego is dazzled by Conchita's beauty and saves her when she faints in the middle of the battle. Ignoring his true identity, when she awakes, she believes he is the "foreigner" who rescued her from the terrible Diego and thus falls in love with him. Without revealing his identity, Diego leaves Campeche, promising Conchita to return. Despite her family's efforts to marry her off, she remains faithful to Diego. A year later, he receives orders from his commander to attack Campeche once again. Devastated and torn between obeying his orders and protecting his beloved, Diego complies with his instructions, making sure Conchita will not be hurt during the attack. The city is set on fire. The population is paralyzed by fear. By accident, Conchita and her little brother are trapped in their house. The heat is so intense that no one dares try to rescue them. Again it is a "foreigner" who appears from nowhere, rushing into the flames and saving them.

Like Ancona's hero, Diego attempts to position himself alongside the Yucatecs. In trying to fend for their interests, he exhorts them to fight and condemns them for behaving like "chickens." He insists they must learn to defend what is theirs. But unlike Leonel, Diego has committed extremely brutal acts among his own people and therefore cannot be part of the Yucatec society, even though he has been unfairly outcast. If violence is to be justified in these novels, it must be directed toward the enemy. It cannot be gratuitous, which is how Diego's actions are portrayed.

Don Fernando, a cousin courting Conchita, confronts the foreigner and discovers that he is his rival, Diego *el mulato*. The two men fight, and Don Fernando is beheaded. Having also killed Conchita's father in a prior attack, Diego realizes that it will be impossible for him to be united with Conchita. Tormented by the thought of living without her, he kidnaps her, and they escape on a small boat. As the fires are slowly extinguished, the Campechanos begin their counterattack and chase the pirates, forcing them to retreat to their ships. Diego tries to avoid

confrontation with the Campechanos. But the proud Americans are enraged with Diego and set out to sea to rescue Conchita. Throughout all
this, Conchita remains unconscious. When she awakes, she is confused
and does not understand why the Campechanos are chasing her. The
vessels crash. Diego throws himself into the sea, and the Campechanos
save Conchita. Realizing that she has fallen in love with her father's and
cousin's assassin, Diego *el mulato,* Conchita becomes insane. The epilogue informs the reader that she was locked in an infirmary for life.

In both of these novels, being of a different color or lacking an evident
Spanish heritage is the cause of rejection that ultimately leads to piracy.
In Leonel's case, piracy allows him to obtain an identity. In Diego's,
we do not know exactly why he chose to be a pirate, though we are
led to believe he did so because he was banned from his own land for
the color of his skin. Hence, piracy also furnishes him with an identity.
Despite being pirates and using violence, both heroes are decent individuals: they fall in love, they wish they did not have to use force, and
they care about their loved ones. They are also forced to become unruly
and commit serious crimes. Leonel kills his own father, assaults Spanish vessels, and escapes from prison. Diego obeys (foreign) orders and
invades Campeche, destroying the city and killing in cold blood anyone
crossing his path. In both cases, each hero has been unfairly treated and
condemned by society. This is what has led them to piracy. Although
they are Americans, they have become foreigners in their own country.

What these two novels reflect is the difficulty Americans had securing
a place within their own territory. In separating themselves from the English and the Spanish, Americans seem to have lost the only acceptable
points of reference; thus, as the cases of Leonel and Diego demonstrate,
they are left to roam the seas, exiled from their own homes. In addition, they are excluded from their land because there is an implicit idea
of what Spanish Americans are supposed to be. Indians and blacks do
not seem to have a place in the continent; neither do those who do not
have an established heritage and past. Yet what both authors seem to
try to underline is that if issues of race and heritage are not addressed
explicitly, Americans will be unable to build a home to house their own
people. Foreign models are inadequate for the consolidation of independent Spanish American nations. Spanish Americans must search within
their spatial boundaries to understand the true nature of their own cul-

ture. In the Yucatán, this proved to be an extremely difficult task, as a foreign concept of progress subsumed the road for national consolidation, and Indians were seen more as a hindrance to progress than as an essential component of Mexican identity.

Read as a corpus, these historical novels dramatize the struggle that underscored the debate to consolidate an American identity during the nineteenth century. As each author looks back into the past in search of a model that will legitimize his or her ideal, England or Spain never ceases to be the central axis. This particular configuration exposes two extremely significant absences in the debate on nation building: that of the indigenous people and blacks. How did these individuals fit into the American project? What role, if any, were they assigned in the national reorganization? Why did these novelists, claiming to discuss what defined the American identity, fail to include blacks and the indigenous cultures present in their own continent?

Acosta de Samper does not ignore the existence of blacks and indigenous people but believes they should be excluded. The following is the candid explanation she offers to justify their absence.

A pesar de la gran mezcla de la raza indígena con la blanca que existe en Colombia, la primitiva tiende a desaparecer; y aunque ésta exista por muchos años aún, la civilización de que gozamos nos viene de Europa, y los españoles son los progenitores espirituales de toda la población. Así pues, a éstos debemos atender con preferencia, si deseamos conocer el carácter de nuestra civilización.[48]

[Despite the great mixture of the indigenous race and the white one that exists in Colombia, the primitive tends to disappear; and although it may exist for many years, the civilization we enjoy comes from Europe, and the Spaniards are the spiritual progenitors of all the population. Therefore, we must listen to them with preference, if we want to really understand the nature of our civilization.]

Acosta de Samper's racist position was shared by the vast majority of the white Spanish American elite. Like most *criollos,* she looked to Europe to find her identity. The national image she reconstructed was one that projected her own Spanish heritage as the most important aspect in defining a national identity. Others, like López, preferred to disregard their Spanish origin and align themselves with England to project a more fruitful and "progressive" national identity. Soledad Acosta de Samper and Vicente Fidel López represent two extremes of the same spectrum. Not surprisingly, in the work of both, the indigenous population appear as inferior people. Indians are represented as either slaves or traitors. They are forced to fight for the Spanish cause but are ready to seize any opportunity to turn against the Spanish. They are defined as untrustworthy and are placed with the enemy. Even authors who claimed that it was important to steer away from Europe, as did Eligio Ancona or Justo Sierra O'Reilly, were trapped within the limits of the same debate. When Ancona calls on the Yucatecs, he is not referring to the Mayans or any other indigenous culture. He is speaking to the *criollos* born in Yucatán. Sierra O'Reilly does the same when he describes the Campechanos chasing Diego *el mulato.* The people of Campeche are determined to defend their territory, making sure only the "true" Campechanos form part of their community. That is why Diego, a mulatto, must be driven away.

Looking at America independently from Europe would have entailed placing blacks and the indigenous cultures within the American project. It would have meant acknowledging their importance. But most *criollos,* fearing perhaps their own displacement, were not able to do so as they took into their own hands the shaping of the nation. Hence, America became a name beyond which lay a number of contradictory projects battling each other to appropriate a meaning and a future—a future that was constantly being torn apart and rebuilt by the *criollo* elite while the pirates were left on the seas, free to embody the enemies and heroes of Spanish America.

CHAPTER FOUR

Nation Building and the Historical Novel

A nation is a soul, a spiritual principle. Two things, which
in truth are but one, constitute this soul or principle.
One lies in the past, one in the present.
—Ernest Renan, "What Is a Nation?"

During the nineteenth century in Spanish America, the historical novel became one of the main literary expressions to play a role in shaping future nations. Blending history and fiction, these novels offered readers a means of understanding their country's history and culture. Following the models established by Walter Scott and Alessandro Manzoni in Europe, and James Fenimore Cooper in the United States, Spanish American writers looked back into their past seeking to unveil moments of glory and honor that would reflect their national heritage and identity. How these historical narratives articulated and legitimized a specific national identity through their use of history and fiction is the main focus of this chapter.

The rise of the historical novel and its importance in the discussion of nation building is undoubtedly related to the role history took on during the nineteenth century. No longer perceived as one vast uniform movement ordering the world's development, history was fragmented into a plurality of histories (biological, economic, linguistic), each with its own complex process of changes governed by certain laws of evolution. Everything was historicized. It became a mode of being; a discipline with its own laws and research methods; a principle of social investigation, even a narrative form. As Foucault notes, during the nineteenth

century, "a profound historicity penetrates into the heart of things, iso-
lates and defines them in their own coherence, imposes upon them the
forms of order implied by the continuity of time."[1] Thus history becomes not only an object of study but also a way of knowledge, an
epistemological principle. This process, a product of the Enlightenment,
crystallized in Europe with the rise of the bourgeoisie and spurred the
desire to retrieve the past, where "man"—and it was generally *man*—
discovered his origins and his own historicity.[2]

The force of history lies in its explanatory power to make the world
intelligible, elucidating its laws and effects on "man." In this sense, the
rereading of the past becomes a way of defining one's nation, as it reveals the individuality of a people and brings to light the great moments
of national honor. This is precisely where the historical novel fits in, as
a response to and consequence of this new conceptualization of history
that extends to literature.

In Spanish America, the need to consolidate a sense of unity and
define an "American" culture propelled the formation of national lit-
eratures and histories throughout the continent seeking to display each
country's uniqueness. Yet unlike England or France, where the distant
past had the ability to awaken a consonant patriotic fervor (as Scott's
Waverley novels did), the colonial past in Spanish America was a much
more controversial period. Viewed by many as an era of brutal domination and exploitation by Spain, "the conquest" and the colonial period
in general epitomized the forces that opposed progress and order, the
two main principles guiding Spanish American nations during postindependence.

Contrary to the historical novels evoking the battles of independence, in which the Americans were clearly portrayed as the heroes,
those novels focusing on the colonial past presented extremely different
heroes. They were Spaniards, *criollos,* indigenous people (as in the *novela
indianista*),[3] and in some cases they were even foreigners. This ambiva-
lence was due to the fact that Spanish American writers looked back on
their past from the perspective of their contemporary political ideals.
Unlike European romanticists who found an inherent beauty in the
Middle Ages, Spanish American romanticists found their distant past
saturated with tyranny, oppression, and corruption. Reconstructions dif-
fered, depending on how that past was explained and who was held re-

sponsible for generating a climate of distrust and fear. Consequently, the historical novels retrieving the colonial period not only reconstructed the past of Spanish America but also echoed the different ideological positions voiced in the debate about nation building during the nineteenth century.

The Beginning

Although there have always been literary interpretations of historical events, the most important influence in the development of the historical novel as a genre was the work of Walter Scott.[4] Hailed as one of the great writers of the nineteenth century, Scott configured the canon of the new genre. With an intense desire to conserve past traditions while arguing in favor of modern life and progress, Scott was the first to offer a "comprehensive vision" of the virtues of the past and those of the Enlightenment.[5] His work was translated immediately into a number of languages and inspired numerous novelists throughout the European continent. Alessandro Manzoni, Victor Hugo, Honoré de Balzac, Alexandre Dumas, and Willibald Alexis are just a few of Scott's many followers. His success was so great that his name became synonymous with praise and merit:

> Walter Scott será para la crítica de todas partes la medida absoluta con que justipreciar los méritos relativos de los demás novelistas. Al norteamericano Fenimore Cooper se le llama el Walter Scott americano; al poeta polaco Alexander Bronikovsky, el Walter Scott de Polonia. Willibald Alexis declara repetidas veces que quisiera llegar a ser el Scott de Prusia, y en 1823 publicó su *Walladmor*, declarándolo "libremente traducido de Walter Scott"; y aunque la crítica ha comprobado luego que no era verdad, sino que Alexis siguió los recursos y procedimientos de Scott (con influencias también de los alemanes Ludwig Tieck y Hoffman), esto mismo es revelador de la omnipresente fama del novelista escosés bajo cuyo pabellón estaba segura de pasar cualquier producción literaria.[6]

[Walter Scott will be the yardstick that critics use to measure the relative merits of other novelists. The North American Fenimore Cooper

is called the American Walter Scott; the Polish poet Alexander Broni-
kovsky, the Walter Scott of Poland. Willibald Alexis stated over and over
that he wanted to become the Scott of Prussia, and when he published
Walladmor in 1823, he declared it to be "a free translation of Walter Scott."
Critics, however, proved him wrong, noting that Alexis just followed
Scott's style and technique (though he was also influenced by Ludwig
Tieck and Hoffman), in any case it reflects the omnipresent fame the
Scottish novelist had over every literary production.]

Spanish liberal émigrés, exiled in England during Fernando VII's despotic regime (1814–1833), were the first to translate Scott's work. Their
translations were published in London, Toulouse, Perpignan, Barcelona,
Bordeaux, and Madrid and circulated rapidly in Spain despite censor-
ship.[7] Scott's popularity extended to America almost simultaneously as
it did in Europe. His success there was soon accompanied by that of
Eugène Sue, Alexandre Dumas, and James Fenimore Cooper. According
to Amado Alonso, Mexican bookstores carried translations of Scott's
novels as soon as they appeared in London. His influence extended to
different levels of the literary sphere, as the numerous theatrical adap-
tations of his novels represented in Mexico and Lima attest.[8]
 Scott's novels created a frenzy in Spanish America and became a
model many writers sought to imitate. It was in Cuba where the legitimacy of this genre was most seriously debated. The Cuban writer Domingo Del Monte fervently praised Scott, highlighting his qualities as
poet, philosopher, and antiquarian, three essential traits that, according
to Del Monte, singled Scott out as a great historical novelist. Carefully
detailing customs and attitudes of a particular period, Del Monte proclaimed that Scott's novels taught readers about the most intimate aspects of their past, clearly surpassing the obvious results history could
only document.[9]
 Scott's acclaim, however, was not unanimous in Spanish America.
Those who identified history with "truth" and "reality" considered the
historical novel a corrupt genre. In 1832 José María Heredia, the famous
Cuban poet and precursor of romanticism in Spanish America, condemned the genre, classifying it as "eminently false," since nothing of
what was actually stated could be proved.[10] Even the well-known Italian writer Alessandro Manzoni, author of one of the most influential
historical novels, *I Promessi Sposi* (1827), defined the genre as a contra-

diction in terms while still claiming that it was the most refined effort to meet the challenge of mixing history and invention.[11]

What distinguishes the historical novel from other fictional genres is its peculiar link to history. The reference to documented events and facts within the narrative seems to provide a singular connection with the "real." Although the historical novelist presents only an *imaginary* portrait of the past, that portrait is assumed to be grounded on a certain accuracy or "truthfulness" that is conveyed by the "historical" events or individuals alluded to in the text. Despite discordant opinions concerning the precise form of the genre, critics agree that what matters most in the historical novel is not so much the "historical" accuracy, but rather that the complete portrait maintain an inner coherence that does not contradict the "historical" events referred to.

Facts and imagination are the two elements involved in determining the place and legitimacy of the historical novel, a debate that takes us back to that well-known "family quarrel" concerning the relationship between history and fiction.[12] The most notable difference between these two discourses is assumed to be knowledge. As Aristotle argues in his comparison of history and poetry, "The true difference is that one relates what has happened, the other what may happen."[13] But how does history prove that what is claimed to have occurred actually took place? The historian appeals to documentation to corroborate his or her claims as factual. But there is another important aspect to consider, for facts do not speak for themselves. As Hayden White explains, they must be emplotted within a specific narrative.[14] To establish a meaning and fill the void of pure series, the facts must be connected, threaded, and this is done through language. Thus, the question of referentiality, of representation, from a literary perspective is crucial in the historical novel, for the same events may convey different meanings depending on how they have been articulated.

Although historical discourse maintains the illusion of having a direct correlation with its referent, of being a faithful "copy" of "reality," it can present itself only as a representation, an image.[15] For history is not only a reconstruction of events; it is also their explanation, so that we, as culturally marked individuals, may somehow make sense of them. In trying to reconstruct, to "document," what must have happened during that past, the historical novelist claims to share a place with the historian.[16]

Insofar as history offers an explanation of events from the outside, and literature lives them from within, many writers found that the historical novel gave them a special freedom that history proper did not. Vicente Fidel López, a historian himself, used the historical novel to portray an aspect that history, according to him, could not reach because it was a much more personal aspect of the past, an aspect he defined as the family or intimate part of life:

> A mi modo de ver, una novela puede ser estrictamente histórica sin tener que cercenar o modificar en un ápice la verdad de los hechos conocidos. Así como de la vida de los hombres no queda más recuerdo que el de los hechos capitales con que se distinguieron, de la vida de los pueblos no quedan otros tampoco que los que dejan las grandes peripecias de su historia. Su vida ordinaria, y por decirlo así familiar, desaparece; porque ella es como el rostro humano que se destruye con la muerte. Pero como la verdad es que al lado de la vida histórica ha existido la vida familiar, así como todo hombre ha dejado recuerdos ha tenido un rostro, el novelista hábil puede reproducir con su imaginación la parte perdida creando libremente la vida familiar y sujetándose estrictamente a la vida histórica en las combinaciones que haga de una y otra para reproducir la verdad completa.[17]

[In my view, a novel can be strictly historical without having to cut or alter one bit the truth of the known facts. Just as all that remains of men's lives is the memory of their great deeds for which they became famous, all that remains of a people's life is the memory of great events in their history. People's ordinary lives, their intimate family life, disappears because it is like a human face that is destroyed by death. But since historical life coexists with family life, just like a man who has left memories once had a face, the talented novelist is able to reproduce with his imagination what is lost. He will be free to create family life bound by historical life and through their combination reproduce the complete truth.]

According to the model established by Walter Scott, the historical novel consists of two structural components: a fictional story set within a historical frame. However, what distinguishes the historical novel as such is not simply the presence of these two elements but the way in which the narrative technique is used to create the artistic object. The historical background, though fundamental, takes only a secondary place; its main function is to determine the setting, establish the limits, and provide a "realistic" background for the fictional story. The fundamental aspect of the narration is the fictional story, where episodes and characters that did not exist but could have existed within a specific context are intertwined with the historical events chronicled. The purpose of the fictional story is to echo the values and "spirit of the time" in a distinct and tangible manner for the reader. In other words, the central point is not to retell the great historical events but, as Georg Lukács stated in his classic study *The Historical Novel*, to enable readers to "re-experience the social and human motives which led individuals to think, feel and act just as they did in historical reality."[18]

To convey a sense of "historical reality," the events and circumstances in which the fictional story is set must be carefully documented, if not well known, so that they may be recognized by the readers. Some critics insist that to ensure the historicity of the events reconstructed, there must be a chronological distance between the narrating act and the events narrated. According to Enrique Anderson Imbert, if the events recorded occurred during the novelist's life, he or she will be unable to present them with the "eyes of the historian."[19] Following this reasoning, he disqualifies *Amalia*, written by the Argentine José Mármol, as a historical novel because it is based on events that occurred during the dictatorship of Juan Manuel de Rosas, which coincided with the author's own experience. Thus, Anderson Imbert asserts: "A novel is historical, not because it presents the past to its readers, but because it is the past for the novelist."[20] Amado Alonso shares this position, citing the same novel as an example of what cannot be considered a historical novel.[21]

The problem with this assertion is twofold. First of all, chronological distance does not make a specific event historical; rather, a particular event is historical because in one way or another it has had a "significant" (causal) effect on the development of the subsequent events.[22] Second, both critics erroneously privilege distance as a way of ensuring that the narrative appears "objective." In doing so, they fail to recognize the narrative techniques through which events are framed to appear inserted within the past. They overlook the interplay between what Emile Benveniste termed *histoire* and *discours*.[23] As two distinct and complementary modes of utterance, *histoire* is a third-person narrative of past events expressed in the definite past tense, whereas *discours* is tied to the time and place of the narrator's telling and assumes a relationship—explicit or not—between speaker and listener. Consequently, events in the historical utterance appear to narrate themselves. The presence of a third-person narrator suggests an "absence of person" and gives the narration of events the appearance of being "objective."[24] Historical facts are related in one voice and tense, but events are judged and commented on in another. However, the historical novel uses both forms of utterance. On the one hand, the reader's attention is directed to the events narrated (*l'énoncé*); on the other, when the narrator brings the events to the present and comments on them, the attention is directed to the act of speaking (*l'énonciation*) and the relation between narrator and reader.

Mármol is conscious of the effect the play of tenses has on the reconstruction of events, and he addresses the issue in his *explicación* preceding the novel:

La mayor parte de los personajes históricos de esta novela existen aún, y ocupan la misma posición política o social que en la época en que ocurrieron los sucesos que van a leerse. Pero el autor, por una ficción calculada, supone que escribe su obra con algunas generaciones de por medio entre él y aquéllos. Y es ésta la razón por que el lector no hallará nunca en presente los tiempos empleados al hablar de Rosas, de su familia, de sus ministros, etc.[25]

[Most of the historical characters of this novel are still alive today, holding the same political or social position they did when the events occurred. But in a calculated use of fiction the author writes as if there were a few generations between him and his characters. This is why the readers will never find the present tense referring to Rosas, his family, his ministers, etc.]

By making explicit that it is not the actual chronological distance that conveys historicity but rather the way in which the events are framed within the narrative, the Argentine author offers a direct rebuttal of Anderson Imbert's argument. Finally, the author of a historical novel cannot be expected to narrate events with "the eyes of the historian." History, in any case, will be looked at and shaped through the "eyes of the novelist."[26]

The most important structural component of the historical novel—

which gives the genre its actual form—is the fictional story, usually a romance or love story, presenting episodes and characters that did not exist, but could have.[27] Although these elements are invented by the author, they cannot be arbitrarily imposed on the historical frame; they must be deeply connected to the historical events portrayed. Amado Alonso emphatically states:

> En la literatura de asunto histórico, legendario o mítico, ya no se dibujan como antes unas vidas personales sobre un fondo arqueológico casi en blanco o indiferente, sino que ahora, con las novelas históricas, el fondo se adelanta con su estructura propia y el autor y el público se complacen en presentarlo y en reconocerlo.[28]

> [In literary texts that deal with historical, legendary, or mythical issues, peoples' lives are no longer portrayed over an indistinguishable archaeological background. In historical novels, the background becomes paramount with its own structure, and, it seems, both author and public enjoy presenting it and recognizing it.]

The point is not simply to reconstruct a period from the outside displaying the lifestyle and manners of that particular time (what Alonso calls the archaeological element) but to penetrate within the realm of the personal and reexperience that past in all its concreteness. The fictional story is the crucial link connecting the personal destinies with the determining context of a historical crisis.[29] It is this link that will offer the reader an understanding of the past. However, as Lukács underlines, the point is not to look at "the past as past" but to provide a representation of the historical process that reveals the present as history. This does not mean alluding to contemporary events, but rather means "bringing the past to life as the prehistory of the present" (53). The relationship between past and present for Lukács is determined by his concept of history. History for Lukács is "an uninterrupted process of changes" governed by progress that has a direct effect on the life of every individual (23). Lukács praises Scott because he presents history as a series of great crises in which progress is represented and defended. It is through these complex struggles between "above" and "below" that the heroism of a people is expressed and the progressive features of a society as a whole become visible. The struggle resides not in the fact that one force must overcome the other but in the dialectical relationship between forces that condition the future and reveal the totality of national life. Thus, what makes the historical novel historical is "the active presence of a concept of history as a shaping force—acting not only upon the characters in the novel but on the author and readers outside it."[30]

Scott succeeds in portraying the complex path of England's national greatness by focusing on the small and seemingly insignificant events. He achieves this through his distinct "middle-of-the-road" heroes. Portrayed as social beings, not as unique individuals, these "typical" heroes bring out the social and human motives of behavior of a particular period. Scott's heroes are caught between a struggle of forces, but they do not belong to either camp; they simply reveal how this struggle affects their daily lives. It is through the "middle-of-the-road" hero that the spirit of a particular time is retrieved and an explanation of the state of affairs that affected human experience is offered. Once this has been done, the great historical hero can make an entrance:

> By disclosing the actual conditions of life, the actual growing crisis in people's lives, [Scott] depicts all the problems of popular life which lead up to the historical crisis he has represented. And when he has made us sympathizers and understanding participants of this crisis, when we understand exactly for what reasons the crisis has arisen, for what reason the nation has split into two camps, and when we have seen the attitude of the various sections of the population towards this crisis, only then does the great historical hero enter upon the scene of the novel.[31]

The prototype of the historical novel essentially begins and ends with Walter Scott. As Lukács sees it, Scott gives the "perfect" artistic expression of a historical defense of progress. After him, even the most important of his followers begin adapting his model to suit their particular needs and specific historical outlook.[32] The dramatic and fast-changing events affecting life in Europe, such as the numerous internal battles and the Napoleonic Wars, undoubtedly marked the development of the historical novel. Thus, from its origin, the genre is constantly evolving. In 1826, Alfred de Vigny introduces great historical heroes as the main characters of his novel *Cinq Mars*, thus altering the concept of the hero. Without completely abandoning Scott's model, Gustave Flaubert in *Salammbô* (1862) focuses much more on the archaeological details such as clothing, food, customs, and lifestyle of Carthage, where the tragic relation between Salammbô and Matho takes preeminence. Until then, the events portrayed in the historical novel did not go beyond the medieval past; Flaubert is the first to include the ancient world as an integral part of the historical novel that becomes exoticized.[33] Others like Victor Hugo would focus on the moral lessons to be learned from history and how they might be rectified in the present. This would be an extremely important characteristic for the historical novel in Spanish America, where events and characters of the past were constantly portrayed and judged in terms of their moral connotations.

The development of the historical novel in Spanish America begins with *Jicotencal*, which appeared the same year as *Cinq Mars*, in 1826.[34] This anonymous text was originally published in the United States, in Philadelphia, an important intellectual and political center for Spanish American liberals during the last decades of the eighteenth century through the early nineteenth century. The novel reconstructs the Mexican conquest, highlighting the confrontation between Hernán Cortés and the Tlaxcaltec hero. Strongly influenced by eighteenth-century rationalism, the novelist frequently becomes an essayist without Scott's poetic power and effectiveness. Although *Jicotencal* reproduces Scott's model, there are already a number of formal traits that will distinguish the historical novel in Spanish America from his. Well-known historical figures, for example, do not necessarily remain on a secondary plane, a requirement Lukács considered essential. In discussing the historical novel in Spanish America, Noé Jitrik underlines the type of characters as one of the three distinctive features that differentiate this genre from Scott's model. According to Jitrik, the characters tend to be well-known figures such as Juan Manuel de Rosas, Henri Christophe, or Pancho Villa rather than "middle-of-the-road" heroes.[35] Although many novelists did focus their reconstructions on well-known historical characters, particularly in texts dealing with the conquest or more contemporary political figures, this cannot be considered a defining trait. At least in the cases of pirate novels, authors such as Vicente Fidel López distinctly maintain the historical characters on a secondary plane, and Vicente Riva Palacios and Justo Sierra O'Reilly, for example, go even further by presenting historical characters and events that are unknown or have been forgotten. This distinction between well-known and "middle-of-the-road" characters might have more to do with the function of history embedded in the text than with the structure of the historical novel itself.

In the novels dealing with piracy, history is used to address issues of national identity; the interest is placed not in understanding one's origin but in defining oneself against other identities, a point that Jitrik strongly underlines. Thus, historical novels in Spanish America during the nineteenth century focus less on universal conflicts, for which Lukács emphatically praised Scott; instead, the novels concentrate on specific, more localized struggles in the hope of defining an identity that is still fluctuating. History is placed at the service of the present to help project the future of the Spanish American nations. Writers in Spanish America did not see the aesthetic function of the historical novel. The idea of contemplating the past in its universal character, beyond both the present and the past, was far from their goal. Instead, they adapted the genre to engage readers in the historical events of the present precisely to eradicate or preserve parts of their past that were judged from a moral perspective.

The main attraction the historical novel held for writers in Spanish America was the possibility of combining a discourse that maintained the illusion of reality while imprinting on that discourse their own values and ideas about the past. And those ideas and values were determined by contemporary politics. As literature during most of the century was closely tied to politics, many writers were also statesmen, politicians, and military men. This obviously influenced the formal techniques and cultural characteristics assigned to the novel.[36] Consequently, the views of the past portrayed in most historical novels were deeply rooted in ideological debates concerning the future of the nation. The focus was not so much to highlight the greatness of the nation but to explain the past from a particular political vantage point. Thus the heroes of the colonial past varied enormously depending on the author's contemporary views. As discussed earlier, those who sought to place their country within the parameters defined by England and France used the past to expose the vices of the Spanish and justify the need to eradicate Spain from their country's future project. Others chose to vindicate the indigenous cultures, and still others highlighted Spain's virtues, arguing that America's identity could not be defined without recognizing its Spanish heritage. The way these different factions were articulated depended on the heroes' moral stands. As a result, the concept of typicality in these Spanish American historical novels is expanded, for the hero is "typical" inasmuch as he or she embodies the moral characteristics determined by contemporary partisan divisions while representing the salient aspects of a historical milieu. In this way, through the depiction of the heroes, writers in Spanish America used the past to expose the characteristics they considered essential to consolidate their projected national identity.

The Liberal Project

In the prologue to *La novia del hereje,* Vicente Fidel López explains the purpose of his text and its value:

> He procurado dar verdad histórica y local a la narración, modestia y buen sentido al estilo, y una decencia estrictamente moral a las situaciones. Así es que lo único de que estoy seguro, es: de que siendo ese un trabajo esencialmente americano en su fondo, y desprovisto en su estilo de toda clase de pretensiones, se escapa por ese lado a las ridículas parodias de las pasiones, de las tendencias y de los estilos exóticos, que tanto contribuyen a quitarnos el conocimiento y la conciencia de las sociedades de que formamos parte. (12)

> [I have sought to give the narration local and historical truth, modesty and a good sense of style, as well as moral decency to the situations. Thus, the only thing I am sure of is that given that this work is essentially American in its depth and lacks any sort of pretentions, it eludes those ridiculous parodies of passions, trends, and exotic styles that deprive us of knowledge and awareness of the societies we are part of.]

Truth, a controlled style, and moral decency are the three main characteristics López emphasizes about his narrative. Historical truth, because he reconstructs national events known and documented; local truth, because he portrays in a reliable fashion everyday life, "family" life, during the colony. López claims that his novel reflects moral decency because he portrays the ways in which the Spanish family and Spanish nation are corrupt and lack moral principles. These are the elements López presents to authorize his novel as a document; they certify that his main purpose is to provide a "genuine" understanding of the American culture, a culture he is determined to defend. In stressing that his work is "essentially American" while disdaining "exotic" styles, López seems to reject all foreign influences. Yet in his prologue, he declares his admiration for the two great foreign historical novelists, Walter Scott and James Fenimore Cooper. Although López alludes to the importance of this genre throughout the continent, he does not name any Spanish American writer, thus positioning himself in the same category as the renowned authors and, despite his apparent modesty, implicitly presenting himself as *the* Spanish American historical novelist.

By underlining the truthfulness of his text and stressing that he has carefully researched the material for his novel, López seems to imply that he has taken the task of documenting the facts he uses very seriously and that his view will be, if not "objective," at least fair. Yet after the first couple of pages, it is clear that whatever neutral narrative voice López might have initially claimed to present is soon displaced by a strongly opinionated narrator who never loses the opportunity to attack Spain. By the third page, the Spanish have been called, among many other things: oppressors, fanatics, soulless warriors, cruel tyrants, and disciples of Torquemada. The narrator constantly interjects negative comments about the Spanish, whose slogan in America was "to conquer, plunder, and oppress." On the other side of this brutal picture stand, vivacious and astute, the English corsairs. Their raids against the Spaniards are presented as a justified vindication of the inhuman treatment the Spanish imposed on America. Hence, their attacks are "like an omen of that future day when people, devastated by such tyrannical supremacy, will step on the shreds of Spain like a doormat" (25).

Notwithstanding his overtly aggressive tone either attacking the Spanish or defending the English, López is obsessed with the need to corroborate the veracity of his reconstruction. Rather than remaining at a distance and presenting the events in a more impartial fashion, the narrator constantly heckles readers in order to impose his own conclusions. The text is consequently stitched with numerous remarks directed personally at the readers, trying to dispel any possible doubts or answer questions that might occur. For example, after describing certain colonial family traditions, the narrator states:

Por extravagantes o incomprensibles que semejantes costumbres parez-
can al lector de nuestros días, le podemos asegurar que ellas han sido
observadas con toda estrictez desde la época de que hablamos hasta los
primeros años de nuestro siglo. (191)

[No matter how extravagant or incomprehensible these customs may
seem to today's reader, we can assure you that they have been carefully
observed since the period of time we are speaking of until the beginning of our century.]

The narrator goes beyond simply stressing the truth of his statements;
he offers proof: thus the numerous footnotes that accompany the text.
Except for a few inconsequential clarifications such as what a "huerta"
is or to confirm that a name or conversation are true—which López corroborates by simply stating "historic" (nn. 48, 50)—most of the notes cite
European sources, the majority of which, needless to say, are British.
When referring to past events in Peru, William Robertson's *General His-
tory of North and South America* is quoted. Documents belonging to the
well-known Hakluyt collection and Purchas are also cited. In addition,
a number of English texts corroborate Drake's activities in the Spanish
Main: the *Penny Cyclopedia*, the *Memoirs* of Walter Raleigh, *The World
Encompassed,* to name just a few. Other works López consulted are the
Histoire de la Réformation du seizième siècle by J. H. Merle D'Aubigné and
Thomas Birch's *Memories of the Reign of Queen Elizabeth.* Yet there is not
one document from the Peruvian archives, and all Spanish references,
which would normally present a contrary view of Drake's activities
on the Spanish Main, are excluded. Only when describing the fear and
alarm Drake's presence provoked among the Spaniards and *criollos* in
Peru does López quote lengthy passages from the famous historical
poem *La Argentina* (1602) by the Spanish archdeacon del Barco Centenera.

López's sources clearly demonstrate that his interpretation of the historical events portrayed in his novel is evidently one-sided. This is no
surprise when one looks at just a few of his historical interpretations.
In discussing the independence movements in Spanish America, for example, López states in his *Manual of Argentine History*—dedicated to pro-
fessors and schoolteachers—that the two revolutions that best marked
the modern nature of contemporary history were those of Argentina

and the British colonies: "They are the two that disrupted the political and commercial system of the old world."[37] That López disregards all other Spanish American revolutions enables him to link Argentina's history to England's. In doing so, López openly exposes his admiration for the English empire, echoing the general attitude that existed among the Argentine liberal elite toward England. Following the historical precepts of romanticism, López believed that the task of the historian was to shed light on progress by establishing the continuity between present and past and to reveal, as he says, "the fight between those who claim they want to detain progress and those who want to undo the ties that restrain their flight towards freedom."[38] For the liberal elite, all ties to Spain represented an obstacle to freedom, to be undone only by the English, as *La novia del hereje* makes explicit.

The negative role of the Spanish is conveyed, however, not by the historical events alone but by the fictional story: the relationship between María and Henderson. In trying to ground this story within the historical context, the narrator makes a point of assuring his readers that Henderson did exist. Soon after the English mariner has been introduced in the novel, the narrator tells his readers:

> Por lo que a mí hace puedo jurar a mis lectores que he seguido, paso a paso, la historia de los acontecimientos que forma el fondo de mi trabajo. No es una invención mía, no, el orden de los sucesos que se ha leído: y ese mismo Henderson cuya gentil figura está destinada a concentrar todo el interés novelesco de este escrito, se halla muy lejos de ser una mera ficción de mi fantasía. (76)

> [I swear to all my readers that I have followed, step by step, the history of the events that make up the essence of my work. I have not invented the order of events; and Henderson, whose gracious figure is destined to concentrate all the novelistic interest of this text, is far from being a mere fiction of my fantasy.]

A footnote follows, directly quoting the *Penny Cyclopedia* to the effect that a number of young noblemen from England did, in fact, embark with Drake on his expedition. We are left to surmise that Henderson could also have accompanied Drake in his voyage. In any case, it is all the proof we are given to corroborate Henderson's existence. This is

López's way of assuring his readers that the love story could have occurred. By carefully threading together what is known (documented)
and what is believable (invented), López admits his reconstruction to be
fictional but at the same time insists on presenting it as a document because of its factual content. Whether Henderson actually existed is not
pertinent to the essence of the novel, as long as his actions are verisimi-
lar. The historical events relative to the text, such as Drake's attack on
Lima, the Inquisition's actions, and the confrontations between England
and Spain, are there to create a realistic background for the fictional aspect of the novel. Henderson's role is to dramatize the contrast between
English culture and values and those of Spanish colonial society on a
more intimate and personal level. As long as López's narrative makes
Henderson's and María's actions believable, their historical existence is
of secondary importance.

By carefully intertwining the romantic plot with documented events
that sustain the portrait of Spanish colonial society presented in the
novel, López's reconstruction of the past and his love story are conceiv-
able. Envisioning the nation as a home, López places at the center of
his text the love story between two families (two nations) to echo his
national project.[39] He focuses on the Spanish home and its despotism to
establish its parallel with the nation, a link he continually stresses:

> Apelamos a la historia para ratificar nuestras observaciones. Cualquiera
> que se tome el trabajo de inquirir el estado doméstico de aquellos países
> y aquellas épocas donde han aparecido grandes y bárbaros tiranos,
> donde la sociedad se ha visto sumida en mayor corrupción, hallará que
> el primero de sus rasgos es el despotismo paterno introducido en las
> relaciones de la casa. Ninguna nación del mundo presenta una serie
> de tiranos más atroces ni más continuados que Roma. . . . Después de
> Roma, la España: allí donde Felipe II ahorcó a su propio hijo en nombre
> de su propia autoridad. (192)

> [We call upon history to corroborate our observations. Anyone who
> takes the trouble of studying the domestic sphere of those countries
> when barbaric tyrants ruled, or when societies were steeped in the great-
> est corruption, will find that the very first characteristic is the despotism
> of the father in the home. No other nation in the world presents a greater

and more continued series of ruthless tyrants as Rome. . . . After Rome, Spain, where Philip II hanged his son in the name of his own authority.]

Concentrating on Don Felipe de Gonzalvo's family, López places at the center of his novel the moral values—which he shows to be corrupt— of the colonial past. Gonzalvo arranges his daughter's marriage to keep his contacts within the Church and has no qualms about making a pact with Drake to keep his personal gold. For López, the conclusion is clear: if this hypocritical despot ruling his family is an example of Spanish family values, one can only expect to find tyranny in Spanish America's society. López transfers the debate of nation building to the realm of the home, stressing the connection between the two. In this way, he encompasses society as a whole, the public sphere as well as the private sphere. Thus the building of the nation becomes both a political endeavor and a private one.

Although historical references abound, the second half of the novel is considerably less historical. When Henderson returns to Lima to rescue María, he does so with the help of another English pirate, John Oxenham, who is caught by the Spaniards and, as we learn in the very last pages of the novel, is tried and hanged in Lima. López adds a footnote— in English—to corroborate the veracity of this event. However, Oxenham (the historical individual) was apparently already imprisoned by the time Drake got to Lima in 1578.[40] Not only does López rearrange the sequence of events to fit the fictional story, but by transcribing the quote in English, he includes a foreign language in his "American project." This displacement of languages echoes a more profound and complex displacement, that of cultures. In the end, the narrator justifies this shift because María's rescue and transfer to England are warranted, for it is only there that she will be able to have a decent, comfortable, and "modern" life. The idea that *América* cannot project itself into modernity without an alliance with Europe is precisely one of the crucial elements that inhibited Spanish Americans from looking at their own countries and idiosyncracies freely. The definitions the elites set forth of national identity were constantly patterned along foreign models, which consequently forced them to become other to themselves and envision a reality that had a particularly unstable anchorage in their own land.

Despite his claims of historicity, López is more concerned about discussing the future of Spanish America, particularly that of Argentina, than reconstructing a complete portrait of colonial society in Spanish America. He uses the past to criticize contemporary Argentina. López knew his readers would see the connection between the ruthless description of King Philip II of Spain as "despotic tyrant" and the figure of Juan Manuel de Rosas, the Argentine dictator who forced López and many other members of the *generación del '37* into exile. He also knew that his readers would easily trace the parallel between the story's blissful outcome (the marriage between Henderson and María—the English and the *criolla*) and his ideal of a nation, a prosperous republic based on a strong union with a Northern European country. In fact, López's novel may be read as an illustration of what Juan Bautista Alberdi advocated for the future of Argentina in his seminal text *Las bases*.[41] Furthermore, when the reference to the present is unclear, the narrator provides the necessary information, either within the text itself or in a footnote. When depicting the open market in Lima, for example, the narrator adds a footnote to make a general comment about other colonial cities and makes a specific remark about the plaza del Fuerte in Buenos Aires (265). In another instance, when describing the physical beauty of María, the narrator includes a note about *Esther*, an unpublished work written by López's compatriot and friend Miguel Cané (347).

If Argentina is at the center of López's thoughts, why then did he choose to stage his novel in Lima, Peru? López himself claims, in his prologue, that what attracted him most about Lima was the way it contained the contradictory elements that defined Spanish colonial society. As the capital of one of the most important Spanish viceroyalties, whose power originally extended from Panama to the Strait of Magellan, Lima was a prestigious focal point for Spanish colonial rule. It was, at the same time, a city where "the fragments of the *Huincas'* empire vibrated while the foot of the victors continued to sink into their flesh" (14), a city where *zambos* and blacks mixed with the rich and the *cholas* and *cholos,* all watched by the ever-present eye of the clergy. Choosing Lima enabled López to present a strong critique of the Spanish for having brutally ravaged the Incas during the conquest. In contrast, the Argentine territory did not provide a rich indigenous culture comparable to that of the Incas. Yet López's purpose is not to defend Inca culture. He merely uses it as a pretext to underscore Spanish brutality. He has no sympathy for blacks and *zambos,* whom he portrayed as untrustworthy individuals. Lima is the "American Babel," a society where blacks, *zambos, mulatos,* and Spanish grotesquely overlap, reflecting the harsh extremes of a colonial society. For López, this pandemonium is the direct consequence of the lack of order he and his compatriots strongly advocated. And it is precisely this lack of order that justifies the need for María to seek a new home far away. According to López, if Argentina is to become part of the "civilized" world, the future Argentine nation must stay away from this model and sever its ties with the colonial past.

Throughout the novel, López uses history to legitimize the fictional plot that, in turn, becomes the evidence that Spanish America needs to reconstruct its future along the lines of his English model. Lima represents what Argentine liberals most feared: a city where cultures and races mix indiscriminately, creating a world of chaos. Cities, particularly capital cities, are "the sites of the rationalization of legal power."[42] They are the crucial spatial settings where laws are generally first discussed, approved, and implemented. In this sense, the law becomes a civilizing instrument and centralizing force. It orders, structures, and protects. But Lima is lawless in *La novia del hereje,* thus the need for a happy ending that occurs in a completely different spatial setting, one with which Argentine liberals strongly identified. This explains why López not only opposes the Spaniards to the British but marries the "American" woman, the *criolla,* to the Englishman so that a new race may begin. López's use of history serves to foreground his remapping of the world and to explain the past in terms of his future project. What is perhaps most disturbing is that rather than reconstructing the colonial past, Vicente Fidel López uses history to advocate recolonizing the future of his country.

A Different Version of the Past

In searching to define her national identity, Soledad Acosta de Samper presents her Spanish heritage as an inherent part of the Colombian identity:

> Todas las naciones del mundo tienen sus héroes populares á quienes respetar, y cuyas hazañas, narradas de padre en hijo, interesan á la

juventud, que aprende así á amar las virtudes de sus antepasados y á odiar á los perversos. Nosotros no tenemos más héroes populares que los de la Independencia, cuyos hechos no pueden todavía ser narrados con suficiente imparcialidad por sus inmediatos sucesores. Es preciso, pues, que volvamos los ojos más atrás, que recorramos con la imaginación los siglos pasados y conozcamos lo más posible á los que, atravesando los mares, vinieron á plantar sus tiendas en estas tierras tan lejanas, y á fundar naciones cristianas en donde reinaban la barbarie, la superstición y la idolatría.[43]

[Every nation in the world has its popular heroes whose deeds are respected and told from father to son, engaging younger generations. They, in turn, learn to love their ancestors' virtues and hate those who are perverse. We have no other popular heroes than those who fought for our independence, but whose deeds cannot be told yet by their immediate successors objectively. Hence, it is necessary to look back and trace the past centuries with our imagination, so that we may know, as best possible, the people who came across the seas to plant their tents in these lands so far away. They are the ones who founded Christian nations where barbarism, superstition, and idolatry once ruled.]

Like López, Acosta de Samper believed that it was essential to know the past to define the true "character" of a nation. Distance is important to Acosta de Samper, not necessarily because it bestows impartiality (those fighting for independence are recognized as heroes), but because it allows her to reach back and highlight the Spanish heritage defining her national identity. The heroes of the independence movement are *criollos,* and Acosta de Samper wants to stress the link between *criollos* and the Spanish, not evoke the rupture between them. Consequently, she sets out to retrieve the colonial past, a period she claims was marked by the glorious and "civilizing" actions of Spain. In a territory originally inhabited by barbarians and idolaters, thanks to Spain, America achieved a more humane way of life and became a Christian world. The essence of the conflict is the same as the one presented by the liberal elites: civilization versus barbarism. The difference is that for Acosta de Samper, Spain represents the civilizing race while England typifies the barbaric force.

Acosta de Samper's main concern is to highlight Spanish conduct during the colonial period, a task she claims that must be carried out with a certain "imagination." Given the disparate historical readings of the colonial past, she stresses that it is impossible to achieve the truth just through facts. Thus, to present her reconstruction of past events as an "objective" and truthful account, she displays the contradictions between different historical sources as proof of her "neutral" position:

> No hay concordancia entre los historiadores españoles e ingleses acerca de los muertos, heridos y prisioneros que resultaron de aquel combate. . . . no ponemos nuestra confianza ni en los partes de los ingleses . . . ni en los de los españoles . . . el lector juzgará de ello lo que le parezca, pues le presentaremos los documentos de unos y otros. (209)

> [There is no agreement among Spanish and English historians about the number of dead, wounded, and prisoners in that combat. . . . we do not place our trust in the English . . . nor in the Spanish versions . . . the reader will be the judge, for we will present the documents of both sides.]

It would seem that the narrator's intention is to introduce only facts and refrain from siding with a particular position. Yet it is clear—as the narrator precisely states—that facts vary according to the sources, for the documents from both sides do not coincide. The Spanish claim that the English, jealous of their rightly deserved riches, attacked Spanish vessels and committed brutal atrocities on the population, looting their churches and homes as vicious heretics that they were. The English, on the other hand, assert that Spain used religion brutally to exploit the continent and, in fact, rightly deserved nothing. Warning that both sides should be mistrusted, the narrator pleads to be an honest and impartial voice, who simply reconstructs events without pronouncing any verdict a priori. Thus the narrator appears to be an omniscient third person, capable of transcending the subjectivity of the first and second persons. It will be the task of the reader to judge the way the facts—the English attacks on the Spanish Main, specifically on Cartagena—must be interpreted, an enterprise the narrator will, nevertheless, make sure places the Spanish among the just and the honorable.

Acosta de Samper's desire to postulate herself as an "objective" witness between Spain and England in a way reflects her personal link to both countries. Her father, Joaquín Acosta, was a dedicated Colombian patriot. He served his country as a general during its fight for independence and became a well-known diplomat throughout the continent. He was also the director of the National Observatory and Museum. He traveled extensively throughout Europe and the United States, where he met many influential politicians and renowned scientists. In addition to numerous scientific studies, he wrote a historical account of the discovery and colonization of Nueva Granada (*Compendio histórico del descubrimiento y colonización de la Nueva Granada*).[44]

Acosta de Samper's mother, however, was far from sharing any Spanish heritage with Joaquín Acosta; Caroline Kemble was born in Kingston, Jamaica, and came from a Protestant family. When Acosta de Samper was twelve, she was sent to Nova Scotia, where her grandmother lived, and then to Paris to complete her education. Throughout her life, Acosta de Samper dealt with contrasting loyalties that never seemed to interfere with her own personal beliefs. She thought of herself as Colombian, though her education was European; her heritage was both Spanish and English, yet she chose one over the other and defended Spain's actions during the colony; she was a fervent Catholic but married an important liberal politician who strongly opposed Catholicism; she lived in a society that confined a woman's place to the home, yet she was extremely outspoken, believed strongly in educating women, and emphasized the importance of their role in their country's history.

Acosta de Samper's crafty narrative technique is reflected in the way she shifts from focusing on the events narrated to the way she addresses the readers and brings them into the text. In her reconstruction of Drake's attack on Cartagena, the narrator begins by portraying him in accordance with the accepted popular description at the time. Known as "the Dragon" throughout Spanish America, Drake is depicted as an extremely violent man who stops at nothing when it comes to brutalizing Spanish Catholics and ransacking their churches. Being Protestant and English made Drake a heretic and a declared enemy of Spain. From the beginning of the narrative, his image of cruelty and violence assumes a predominant position that, by mere opposition, highlights the goodness and courage of the Spanish who dare confront him. The narrator claims no responsibility for the extremely negative picture of Drake. The image is presented through a series of dialogues that have been recorded by an "objective" or external voice. By simply claiming to transcribe the fear and hatred of the pirates the Spaniards express in their own words, the narrator conveys an emphatically bleak picture of the assailants while remaining at a distance, avoiding having to corroborate or question the truthfulness of the account. This same narrator, however, goes on to reconstruct events that implicitly end up ratifying that initial image of cruelty.

By maintaining the position of an external narrator and shifting the focalization in a subtle way—in other words, playing with the relationship between the vision through which elements are presented and the identity of the voice that is verbalizing that vision—Acosta de Samper is able to praise the Spanish while still being historically accurate.[45] The narrator begins by giving a general overview of Cartagena during the period the events are to take place. She then proceeds to portray the main characters in action, recording their words and thoughts. As one would expect from a "historical" account, the presentation appears to be articulated from an external and impartial perspective. But soon the narrator, though never appearing as a character within the text (that is to say, never articulating an "I"), begins to provide explanations that branch away from an impartial voice and are implicitly aligned with the Spanish outlook. This is where the focalization shifts and becomes double, letting the anonymous focalizer give way to a narrative agent who is partial to the events narrated. Describing Jimeno's agony when fighting against the French pirates, the narrator observes: "Sancho Jimeno's situation was distressing. How to defend oneself from that army of men who feared not God nor the devil; who cared little about dying . . . ?" (88). Although this is presented as an objective depiction, the narrator is in fact articulating Jimeno's thoughts about the pirates. At other times, the narrator will simply insert a more personal comment within the description. In relating the agreement between Pointis, the French captain, and Ducassé, the head pirate, to pay the freebooters the same amount as the king's troops, the narrator adds in the same sentence quite matter-of-factly, "Quite an embarrassing thing that would surely dishonor any government today" (75).

Acosta de Samper uses the serious controversies that existed between Pointis and Ducassé to differentiate between the more "civilized" Frenchmen and the unruly pirates. The historical events described in this episode are considered by C. H. Haring as part of the "last great expedition" of piracy in the Caribbean. The enterprise was backed by the king of France, who ordered Jean Baptiste Ducassé, governor of French Hispaniola, to aid Sieur de Pointis in his venture to the Mexican Gulf. According to Haring, the buccaneers led by Ducassé opposed the project from the beginning, but the governor held his men together.[46] During the expedition, Pointis is said to have been extremely jealous of his countryman, especially since he could not control the unruly pirates. Acosta de Samper astutely uses this episode to contrast the cruelty of the pirates, who pillage the city, with the more "gentlemanly" action of Pointis, who simply takes the ransom and leaves. By differentiating between forces, the narrator is able to present an "objective" reconstruction while simultaneously slanting the portrayal toward the Spanish outlook and ultimately place Spain on the side of the justice.

Despite Acosta de Samper's strong defense of the Spanish, the events she reconstructs in her text are corroborated by both Spanish and English sources, though she cites only Spanish references in the footnotes scattered throughout the episodes. Incorporating English references would have meant acknowledging a certain authority to that nation's view (as López did), which was clearly not a part of her project. In addition, the absence of explicit references that do not coincide with her reconstruction gives Acosta de Samper a little more leeway in validating her support for the Spanish.[47] When alluding to the English version of events, the author prefers to summarize the general position rather than provide the actual reference, even when it is to corroborate Spain's seemly actions, as in Admiral Vernon's defeat: "The English confess in all their official histories and documents that the Spanish treated the prisoners with the utmost humanity" (211). There is no proof of this assertion, just the narrator's statement.

To convey the sense of a realistic and accurate representation of the past, the narrator does not portray all Spaniards as courageous and noteworthy fighters. In fact, only Catholic bishops and a few singular individuals fit that description; most of the higher-ranking political authorities, such as the governors, turn out to be corrupt. Hernán Mejía Mirabal, the young hero willing to sacrifice his life in the battle against Drake, embodies the virtuous Spanish soldier, as does the protagonist of the third *cuadro,* the Castilian Sancho Jimeno. Lacking the support of his governor, Jimeno must rely on his own men to defend the fort of Boca Chica he has been entrusted. He displays such bravery that he is spared by his adversaries when they finally overcome the Spanish forces. In contrast, the higher-ranking Spanish officials are the ones to blame for their defeat. In both instances, the governors behave irresponsibly and neglect to take the necessary precautions to defend their people.

The indigenous people are also among those guilty of undermining the Spanish victory. As one Spaniard refers to the events related to the fight with Drake, he affirms that the Indians proved to be useless soldiers because they refused to fight during the night. Blacks, too, share the guilt for the tragic outcome in Acosta de Samper's reconstruction of the past. They are traitors who take advantage of the pirates' attack to seek their own freedom. They are the first to confess where the Spanish have hidden their valuables. As one Spaniard asserts, "These Africans take pleasure in harming their masters." This affirmation is attenuated by the narrator's assertion that a few black slaves did, in fact, try to defend the interests of their owners (60). But the narrator does not argue against or contest the negative view of the Indians.

Placing the Spanish bishops and the noble heroes on one side while positioning the blacks and the indigenous people with the corrupt Spanish authorities and the English on the other reflects the distinct configuration of Colombian society endorsed in Acosta de Samper's reconstruction. In this way, she is able to substantiate her conviction that the only individuals who should be included in Colombia's nineteenth-century national project are those who are Catholic and of Spanish descent. Her portrayal clearly responds to the specific issues liberal intellectuals brought forth when they criticized Spain for being the emblem of backwardness—thus the oppositional analogy between Acosta de Samper's and López's portraits of the Spanish.

Yet rather than capriciously twisting the historical events so that they fit the reconstruction as López did (especially in the second half of his novel), Acosta de Samper is much more careful with her manipulation of events. In addition to shifting the focalization, she plays with the time frame of her narration, allowing her to present an unusual, though historically accurate, depiction of the encounter between pirates and Spanish troops. As discussed in the previous chapter, she tends to extend the time span of the events portrayed in order to highlight the eventual superiority of the Spanish. Thus, when Drake attacks Cartagena, she does not end the episode until his death, ten years later, regardless of the fact that the episode in question (as were many other of his attacks) was devastating for the Spanish. Instead, she presents his death as a just punishment for his cruelties and the confirmation that the Spanish were right to oppose him. A similar pattern occurs in her portrayal of Henry Morgan; the *cuadro* concludes years after his attack on Cartagena when Morgan decides to abandon piracy and requests the blessing of a Catholic priest. Acosta de Samper's manipulation of events lies in the elimination of causality; by simply juxtaposing events, she is able to re-direct the reading of history to fit her defense of the Spanish.

Nevertheless, as with López, what enables the narrator to portray certain individuals as immoral and cruel is the fictional aspect of the reconstruction. This is what Acosta de Samper means when she refers to "the imagination" required to retrieve the remote past. Both López and Acosta de Samper know that they must frame history within their cultural and ideological paradigms if they are to be successful in their reconstruction. Thus, history in these novels is a marker of legitimacy used to provide the setting for the fictional plot that carries the true weight of the narration.

One of the most striking aspects of Acosta de Samper's reconstruction is the way she highlights the role women have played in the develop-ment of their country's history. Without failing to comply with the "tra-ditional" feminine portrait, which depicted women as fragile beauties who easily faint when first confronted with danger, her female char-acters—specifically Clara Bustos and Albertina de Leyva—hold strong moral values and are not afraid to act accordingly. In their own way, they too become heroines.[48] While hiding with the rest of the women during Drake's attack, Clara Bustos, the governor's daughter, is joined by her fiancé, a cowardly captain who escapes the scene of the battle, claiming to be worried about her. Ashamed at his action, Clara openly belittles him, saying that a true soldier never abandons an occupied city to attend to personal matters. Clara's rejection of the captain and her de-cision to take charge of a group of frightened women and help them to safety reflect an inner strength aimed at reminding readers the impor-tance of including women within the national project. A man of honor, she adds angrily, would "die defending himself, or run to his compatriots to fight for the king and his country! . . . A true gentleman prefers death to dishonor" (57).

Albertina de Leyva has an even more striking role in the last *cuadro*, which reconstructs Admiral Vernon's expedition to Cartagena in 1738. Having been kidnapped by an English captain, Albertina finds herself living in England amid the future assailants of her country. Refusing to carry on as a simple bystander, Albertina manages to alert the Spanish forces of the English attack. Hence, she too becomes a patriot, risking her life for Spain. In addition to the internal conflicts among the English forces, in Acosta de Samper's portrayal, it is ultimately Albertina's revelation that allows the Spanish to prepare their troops and defeat the English. Although Albertina de Leyva is a fictional character, her actions do not contradict the traditional portrait of women, nor do they alter the historical events relating to Vernon's documented defeat. In fact, this particular *cuadro* has the most extensive historical explanations, detailing the economic and political circumstances behind the confrontation between England and Spain; the narrator even includes, in a footnote, a list of the ships under English command. The *cuadro* is emblematic of the way history is used by Acosta de Samper; it is primarily a point of reference, a means of grounding her fiction in Colombia's history and legitimizing her vision for the future.

Los piratas de Cartagena has been dismissed by Donald McGrady for containing too many historical references. Furthermore, he faults the author for subordinating the fictional aspect of the narration to the historical events presented.[49] Indeed, Acosta de Samper is perhaps the novelist who most attentively confines her reconstruction to historical accuracy. Yet she brings life and drama to the characters and events portrayed, whether historical or fictional. The historical account of the events she presents underlines specific moral attributes she believes Colombians should rescue from their past. By constantly displacing all those who are not good Spanish Catholics, the voice of the narrator, denouncing liberal ideology, overshadows the "impartial" voice claiming to present only the facts. As the novel concludes, the values Spain called on during the colonial past to stand apart from all other European forces are the same values Acosta de Samper claims Colombians should embrace. In addition, the author introduces, discreetly, her concern for women and their role in society. Her female characters are a distinct testimony of the importance women have in consolidating a national identity because they too transmit those essential moral values. Thus Acosta de Samper reminds her readers that women are also protagonists and should not be excluded from history.

Turning Away from Europe

In Mexico during the second half of the century, more precisely after the fall of the emperor Maximilian in 1867, the need to consolidate a sense of national unity became a central project for writers and politicians alike. The numerous wars that had ravaged the country since independence left Mexicans with a painfully crippled nation.[50] Among the intellectuals, Ignacio Altamirano took an active role in fomenting a new type of narrative that he believed would bring Mexicans together and forge a strong national literature. He urged writers to focus specifically on American issues and warned them of the consequences if Europe continued to be looked on as a model:

> Mientras que nos limitemos a imitar la novela francesa, cuya forma es inadaptable a nuestras costumbres y a nuestro modo de ser, no haremos sino pálidas y mezquinas imitaciones, así como no hemos producido más que cantos débiles imitando a los trovadores españoles y a los poetas ingleses y a los franceses. La poesía y la novela mexicanas deben ser vírgenes, vigorosas, originales, como lo son nuestro suelo, nuestras montañas, nuestra vegetación.[51]

> [As long as we continue to imitate the French novel, which cannot be adapted to our customs or way of being, we will only produce pale and wretched imitations. Just as we have only produced ordinary lyrics by imitating Spanish troubadours as well as English and French poets. Mexican novels and poetry must be pristine, vigorous, original as our soil, our mountains, and our vegetation.]

Literature, for Altamirano, had a patriotic mission. He was adamant that Mexicans no longer let Europeans describe Mexican customs, virtues, and vices. It was the Mexicans' responsibility to explain what being Mexican was all about; no one else's. Part of that project meant reclaim-

ing the distant past, the times of Huitzilopoxtli, of Cinanteutli and Mit-
lanteutli, a period Altamirano characterized as "an endless mine," which
the garrulous foreigner simply corrupted into "ridiculous legends" (10).
Altamirano's project was to stimulate a national narrative, and his articles, published as *Revistas Literarias de México*, constitute the first serious
project of organizing the literary production in Mexico after independence.[52]

Altamirano's ideals are echoed in Eligio Ancona's introduction to *El
filibustero*, where he strongly criticizes those who seek inspiration in
European models:

> El campo es vasto y seductor para el historiador, para el poeta y para
> el novelista. Desgraciadamente la mayor parte de los escritores latino
> americanos, en vez de cultivar este campo casi virgen todavía, han ido,
> como Calderón y García de Quevedo, á buscar sus inspiraciones á la
> vieja Europa.[53] (viii)

> [For the historian, the poet, and the novelist, the terrain is vast and
> seductive. Unfortunately the majority of Latin American writers has fol-
> lowed Calderón and García de Quevedo in search of inspiration from
> ancient Europe instead of cultivating this virgin land.]

As a historian, Ancona believed it was necessary to be well documented
and record as much information as possible to give a complete reconstruction of the events. History was to be written with impartiality;
taking sides was out of the question. His well-known, extensive com-
pendium of Yucatán's past, *Historia de Yucatán*, remains an example of
his precepts about the writing of history. Yet Ancona also believed that
the historian had a much more important task than just providing a detailed description of the events occurring in a particular country:

> La historia para llenar el importante objeto que tiene en la vida social,
> no debe limitarse a una relación más o menos detallada de los sucesos
> acaecidos en el país de que se ocupa. Debe comprender además un
> cuadro tan completo como sea posible, de las índoles, de los usos y
> costumbres de cada una de las razas, que en diversas épocas lo han
> habitado; de su religión, de sus leyes, de sus dotes morales e intelectu-
> ales; de las causas que han influído en sus revoluciones, de las cualidades

que posea para elevarse, de los obstáculos que le impiden su desarrollo; de todo aquello, en fin, que pueda utilizar algún día para engrandecerse y mejorar su posición.[54]

[In order to fulfill its important role in social life, history must not be limited to reproducing in more or less detailed fashion the events that took place in a particular country. History must also offer as complete a portrait as possible of the practices and customs of the different races that have lived in that country throughout time. It must reflect its religion, laws, moral qualities, intellectual characteristics, the causes that influenced its revolutions, a country's disposition to progress and the obstacles to its development. In other words, everything that some day might help that country flourish and improve its standing.]

History, according to Ancona, is geared toward the future. Its main purpose is to teach individuals about their society so that they may engage in improving, correcting, and ennobling their country. Each race seems to have a purpose. Yet in this novel, Ancona does not assign any particular importance to the Indians and their culture, whose presence in the Yucatán was extremely significant, nor to blacks. Although the author is referring to the role of history in this passage, it was the novel, rather than history, that he thought best presented a complete portrait of society to the average reader.

In *El filibustero,* Ancona pays little attention to historical accuracy. Instead of presenting well-known, documented events and characters from the colonial period (as most historical novelists did even if their reconstruction was not entirely historical), he chooses to focus on a completely fictional aspect of that past, the life of a well-meaning orphan, Leonel, and his life as a pirate. Nevertheless, the first two pages of Ancona's novel are dedicated to citing the sources he used for his reconstruction of the past. He states that the first part of his novel, which describes life during the colony, is strongly indebted to the portrait presented by the Spanish poet García Gutiérrez in *Los alcaldes de Valladolid.* Ancona goes on to highlight the main difference between both texts, claiming that the central subject of his novel only touches on history "accidentally," whereas Gutiérrez's novel is submerged in it (2).

Despite the claim that his novel is only fortuitously historical, Ancona inserts a number of historical references throughout the text to create a realistic background. But the narrator prefers not to cite the actual sources of information, with two exceptions: an article by the liberal historian Justo Sierra and a history of the Yucatán written by the friar Diego López de Cogolludo.[55] The information is generally summarized, or else facts and dates are simply asserted without any reference to specific documents for corroboration. Furthermore, most of the historical information presented in the novel is anecdotal: the names and dates of a few governors, the number of councilmen a city hall had, or the date a specific convent was constructed. The overall portrait of colonial life is quite varied. The narrator gives a general description of the different attitudes and lifestyles that coexisted at the time, from those of the religious and political authorities to the hardships of everyday life of the economically less fortunate. This portrait is presented from a distinct ideological position, despite the few comments interspersed assuring an "impartial" view, as the following observation comparing past and present institutions indicates: "Nosotros no abogamos en favor de uno ni de otro sistema: conocemos las ventajas y desventajas de cada" [We do not plead in favor of one system in particular: we know the advantages and disadvantages of each] (202).

Readers know from the introduction and the very first pages of the novel that the narrator has extremely strong feelings about the colonial system and its impact on Yucatán. In fact, there seems to be a tacit solidarity between the narrator and his audience. In the first place, the implied readers have a specific identity, one that is shared with the narrative voice; they are referred to as "hijos del ardiente suelo de mi patria" [sons of my spirited homeland] (302). In addition, the illusion of intimacy between the narrator and the readers is enhanced as the introduction begins with a reference to Ancona's previous novel, *La cruz y la espada*, a historical narrative set during the conquest that appeared the same year as *El filibustero*. Picking up where this novel ended, the narrator proceeds to fill readers in on the events that occurred in Yucatán during the 160 years that separate the settings of both texts. It is as if the narrator were carrying on a conversation with his readers, hence, the rhetorical questions interjected to reaffirm the contact and thread the numerous subplots in the novel: "¿Te acuerdas, lector de aquel bueno de Cifuentes?" [Do you remember, reader, that good old Cifuentes?] (299). These side remarks reinforce the closeness with the readers, guiding their connections as they fill in the blanks in the narrative.[56]

For Ancona, the purpose of reflecting on Yucatán's past is to learn about its civilization and distinguish positive traits from "poisonous" ones. In this way, readers will be able to identify whatever negative elements have survived from the past and hopefully eradicate their influence from their society. Consequently, Ancona highlights specific elements, particularly those related to the abuses of the Inquisition, and contrasts them with the present.[57]

The abuses and corruption governing colonial institutions are what force Leonel to become a pirate. As this fictional hero confronts Spanish family values, in addition to religious and political authorities, he discovers the multiple facets of injustice and immorality. The narrator not only describes Leonel's feelings but also inserts certain remarks to reinforce the tyranny of the Church as well as that of the judicial system. In doing so, the narrator appears to refrain from using a harsh tone. When Father Hernando, Leonel's tutor, is introduced, the narrator ironically states that he originally came to the Yucatán "en una de tantas remisiones de frailes, que no sabemos si para bien ó mal de la colonia, nos enviaba de cuando en cuando el católico celo de los monarcas españoles" [in one of those many shipments of friars that the Spanish monarchs with their Catholic fervor sent us, we do not know if for better or for worse] (6). As the story develops, it is evident that the presence of friars had a negative effect on the colony, for many of them, as Father Hernando illustrates, were extremely corrupt and immoral. This image is not so much the result of documented proof as it is of the fictional story and of Ancona's effective use of ridicule and satire.[58] For example, the honoring of saints with bullfights, a custom the narrator defines as barbaric, is ridiculed by the interjection "strange way of giving thanks." This mocking is further enhanced as the narrator states that the Inquisition accused an innocent merchant, Pedro Cifuentes, of being a Jew because he wore clean clothes on Saturdays.

The most interesting aspect of Ancona's novel is the way he transforms Leonel's conversion to piracy into a crusade of national vindication. Ancona had already stated in his introduction that among the torments that assailed his country, one was unquestionably piracy:

Las huellas que dejaron [los piratas] sembradas en la península aun se conservan bastante vivas en la memoria de todos para que creamos necesario recordar aqui los templos que profanaron, las riquezas que fueron objeto de sus rapiñas, las poblaciones que saquearon y redujeron a cenizas y el reguero de sangre con que marcaron su transito donde quiera que se posaron sus inmundas plantas. (vi–vii)

[The traces [pirates] left in the peninsula are still alive in everyone's memory enough to warrant remembering the temples they desecrated, the riches they stole, the towns they ransacked and burned to the ground, and the blood they left marking every step of their way.]

Despite this assertion, the only individual who actually fights for the well-being of Yucatán is Leonel, a pirate. Only as a pirate is he able to confront the Spanish authorities, demand justice, and make sure they comply with his requests. But it is only by abducting the future governor and captain general of the province, Meneses Bravo de Saravia, that Leonel's voice can be heard. As a pirate, he does not fulfill the traditional image identified with these individuals or with the author's initial description of piracy. In fact, the strongest criticism of colonial institutions is voiced by Leonel as a pirate. Piracy in this text becomes a form of empowerment. It allows Leonel to fight for the justice he has been denied. Ancona is able to articulate this peculiar twist by connecting the fictional story of Leonel and Berenguela to the existence of Barbillas, a pirate who kidnapped Governor Meneses in 1708 but whose origin is unknown.[59] Ancona gives Barbillas a past and an identity in his novel while offering a patent example of the effects colonial institutions had on Yucatec society. This is essentially Eligio Ancona's goal; history is only a loose frame to portray, in a more intense and personal way, how Spanish institutions damaged the life of Ancona's native Yucatán.

Ancona's use of colonial history was undoubtedly influenced by another well-known Yucatec writer, Justo Sierra O'Reilly, who in 1842— twenty-two years before Ancona—had published his historical novel *El filibustero*. Although Sierra O'Reilly did not actually write a formal history of Yucatán, it was one of his preferred topics. In addition to novels having to do with Yucatán's past, he published and edited numerous historical works, most importantly Diego López de Cogolludo's *Historia de Yucatán*.[60] This text concentrates on events that occurred in the Yucatán from the sixteenth century until the beginning of the seventeenth century. López de Cogolludo's work was considered essential for any subsequent study of the history of the Yucatán and was published twice during the nineteenth century (in 1842 and 1867). Sierra O'Reilly was in charge of the second edition, which appeared in 1842. He also planned to continue López de Cogolludo's work until the time of independence, but only the second volume appeared in 1845. Another significant contribution to the understanding of Yucatán's past that Sierra O'Reilly made was to translate John L. Stephens's study based on his archaeological explorations of the ruins in the peninsula.[61]

Sierra O'Reilly begins El filibustero, subtitled "A Legend," with a footnote—the only one in the entire text—certifying that "this legend is completely historical even in its most insignificant circumstances" (3). However, except for the name of Diego el mulato and a few dates specifying his attacks on Campeche, there are no explicit historical references. Sierra O'Reilly reconstructs Diego's actions, focusing on the terrible image this cruel pirate conjured up for the population during the seventeenth century. He adds a certain complexity to the character of Diego by including a fictional ill-fated romance. The romance allows Diego to be portrayed as both violent and sensitive, brutal and considerate, as he attacks the Campechanos with rage and yet is determined to protect his beloved from any possible harm.

Historically, the few documented references to Diego el mulato are varied and at times confusing. In Philip Gosse's Who's Who of piracy, a pirate by the name of Diego or Diego Grillo appears to have been active during the 1600s, although he is said to have been a mulatto from Havana. Among his accomplishments, he defeated three armed ships that had been sent to capture him in the Bahama Channel and massacred all the Spaniards he found among the crew. He was eventually caught in 1673 (which is precisely when Sierra's story ends) and hanged.[62] According to Juan Juárez Moreno, Diego el mulato did attack Campeche on August 11, 1633. Juárez Moreno claims that Diego knew the area quite well, for he had lived in Campeche before becoming a pirate, but the captain leading the attack on Campeche was "Pie de Palo," a Dutch pirate whose real name was Cornelio Jol.[63]

Sierra O'Reilly's novel implies that Diego is from Campeche, since Captain Galván, the man in charge of defending the city, is Diego's godfather. But most records, if in fact they mention his origin, state that

Diego was born in Havana and worked for the Dutch. Whether or not Galván was his godfather is unclear, since most references do not mention him.[64]

Another historical reference is to be found in Thomas Gage's chronicle of New Spain. Gage was an Irish friar who entered the Dominican convent in Valladolid, Spain, at a very young age. Eager to travel, he was allowed to go to the Philippines to continue catechizing and arrived in Mexico in 1625. Preferring the joys of secular life to the quiet and isolation of his cell, Gage abandoned his religious teachings and embarked on a trip to Guatemala. He continued his travels, accumulating pearls and riches before returning to England. Unfortunately, on his way back, his ship was seized by Diego *el mulato,* who, according to Gage's report, allowed him to keep certain books and paintings but confiscated all his money and precious stones. Gage states that when he realized he would not be able to recover his belongings, "I commended myself again to God's providence and protection."[65] On his way back to England, Gage stopped in Havana and claimed to have visited Diego's mother, but he does not describe her or add any further information. According to Gage, Diego was mistreated by the governor of Campeche, for whom he had been working. This led him to enlist with the Dutch forces he dutifully served. But Gage does not explain why Diego was in Campeche. After gaining respect among the Dutch, Diego became captain of a ship under the well-known and extremely feared Dutch pirate Pata de Palo and, seeking revenge, attacked Campeche. A similar version is presented in Diego López de Cogolludo's *Historia de Yucatán.*

There is presently no documented reference for the romance between Diego and Conchita that Sierra O'Reilly presents in his novel. There is, however, a curious rescue Diego apparently made, in which a woman was involved, documented by López de Cogolludo.[66] After Diego's attack on Campeche, the viceroy of Nueva España replaced the governor of Yucatán, General Fernando Centeno. Furious with this decision, Centeno left for Mexico to file his complaint but died off the coast of Campeche. His wife, Doña Isabel de Caraveo, decided to proceed with the trip, but her ship was attacked by Diego's men. Informed who Doña Isabel was, Diego freed the widow, ordering his men to escort her back to Campeche. This event, recorded by López de Cogolludo, adds a certain complexity to Diego's character and is perhaps what inspired Sierra

O'Reilly to create a romance between the pirate and Conchita in *El fili-bustero.*

The novel opens with Captain Domingo Galván exhorting his men to defend their city, a powerful plea addressed to the Campechanos to guard their homes and to do it in their own interest, not for the king.

> A las armas, valientes campechanos! los bárbaros vienen a robaros, a insultaros, a saquear nuestras casas, a violar nuestras hijas, y a incendiar la población. ¡El rey! ¡qué es el rey cuando se trata de conservar el honor y la existencia de lo que tenéis de más caro en la tierra? ¡no! la causa del rey, no es la que vais a defender: es la vuestra, es la causa de Yucatán: es la de la muy noble y leal villa dé Campeche. (1)

> [To arms, courageous Campechanos! The barbarians come to rob you, insult you, ransack our homes, rape our women, and burn our town. The king! What is a king when what is at stake is the honor and defense of everything you hold dear? No! You are not going to defend the king's cause; it is your cause, the cause of Yucatán, the cause of the noble and loyal city of Campeche.]

The difference between Spain and Spanish America is clearly defined from the beginning. But the division is not bipolar; it is more complex. On the one hand, the Yucatán stands apart from Spain and its king be-cause they do not share the same territory. For Spain, America is not a home; it is only a colony with riches that the Spanish believe they have the right to exploit and a duty to protect, whereas for the Ameri-cans, their land is their home. Consequently, it is the responsibility of the local forces to defend what is truly theirs, not the Spaniards. On the other hand, the Yucatecs and Spanish have, in addition to their heri-tage, a common enemy: the pirates, the ruthless barbarians who rob them of both their homes and their riches. In this novel, those defending the colonies against their invaders are not the Spanish but the Yucatecs themselves. All others are foreigners. Galván's opening harangue is that of an American patriot, not a Spanish captain of the seventeenth cen-tury.[67] Sierra O'Reilly does not revere the Spanish or the English, but rather the Americans; they are the heroes of their history.

But America is not a consolidated unity; in fact, Spanish Americans are struggling to secure a particular image of their nation and continent. This becomes clear as Sierra O'Reilly places the issue of race at the center of the novel. Diego *el mulato* turns to piracy because in spite of being a *criollo*, he has been rejected from society because of the color of his skin. Diego's father is also positioned at the periphery of this society. He is a fisherman living on the outskirts of Campeche, alone, removed from the rest of the residents, bothering no one. The narrator's description leads us to believe that he is a foreigner, though we do not know of what nationality: "Some said he was Italian, others, Portuguese, and others thought he was Dutch. The truth is that no one knew" (4). His green eyes and olive complexion seem to characterize him as a Mediterranean. He is guilty of rejecting his own son and leading him to the crimes he has committed. However, the novel does not explain why he was rejected or why Diego harbors a passionate violence toward Campeche. Chroniclers seem to agree that he was offended or mistreated by an official of Campeche, but little is said about the specific event.[68] In any case, the novel portrays as foreigners all those who are not Campechanos. Still, we are never told what defines a Campechano.

The narrator of *El filibustero* dramatizes the events and characters in the novel. Contrasts of light and darkness magnify sensations and actions within the text. Conchita sees Diego for the first time in a tiny chapel where a flickering, pale light projects Diego's gigantic shadow on the altar. Her fear overwhelms her, and she faints. The evening Diego and his men attack Campeche, the night becomes dark and somber, almost as a warning of the tragic events to come. And as Diego and Conchita begin their escape from Campeche, a forceful storm disrupts the sea. Every event is depicted in terms of black and white, good and evil. Except, perhaps, Diego's impressive gaze. His eyes have an inexplicable gleam, fascinating and insinuating; his look is both divine and fiendish. This mysterious glow makes him a frightening being with moments of tenderness and adds a certain complexity to the narration.[69]

To emphasize the suspense throughout the text, the narrator reports the events as they occur, watching closely, almost possessed. Hence the use of the present tense and the profusion of exclamation marks and ellipses. When the pirates arrive, Conchita prays for protection but is abruptly interrupted:

> ¡Santo Dios! súbitamente oye tocar a arrebato las cornetas, trompas y añafiles dan la señal de la proximidad del enemigo. Trémula, escucha la voz del capitán Galván, que manda a hacer fuego. . . . . ¡¡¡Poumb!!!

un tiro de artillería venido del mar. . . . : las balas se cruzan. . . . . el tiroteo se generaliza. . . . . . Conchita cae sin sentido desmayada en el templo, sin un solo testigo, sin una sola mano que la socorriese. (6)

[Oh my God! Suddenly she hears horns, bugles, and trumpets announcing the enemy in sight. Trembling, she hears Captain Galvan's voice ordering to fire. . . . . Boom! Artillery discharge coming from the sea. . . . : bullets zooming above . . . . . the firing is general. . . . . . Conchita falls unconscious in the church, without any witnesses, without a hand to help her.]

The narrator takes the readers step-by-step through the events without excluding any feelings the main characters may have. The result is a narrative with an overtly melodramatic tone shifting constantly between extremes: from the solitary beaches where Diego disembarks to the turmoil of the city under attack; from the safety of the fisherman's home to the streets inundated with fear and death; from Conchita's angelic looks to Diego's savagery and violence. Mysterious appearances, promises, battles, shipwrecks, frightening dark skies, struggles between love and duty, all these elements are condensed to create the striking legend of Diego *el mulato.*

History in this novel remains at a distance, displaced by romantic descriptions and a tragic love story. Sierra O'Reilly's liberal views are for the most part silent. His discussion of the future of the Yucatán seems to be absent. Yet *El filibustero* echoes his interest in retrieving the Yucatán's history and the forces involved in its struggle to come into being. Documenting its past, legends, and myths, and placing the Campechanos at the center of his text, Sierra O'Reilly makes sure the Yucatecs appropriate their own legends and history.

Throughout the historical narratives discussed, the factors involved in the struggles presented never really affect society as a whole. The totality of national life is, in fact, reduced to the *criollo* elite. The *criollos* are the central characters, embodying heroes and villains. Unlike the average, independent, "middle-of-the-road" heroes Scott had portrayed, these heroes are politically committed individuals who take a stand in the struggle of national identity, if not explicitly, at least through the values they represent. The past that is reconstructed in these novels has little to do with establishing a common heritage for the whole population. Instead, it reveals the issues that were at stake for the elites of the newly emancipated countries. Through their emplotment of history and the values being questioned, these novels present the *criollos* as the subjects forming the body of the nation; it is from their perspective that the forces "detaining progress" are viewed. Hence the historical reconstructions portrayed reflect only the positions and relations that the *criollo* elites perceived as definitive in constituting their national identity.

CHAPTER FIVE

The Force of Melodrama

Le mélodrame, au premier chef, est considéré comme "persona non grata" de l'histoire littéraire. Honni de tous, drame de la démesure, il est devenu synonyme de mauvais goût.
—Jean-Marie Thomasseau, *Le Mélodrame*

Melodrama has been discussed in diverse and often contradictory contexts: from its original theatrical form to contemporary soap operas.[1] As a genre, it is located within specific cultural and historical boundaries significantly developed by Guilbert de Pixérécourt, known as the father of melodrama. The presence of stock characters personifying moral qualities through their physical appearance and exaggerated gesticulation and a confrontation of extremes with a happy ending are the essential elements reinforcing the hyperbolic visual effects of this sensationalist spectacle that mesmerized popular audiences during the nineteenth century. Although it remains associated with a "popular" form of entertainment, melodrama's impact has extended across genres far beyond the dramatic form of its time, and thus today the term is most commonly used in a descriptive sense.[2]

In its origin, melodrama provided popular classes a way to dramatize the intensity of the violent events of the French Revolution while reestablishing at the same time order and stability as justice triumphed in the end. In spite of the cultural and political differences within Europe, the popularity of this dramatic form enabled it to reflect the intense social and economic changes stemming from the large-scale industrial production of the nineteenth century and the breakdown of two important institutions: the monarchy and the Church. Traditional values society had held until then as imperatives were violently questioned.

As a response to the void formed by the crude dismantling of precepts and traditional lifestyles, melodrama presented itself as a unifying and structuring expression. Looks, signs, and gestures became the defining traits of this dramatic form, which staged conspiracies against innocent victims and filled its sets with prisons, dungeons, violence, and blood. In the end, order and justice would be restored, and the evil traitors plotting against the innocent would have to pay for their criminal acts. Through its extremism, melodrama sought to configure a specific order and alleviate the sense of rupture. The need to dramatize and present extremes was purposefully used in melodrama, in both its dramatic and its narrative forms, to ensure the audience/reader's immediate engagement in expelling "evil" from the social order established.

Because of its idealized and simplified vision of the world, where happy endings prevail and the hero is reunited with the heroine, Michael Booth has defined melodrama as "a dream world."[3] It is an allegory of human experience ordered as it should be rather than as it is precisely because the world portrayed is essentially the one its audiences/readers want in the end but cannot get. In looking at the ideological connotations of melodrama, Peter Brooks sees in this restoration of justice a conservative didactic intention:

> Thus with the triumph of virtue at the end, there is not, as in comedy, the emergence of a new society formed around the united young couple, ridded of the impediment represented by the blocking figure from the older generation, but rather a reforming of the old society of innocence, which has now driven out the threat to its existence and reaffirmed its values. Nor is there, as in tragedy, a reconciliation to a sacred order larger than man. The expulsion of evil entails no sacrifice, and there is no communal partaking of the sacred body. There is rather confirmation and restoration.[4]

In Spanish America, however, the strong moral lesson embedded within the events portrayed and the eventual happy ending of melodramas do not necessarily imply a reinstatement of the values of the old society. In fact, during postindependence, the existence of inequalities and undemocratic sensibilities was displaced onto the past, in order to allow a new staging of success, which coincided with a new political order brought about with independence. Thus, the union of the young couple, typical in melodrama, is possible only with the formation of a new societal order—and whether this order can be achieved is a question left unanswered in some of the narratives. Although melodrama may not have been able to effect a fundamental change in any culture's political and economic structures, it staged the tensions and social conflicts that existed between classes.[5] But to the extent that this conflict was articulated by the educated members of the ruling class, and not the lower classes themselves, melodrama should also be seen as a reflection of the way the ruling class regarded the role of the popular classes.[6]

Throughout the first part of the century, the melodramatic conflict in Spanish America was articulated between the *criollo* elites and their European heritage. When dealing with issues of nation building, many authors, as members of the established elite, used the domestic melodrama to articulate their own fears and reasons for securing a specific societal order in which certain European models were either rejected or endorsed. Placing the conflict within the home enabled writers to illustrate effectively the impact the dramatic changes resulting from the wars of independence had or would have on the population without directly addressing social inequalities. The home was a site that everyone, regardless of class or racial differences, could relate to. It enabled the personal, staged through moral conflict, to take preeminence over everything else. By staging political differences through moral conflicts in the home, writers avoided dealing with concrete aspects of the political programs they endorsed and could present an all-encompassing view of the new nation. Morality, and consequently melodrama, was the ideal means to plot the nation, for it subsumed political conflict and erased class differences. Furthermore, in positioning the home as center stage, the conflict between domestic and foreign was also addressed as national borders were extended through moral alliances with European countries.

The historical novels analyzed in this study are not melodramas in the generic sense, but the theatrical substratum of the genre is evident in their structure and use of stereotypes. Furthermore, by simply observing the types of homes and values presented, it is evident that these novels, while exemplifying what Peter Brooks defined as the "melodramatic mode," a way of making sense of experience, are not directed toward popular audiences.[7] The popular classes are included tangentially and only because they are part of the social order, but they have no real voice. These novels constitute part of a fictional system, "a field of semantic force," through which the elites articulated the discussion of nation building in their own clear and manifest terms. How this discussion was structured through the domestic melodrama is precisely the focus of this chapter.

The Family as Nation

Writers found the home to be the ideal setting for their novels because it enabled them to illustrate the consequences of endorsing a specific model of nation and promote specific societal values. In fact, it was within the parameters of the home that the ideals and morals of the newly formed nations would be first enforced. López, for example, stressed throughout *La novia de hereje* the correlation between the family and the nation, drawing strongly on the parallelisms between the tyranny and corruption of the Spanish home and nation in contrast to the refined and caring atmosphere of the English home and nation. The need to redefine the home and the family during postindependence was not only legitimate but crucial. In that process, López redefined national alliances and political boundaries he thought were important in consolidating a future for Argentina. Hence the home became the site of the new social and emotional configuration of the nation, where the personal blended with the political, thus charging the family with a symbolic potency.[8]

As writers and statesmen underlined the importance of the family, women, placed within the domestic sphere, acquired a significant role in ensuring the well-being of the nation. Although they were excluded from an active political role in the public sphere, their task was to ensure the development of healthy future citizens within the sacred and confined realm of the home. Defined solely by their emotional association to the nation, women were nevertheless recognized as participants in the process of nation building. As future mothers of citizens who would inhabit and shape society, women were positioned within the nation but restricted to the secure and private domain of the home. Their task was to reproduce—translate—the beneficial effects the political values defined by men had in the forging of a happy household, which in turn would ensure a healthy and prosperous nation. Yet as melodramas plotted the ideological conflicts within the domestic sphere, women were immersed in the political configuration of the nation, and their role began to transcend their domestic boundaries in the same way that the boundaries of the home were extended across the Atlantic. Family happiness was a consequence not only of healthy feelings but, more importantly, of specific political ideals that built and sustained the prosperity of a blissful home. Hence the private world of the home became deeply entwined with the public world of politics. It is precisely this overlapping of spheres (the sentimental and private versus the political and public) that exposes the contradictions embedded within the social framework of the nation imagined during postindependence, as well as the role women were assigned in the process of nation building.

Focusing on women's emotional confinement, Doris Sommer has studied in depth the relationship between the love story or "romance" and the nation.[9] Sommer analyzes a number of "historical romances," mostly of the nineteenth century, focusing on how the desire for domestic happiness that is fueled in the texts "runs over into dreams of national prosperity." Hence, her reading is geared toward locating the erotics of politics and showing how the national ideals are grounded in "natural" heterosexual love and in marriages that provide a figure for "apparently" nonviolent consolidation during the midcentury conflicts.[10]

Sommer's work is important, for it illustrates how the political conflicts of nation building during postindependence were negotiated in their fictional emplotments. Through the political positioning of those involved in the relationship, the "ideal" marriage came to symbolize the realization of the ideal state. In some of the pirate novels, the correlation between the founding of an "ideal" home and that of the "ideal" nation is obvious (Acosta de Samper, López). At other times, the texts are unable to prescribe the ideal relationship but expose somewhat haphazardly specific elements that hinder the formation of a good home (Sierra O'Reilly, Ancona). Building on Sommer's provocative reading of nation building, my objective is to expand the relation between the love story and the nation by concentrating on the texts' melodramatic aspect in order to thresh out the cultural and ideological frameworks, representations, and discourses that reflect how the nation is imagined and, more importantly, explore how women are positioned in that imagining. By focusing on the melodramatic mode, the contradictions of the political projects debated during postindependence, mirrored in the structure and narrative mode of these novels, become apparent.

For the melodramatic plot to take shape, a heroine must be part of the conflict to maintain the triadic structure of hero, villain, and heroine. Placed in the home and defined fundamentally through their emotional bond to men, women are portrayed as daughters, wives, and mothers who can fulfill their role only through love. Hence, the significance of the love story.

But pirate novels are not love stories; they are about adventures, tempestuous battles, struggles for individuality, and the freedom of choice. In fact, the love stories in these novels are a result of the melodramatic form and only take a secondary role. It is the pirate, with his Janus-like embodiment of hero or villain, who is the springboard and controls the plot. The pirate novels in this study underscore the possibility of a relationship between hero and heroine, but that relationship can materialize only if the political and moral factors that make up the home permit it, and if the hero can overcome all the political obstacles. His trophy is the heroine. Hence, more than the love story itself, the novels focus on the violence embedded within or surrounding the home, which reproduces the battles of national consolidation that hamper the possibility of a romantic union. As the pirates' adventures invade the home, women, though positioned as spectators, are consequently endowed with a political responsibility. And it is within this context that we may find challenges to women's confinement within the domestic realm of the nation as well as the discursive difficulties writers had in imagining their future and the role women were to have.

Domestic melodrama internalizes the ways in which transformations of the outside world affect the family structure, while giving preeminence to the ideal of domestic happiness. In her discussion of the English domestic melodrama, Martha Vicinus notes that family disasters are caused by the economic, social, and religious changes brought on by capitalism. Corruption in these texts is generally linked to aristocracy and capitalists who exploit their workers, but the happy ending ensures that the wicked will eventually fall. Consequently, when a factory burns down, it does so because the owner is greedy; or when a ship sinks, it does so because the captain is cruel; and although their laborers also suffer, somehow the virtuous worker is always saved in the end. Thus Vicinus asserts:

> The family became the refuge from change and the sustainer of familiar values. But as melodrama so tellingly documents, it also became the arena for the most profound struggles between good and evil. The strength of the home and of domestic ties is tested under extreme conditions. Yet these struggles also reassure because they show virtue defeating villainy and—in characteristic Victorian fashion—being rewarded with love, wealth, and security. (131)

In the domestic melodramas of Spanish America, however, instead of providing comfort or some form of reassurance, the home becomes the center stage for the political conflicts taking place within a country. Unlike the European model, the home during postindependence is not a refuge from the changes and difficulties of everyday life, but rather the domain where these changes are openly articulated and where the need to assert a new value system becomes vital; it is where the nation-state defines itself as such. Domestic happiness is possible only if the morals governing the home mirror the ideals of the emancipation movements; if they do not fulfill this requirement, that particular home will most surely have to be destroyed, or a new one must be created, as López so effectively shows us. In this sense, the domestic melodrama in Spanish America is more about rupture or the dangers provoking that rupture than about healing.

In general, the confrontations in domestic melodramas are of two types. The villain, who actually initiates the conflict, may be within the family itself, for example, a tyrannical father who unjustly banishes or hurts his son or daughter. When the villain does not belong to the family, he is nevertheless the one who sets off the clash between family members. In the first instance, the father must repent to restore the family's happiness. If this is impossible, a new family must be founded. The second type of confrontation exposes, in the end, the internal strength and moral values a family is capable of drawing forth when faced with adversity. Whatever the cause of the conflict, it is staged between the parents and their children. It is the battle of the rebellious generations defying their tyrannical parents in search of a new order and freedom, as Spanish America took up arms to free itself from Spain's control. The parallel between the American nations rising to quell their oppressive colonial past is echoed in the young children rebelling against their parents' arbitrary ways. Only in Acosta de Samper's reconstruction is there a continuum between parents and children, as she stresses the importance of the Spanish heritage in America. Ultimately, the family home is the setting where the Oedipal conflict takes full force, reproducing not only the generational conflict but also the clash between the young Spanish American countries and their *madre patria.*

In the historical novels dealing with piracy, the battles with the pirates do not remain exclusively at a national level as they did during the colonial period; they are much more than confrontations between different nations or political projects. The conflict of national imaginings is internalized as the pirate penetrates the realm of the home, and the political confrontation inherent in his national identity is relocated within the domestic sphere. The pirate is an intruder who disrupts not only the economic and political "well-being" of a society but also the family, a more personal and sacred realm. If that home is ruled by fear and injustice, the pirate will be cast as the hero for liberating the heroine from the cruel hands of her father or a sinister future husband as in *La novia del hereje.* If, instead, the family lives in harmony, the pirate becomes the villain and must be persecuted and punished to protect the home. His death in these cases is therefore well deserved, as Acosta de Samper's narrative portrays. The real difficulty of establishing the emotional and political boundaries of the pirate occurs when he is not an outsider but instead belongs to the home (as in Ancona's and Sierra O'Reilly's novels). He is already part of the inner visualization of the nation. His presence uncovers the internal conflict within the home as well as within the nation. Hence, the reasons for being outcast (race, class) can only be hinted at in these texts because one of the central traits of melodrama is to expose the conflict in a universal dichotomy, annulling all contradictions. Furthermore, Spanish Americans wanted to avoid addressing differences of class and race in order to unify their political projects and present them as unifying and all-encompassing.

On the surface, melodrama presents an overly simplistic view of the world, where perplexity and doubt are completely absent. It is a world in which justice must ultimately triumph and a moral order must be secured, however fragile it may seem. Whatever the temporal obstruction—be it violence, natural disasters, killings, poisonings, shipwrecks, tortured heroines, or persecuted heroes—in the end, virtue must somehow prevail.[11] The exaltation of victory and the scorning of wrongdoing during a time of rapid change is undoubtedly one of melodrama's most distinct attractions and explains its rise and rapid success in Europe as well as in Spanish America. But melodrama is much more than a simple exteriorization of archetypes. As a spectacle, it stimulates immediate recognition and identification, steering the audience/readers to share the injustice committed against a character and thus persuading them to identify with the hero's or heroine's revolt against such unfair treatment.[12]

When the cause of that unfair treatment encompasses specific ideological and moral principles identified with the villain, what is being rejected is not only the villain himself for being morally despicable but also his political beliefs. In this sense, Heilman states that melodrama is "the principal vehicle of protest and dissent," a form of dissent that novelists in Spanish America were quick to appropriate.[13] Whereas tragedy is said to focus on the conflict within the individual to choose what is right, melodrama exteriorizes the conflict by confronting opposites; thus, the action lies within the sociopolitical realm, not the individual. But as that sociopolitical sphere enters the home, the clash between forces becomes both personal and political. At a time when most Spanish American nations were trying to overcome their internal struggles and institute a state model, domestic melodrama provided a way to dramatize the confrontations between political projects while forcing individuals to understand the relevance these projects had or would have in their personal lives. It was, in other words, a way of inciting the development of a national consciousness.

Delimited by their melodramatic structure, the confrontations presented in these novels are cast between individuals embodying different political forces; but it is through the characters' behavior and ethics that a particular political project becomes good or bad. This explains why the clash between the conservative and liberal parties in these Spanish American melodramas is not formulated in terms of their economic or political policies, but rather by highlighting the moral differences and conduct of their members. Each character in these texts is distinctly aligned with an ideological position, but what makes that position loathsome is the character's moral attributes. Hence, the heroes in these domestic melodramas do not represent just political ideals; they also embody forms of virtue and justice associated with those political ideals.

Although each character has a distinct role within the conflict, character development in melodrama is practically nonexistent. The apparent flatness critics complain about is due to the lack of psychological depth. This is precisely one of the central criticisms that McGrady makes of Acosta de Samper's narrative:

> These moral traits correspond to the physical features of a character; hence, upon seeing a particular character, we know what to expect. These characters always act in accordance with the first traits the author gives us. Thus, the reader is never surprised.[14]

Unlike their counterparts in a tragedy, melodramatic characters do not have inner conflicts. Everything is exteriorized, the confrontation is located between the two central characters (the villain and the hero) or between the hero and the forces beyond his individual control (natural disasters such as earthquakes, storms, and wars). Each character represents one fundamental emotion that is determined by the individual's moral stand. Resolving the conflict means overcoming the obstacles that have been thrust forward. These characters have no contradictions, no uncertainties, no unique personal qualities. They are essentially the same: either good or bad. It is this sense of wholeness or "monopathy" that distinguishes the melodramatic characters.[15]

As melodrama exteriorizes the conflict, physical traits become significant, not only because from the outset they position each character as good or evil, but most importantly because those physical traits express the ideal looks of the future nation. Looks are intimately tied to moral values, which reflect political ideals. The three main characters of every melodrama—hero, heroine, and villain—all have well-defined corporeal traits, so that as soon as they appear, they will be unmistakably identified without even having to utter a word. The hero, for example, is commonly portrayed as a young and handsome man, eternally devoted to his sweetheart or wife with an inner strength and determination capable of overcoming all the ghastly machinations of any villain. One has only to recall López's portrait of his hero:

Henderson era un joven rubio que apenas contaba con veintitrés años. Su brillante cabellera caía a la moda de aquel tiempo en tostados rizos sobre sus hombros. Una tez limpia y rosada daba a sus miradas juveniles una expresión particular de viveza y de petulancia amable. Sus cejas eran como dos líneas rectas sobre sus ojos que venían a borrarse en el delicado arranque de la nariz; y de su boca, pulida como una obra de arte, y airosamente entreabierta, salía franco y fácil el resuello de su noble corazón. (62)

[Henderson was a blond youth, only twenty-three years old. Following the fashion of the times, his long silky hair reached his shoulders in curls. His clean and blushed complexion gave his youthful looks a particular liveliness and amicable petulance. His eyebrows were two straight lines draped across his eyes disappearing toward the delicate bridge of his nose; and from his lips, polished like a work of art and slightly apart, came a frank and noble heartbeat.]

Youth and beauty, which bestow strength and vitality, are consistently united and are presented as essential qualities to defeat any opponent or engage in the building of a new project. It is also a trait that implicitly excuses the hero's slight presumptuousness, for if he is a little too bold or arrogant, it is only because he is young and overconfident in his beliefs. Goodness is another quality stressed through physical features: Henderson's clean complexion and golden locks allude to his purity. Soft, light shades are the colors linked to his description. Based on the physical description of each character, there is no doubt as to the role that he or she will have in the novel. In these texts, aesthetics carry political meaning; nothing is left undetermined.

Opposing the model of heroism is the villain. Michael Booth identifies two types of villain in the English melodrama: the "white" villain, who is generally cool and calculating, appearing more often in the melodrama of the late nineteenth century, and the "blustering robbers and bloodthirsty pirates of earlier melodrama" (20). Pirates, according to most critics, belong in the category of villains. They are the utmost symbol of chaos and lawlessness, insurgent and violent trespassers who cause pain and anguish to their victims. In fact, the mere revelation of their presence nearby is enough to set off the whole population in a panic, as this passage from Sierra O'Reilly's El filibustero reveals:

¿Qué hay? ¿son enemigos?—sí. . . . pronto . . . . a las armas. . . . . . es,
no hay duda, lo. . . . . he reconocido bien. . . . . . es. . . . . . DIEGO EL
MULATO . . . ¡DIEGO EL MULATO! ¡Santo Dios! ha sonado ya para nosotros la hora final: ¿quién resiste a DIEGO EL MULATO? ¿qué puede
embotar el filo de su espada? ¿quién contiene su brazo exterminador?
¿qué mitigará su insaciable sed de venganza y de sangre? (4)

[What is it? Are they enemies?—Yes. . . . quick . . . . to arms. . . . . it's
without a doubt. . . . . I've recognized him. . . . . . it's. . . . . . DIEGO EL
MULATO . . . DIEGO EL MULATO! Dear God! Our final hour has come:
Who could resist DIEGO EL MULATO? What can restrain his sword's
blade? Who can hold back his exterminating arm? What could mitigate
his insatiable thirst for vengeance and blood?]

Pauses and changes of print in this passage, combined with repeti-
tions and rhetorical questions, convey a suspense and emotional spirit
proper to dramatic performances. The stress on the name emphasizes
the sensation of fear and horror, magnifying the alarm. In this case, the
villain is not an anonymous individual; he is an intruder well known for
his cruelties, and the population immediately realizes the dangers that
lie ahead. Without yet appearing, the trespasser has already been identified and linked with death, and the readers have been well prepared
for the subsequent events.

Given the stereotyped representation of heroes and villains, the sym-
bolism behind the pirate in the domestic melodrama is intriguing. In
La novia del hereje, though Henderson is accompanying the famous and
feared rogue Francis Drake, from the initial description of both pirates,
the reader knows they cannot be villains. Henderson is graceful and
elegant—traits the author praises and which consequently place him
far from any emblematic portrait of evildoers. This redefinition of the
pirate reflects the need to spell out the relation between looks and moral
values and becomes evident as pirates enter the domestic realm. Given
that the Spanish home is corrupt in La novia del hereje, the outsider becomes a positive force that is underlined by his looks, despite being a
pirate. In Ancona's novel, Leonel, the orphan turned pirate, is the hero.
He is young, well built, slightly brown skinned, with dark black eyes
and a bushy dark mustache.[16] His portrait reflects his Spanish heritage,
which in this case is identified with his unscrupulous parents, the repre-

sentatives of a colonial way of life that must be eradicated if happiness is to exist in the Yucatec home. Despite his slightly darker complexion, Leonel is endowed with "a thousand outstanding qualities": he is gentle, yet robust, courageous and energetic, attributes that help "compensate the shame of his birth" (5). On the other hand, Acosta de Samper's description of Drake is not overtly negative: "He was a short man, of elegant forms, white, blue and penetrating eyes, with a very blond beard, accompanied by a proud and audacious expression" (53). Drake's description, however, comes late in the text, when many negative images regarding him have already been asserted and will subsequently be confirmed. Hence, at a time when nations are being reshaped and designed, looks must also be redefined according to moral values. Looks in themselves no longer define the enemy or hero in the same way that being a pirate can no longer be identified with an evildoer. As national models and values are being negotiated, so must the looks each hero is to uphold. This explains why the prototype of the pirate is distorted in these melodramas as the political and moral coordinates of the plots fluctuate.

Nevertheless, with the exception of López, who presents his hero following the traditional European model, most authors make a point of depicting their hero (whether pirate or not) as an incarnation of an "American" beauty. This "American" type, which authors refer to explicitly, is unquestionably influenced by the Spanish model. Ancona's Leonel, as well as Acosta de Samper's heroes, generally have dark eyes and a slightly darker skin complexion. Although one might expect the American ideal to reflect a racially mixed portrait, it does not. The limits to the racialization of difference are clear once the plots develop. Racial mixture is not part of the cultural imagining of the elites; *mestizos* and *mulatos* are excluded from embodying heroes and, at most, occupy secondary roles. Ancona and Sierra O'Reilly underline the importance of including the whole American population, but the heroes and their values in the novels do not reflect or include a racially diverse population. Only Diego *el mulato* is a hero of mixed blood, and it is precisely because of his "darker" skin that he is ostracized from society. His revengeful and brutal actions, furthermore, confirm his violent nature and justify society's rejection of him. Highlighting a slightly darker complexion establishes a distinction between *América*'s identity and Northern Europe's oppressive brutality, signified by whiteness. (Spain, here, stands apart from Northern Europe, as Sarmiento so tellingly made clear.) But none of the authors actually addresses racial diversity. By unifying the portrayal of characters through formulaic external traits and highlighting their moral qualities, the melodramatic mode facilitates avoiding the need to explicate the role racial and class differences played in the cultural imagining of Spanish America. The melodramatic plot in these pirate novels enhances the portrayal of a homogeneous society where morality is the unifying force.

As the looks of the heroes are redefined, so are those of the villains, the mobilizing force of melodrama.[17] When transferred to Spanish America, the physical characteristics of wickedness in English melodrama—the dark stereotypes—give way to different models. At times villains are represented as the traditional black scoundrel, identified by his swarthy complexion, dark hair, and intense black eyes glowing with sinister malevolence; but depending on the physical portrayal of the hero, it is more common to find the villain pictured with fair skin and blue eyes, governed by his desire for vengeance and greed. Whatever their skin color, the villains are always easily identifiable and are invariably surrounded by an atmosphere of fear and deceit. When the villain is embodied not by an individual but rather by certain societal values, these create a hostile environment that frustrate the existence of a comforting home for the characters involved (Sierra O'Reilly).

The role of the villain is crucial, for he is the one who acts: he presents the strife, conceives a plan, and moves toward his goal. The hero only responds to him, hoping to rectify his actions, repair the damage, or regain his beloved. In fact, the focus of most melodramas is the villain's action. The hero of *La novia del hereje* appears only at the beginning of the novel and at the end, when he makes his heroic show to save his sweetheart. The greater part of the novel, some five hundred pages, focuses instead on the intricate plots construed by villains such as Romea, who plans the imprisonment of his fiancée, and Father Andrés or María's father, who are interested only in saving their own honor, whatever the cost. We are constantly shown evil at work. By the end of the novel, the readers are just as anxious as Henderson to punish the villains. Hence, as the novel finalizes, in their urge to connect with the hero's fight against the evildoers, the readers also become heroes. This is the attraction of the melodramatic pattern.[18]

In Ancona's novel, the action is centered around Leonel, a hero who resembles more a rebellious victim. We see the cruelty and injustice governing colonial society by the way it affects him directly. Instead of witnessing the villains plotting, the reader discovers their dirty schemes in unison with Leonel, precisely as they unravel and disrupt his life, marginalizing him from society. Consequently, what we observe is not Leonel's heroic triumph against evil but his heartbreaking fight for survival. Through his journey, Leonel faces the corruption of politicians who tend only to their personal interests; the hypocrisy of the Church, embodied by his father, a Catholic priest who has committed adultery and plots against his own son to save his reputation; and the discrimination of the *"nobles encomenderos"* toward all those who are not Spanish born, fair skinned, or rich. Rather than becoming a national emblem, Leonel is the reminder that there is little space for actual change in a world governed by repressive colonial precepts. As the narrator presents it, Leonel's death is a telling example of the racism and hypocrisy embedded within colonial society, yet there is no direct rebuttal as to how that racism will not be repeated.

The same occurs with Diego *el mulato,* the feared and vicious pirate, who is both a villain and a defeated hero. Although it is not explicit, his actions toward Conchita and the harsh criticism he directs toward his father for rejecting him suggest not only that Diego was forced into piracy but that he is capable of having noble sentiments. His feelings for Conchita are genuine; he not only protects her throughout the pirate attacks but cannot bear to live apart from her and is willing to risk his life for her. In a much less visible way than in Ancona's text, the villain in Sierra O'Reilly's narrative is also identified with the Spanish ruling elite, whose intolerance toward those who are not of "pure" Spanish descent is the cause of Diego's exclusion from the colonial social order. The complexity of this short text is that although Diego has been "forced" to become a pirate, he ends up personifying the violence and brutality he is accused of commanding.

Behind the villain lie all oppressive political forces; they bring about corruption and despotism, instilling fear among the population. This transforms the hero into a freedom fighter and a defender of the persecuted. In *Los piratas de Cartagena,* Sancho Jimeno is battling not only against dangerous pirates but against the French and English, whose primary interest in the Spanish Main is to rob Spain of its riches. Henderson does the same as he tries to save his fiancée; he is fighting against the evil embodied in colonial society represented by the Spanish forces. Whatever the case, the heroes become national emblems as they embark on ideological battles, and their virtues stand out, upheld by their physical portraits.

As each text defines the aesthetic categories of society in relation to a distinct political project, the representations of both heroes and villains necessarily fluctuate. Being a tightly closed world in which good and evil are intimately united with the beautiful and the ugly, the melodramatic structure is the ideal setting for the aesthetic to fulfill its political function. The aesthetic judgments define and articulate "the moral occult" or spiritual values identified with the social order promoted in each text. Hence, through melodrama, the soul and body of both individuals and nations are linked into one signifying political force embedded in the novel.

Women's Invisible Presence in the Melodramatic Plotting

As heroes and villains battle each other throughout the pirate novels, their encounters are provoked by the heroine. She is the link between the two forces; it is through her and because of her that these different powers actually confront each other. However, she does not have a major active role in the development of the plot. Contrary to the diverse images of the hero and the villain, the portrayal of the heroine remains surprisingly consistent throughout the novels. Regardless of her origin, whether Spanish or *criolla,* she is generally described in a similar fashion as a young, beautiful, light-brown-skinned woman with striking dark eyes. Whereas each author presented a different ideal of the male hero depending on his political alliances, the portrayal of the ideal woman is strikingly similar throughout the texts analyzed: she is an "American" beauty. Berenguela, the innocent heroine of *El filibustero,* is characteristic; the young *criolla* is "de talle esbelto, de cabello y ojos negros, de moreno cútis, de frescas mejillas, de boca preciosa, de sonrisa angelical y de mirada divina" [slender, black hair and eyes, brown skinned, rosy cheeks, beautiful lips, angelical smile with a divine gaze] (3). Clara Bustos, one of Acosta de Samper's heroines, is a beautiful *morena* (brown skinned) with dark, expressive eyes, and thick long black hair, braided in Moorish fashion (41). Even López, who looks up to the English model, mirrors Berenguela's description, expanding the depiction of his heroine even further:

> Tenía lo que llamamos en América *un lindo cuerpo*: . . . Su tez no era blanca: era más bien de un color sombreado pálido. Sus ojos eran negros, grandes y vivos; el brillo de su mirada se hallaba realzado por dos de esas melancólicas y misteriosas sombras que llamamos ojeras, y que tan profunda y tan ardiente ternura dan al ojo de la mujer bella. Tenía una nariz muy fina, graciosamente ondulada desde su arranque. La boca era pequeña. Sus labios un poco gruesos y notables; pero como eran cortos y del tinte de la rosa servían al mayor esplendor de la fisionomía. (37)

> [She had what we would call in America a *beautiful body*. . . . Her skin was not white but rather a pale tinted shade. Her eyes were black, big, and lively; her gaze sparkling, highlighted by two mysterious and melancholic shadowy circles that bestow upon beautiful women's eyes such a deep and intense tenderness. Her nose was fine, graciously curved from the bridge. Her mouth was small. Her lips, slightly full and noticeable; but as they were modest and rose-colored they gave her looks great splendor.]

Although López presents an "American" beauty, he still holds the traditional fair-skinned European image as the ideal model inasmuch as he makes a point of carefully attenuating specific features that set María apart from that model. Instead of explicitly describing her skin color, López prefers to shadow it; the pale tint of skin hue allows him to hint at color rather than define it. María's generous lips are constrained by her small mouth, diminishing any attributes that might resemble the more "typical" features identified with the black or indigenous populations.[19] Although *morena* means brown or dark skinned, its use varies significantly depending on the context as well as the country where it is used. Furthermore, a person may be *morena clara* (light) or *oscura* (dark), and depending on the context, the adjective may or may not carry negative connotations. The point of these portrayals is to underscore primarily a skin color that is *not* white, thus marking the difference with Northern

Europe. However, other specific signifiers often associated with black features, such as noses and hair (except for full lips), are not found among the main female characters of these novels. Neither are indigenous attributes (which, of course, vary depending on the specific country). The "refined" aesthetic features identified with the European model have been transferred and reencoded in the *criolla*, who distinguishes herself only by a slightly darker skin hue. Again, the reference to a light shade of color alludes to a hybridity that is in fact absent in these cultural imaginings of the nation. Furthermore, it reflects a class-conscious portrayal of the American beauty that straddles two cultural models (the European and the "other"—indigenous or black) and noticeably avoids addressing how ethnic differences are played out in the social structure of the nation.

That these authors choose to identify their heroines as "American" beauties is telling. No matter what political project is endorsed within the novel, what anchors that project is the woman. Women, in other words, provide the foundational grounding to conceive the nation, yet the recognition for their participation in any political project is almost inconspicuous. It is as if they had no "real" participation. They are the stabilizing force, but they are static, immobile, fixed. This lack of motion transforms women into part of the landscape that will be inhabited, signified, by men. As Hillis Miller explains, landscape is not a preexisting thing in itself; it is made by the living that takes place within it, and only then does it become a humanly meaningful space.[20] Consequently, the moral values of the men and the kind of relationship women establish with men will determine the type of home women are able to construct. Women are enclosed within the domestic space of the home, but its style and meaning will be determined by the men.

By articulating one cultural representation of society over another through explicit differentiation, these novels endorse a specific political project while constructing specific social relationships that determine a hierarchical organization of the world. Within this construction, gender plays a structuring role, for it is used to legitimize hierarchies and institutionalize authority.[21] Women's contingency on men locates them in a hierarchically inferior position. Their individual identities matter very little, which explains the physical similarities among the different female characters of the novels. Women anchor the political projects defined by men within the domestic sphere. Their role is to ensure the production and reproduction of the imagined landscape. In other words, whatever the plotting, the home they form or seek in these novels will always be the projected American home.

Through its severe extremism and gendered stereotypes, melodrama enhances the process of differentiation, fixing the normative concepts at the center of the social relationships, which in turn determine the role and position of women. As we read through these historical novels, it is clear that the symbolic representations of good and evil are embodied by different male figures. The battle to occupy a position of power is a battle between men. Women are secondary; they induce and locate the confrontation, but they do not occupy a position of power themselves. They symbolize the future of the political project but do not define it. This becomes evident as we observe how gendered identities are constructed in these novels.

From Justo Sierra O'Reilly to Acosta de Samper, women are manifestly characterized by their beauty and youth. They are heroines who suffer and endure the villains' wickedness, but they must wait to be rescued by the hero, who is the only one capable of deriding the villain's actions. The women portrayed in these novels are *criollas* who belong to wealthy Spanish families (except for Acosta de Samper's heroines, who are Spanish) and have been educated to fulfill a specific role in the social order. Their duty is to marry well to preserve and continue their family's values. Their space of action is restricted to the family, set within the home, first as daughters and then as mothers. The preeminence assigned to women's bodies in these texts underscores their reproductive capacity. As bearers of future generations, their bodies become the sites for different political projects. Women have no independent position in the nation. Through their pairing, they will be identified with liberal advocates like Henderson or trustworthy Spaniards like Hernán Mejía Mirabal in Acosta de Samper's narrative and thus come into being. Their spouses, as their fathers before them, will be the ones to define the values they, as women, will be identified with and transmit in the domestic realm.

The conditioning of their bodies and the relational positioning of women ensures their subordination. Men will voice their thoughts independently and penetrate an unlimited number of realms. Through their discussions, actions, and decisions, they shape the world according to their own image.[22] Women, on the other hand, are denied the possibility of articulating a voice of their own; molded, altered, shaped by others, they are to fulfill their place defined by men's law.

The subordination of women in Spanish America, however, though general, did not occur to the same degree. As the history of both colonial Spanish America and Brazil evidence, the racial component played an extremely important part in articulating the complex hierarchy of the colonial society. This applied to both men and women. White women, for example, either *criollas* or *peninsulares,* were superior to Amerindians of both sexes or anyone of mixed race. White women were equal to Spanish men—the "superior status"—only in terms of race, for they were legally subordinated to them and could not hold any public office. Considered the weaker sex, women were banned from positions of authority, thus subjecting them to the same restrictions that applied to slaves and Indians.[23] *Mestizos,* on the other hand, who were inferior to whites because of their mixed racial ancestry and because they worked, could hold certain public offices. *Mestizas,* however, could not. This distinction between men and women also applied to the Amerindians and black slaves.

Whatever their ethnic origin or class, during the colonial period, women were legally considered minors, sharing the same status as Indians, slaves, criminals, and the mentally retarded. Only in the late eighteenth century was the societal role of women—specifically, of the elites—seriously discussed and reviewed in government forums, though most restrictions were still maintained. Although women participated in the fights for independence—as did *mestizas* and Indians—there are no indications of their expectations of becoming "citizens." After 1808 the discussion of women's rights was excluded from the political debates. Hence, it was not until women themselves demanded their own rights that their position in society would actually change; this would occur in the twentieth century.[24]

Considered only in terms of whom they married, women could not be perceived—nor dared to perceive themselves—as true independent citizens. As a result of this subordination, of their lack of sovereignty, and their definition as mothers, Mary Louise Pratt states that women have been cataloged as "other to the nation."[25] Using Benedict Anderson's concept of "imagined communities," Pratt argues in her essay that women in modern nations in Spanish America were never imagined or invited to imagine themselves as part of "a horizontal brotherhood." She mentions, among other examples, that they lacked the right to die for their country.

Cataloging women as "other," however, undermines the ways in which they related to the politically charged environment during the wars of emancipation as well as during postindependence. It reinforces the binary gender representations and inhibits the possibility of disrupting the fixity of this concept. Women did fight and die for their country, but being excluded from that "horizontal brotherhood," those who did give up their lives for their country were perceived to do so as devoted spouses or daughters, not as dedicated citizens. Nevertheless, despite their apparent invisibility and public marginalization, women could not ignore the effects the internal conflicts of nation building had in their lives.[26] Undoubtedly, they did not hold the same position as men, yet even in these texts where women are portrayed as passive individuals whose purpose seems to be simply to activate the melodramatic plot, they have a distinct function.

As mothers and producers of "real" citizens, women not only must marry correctly but, in these texts, must choose who they will marry. This is the most important—though implicit—responsibility they have been assigned. Disregarding the laws and customs of the time, in these novels, women choose and bear the responsibility of their own actions. Yet their choice is predicated not on patriotism or political ideals but rather on love. Marriage, however, throughout the colonial period and even most of the first half of the nineteenth century, had little to do with choice or love; it was primarily an alliance between families seeking to consolidate their patrimony and social position.[27] As an insoluble institution, marriage not only secured family ties—of fundamental importance for the elites—but endorsed a particular concept of family in which the roles of both men and women were clearly defined. To break this established order was a serious violation, yet in these novels, women are seen more than once disobeying their fathers and apparently taking their lives into their own hands. This anachronism reflects the nineteenth-century ideology of love and the new positioning of women transferred to the colonial context.

In *La novia de hereje,* María not only disobeys her father when he decides she should marry the arrogant and selfish Spanish suitor but is even imprisoned because of her determination to respect her feelings and reject Romea. Although her father does not acknowledge Romea to be the villain he really is, María has no doubts about him and adamantly stands up to her father. Her battle is to endure Romea's evil plottings and wait for Henderson, her true sweetheart, to free her. María's decision is an undeniable rejection of her family's values. Because they prove corrupt, her decision is confirmed by the narrator as the correct one. The new family she will begin with Henderson will be founded on "equality" and the well-being of its members. This becomes explicit as the narrator ends the novel with a portrait of a beautiful family scene in which mother and daughter, both elegantly dressed, converse openly while a young mischievous boy sits on his father's lap waiting to be told a story. And even when the child is scolded, there are no harsh words, and the little boy shows "no sign of fear."

María's decision to build a new and progressive family—one in which individual freedom is respected and where authority is not imposed through force as it is in the Spanish household—is by no means based on a political stand, but rather on love, a pure and noble sentiment identified with women. But López makes a point of stressing the link between this "natural" and virtuous feeling and the political beliefs of the individuals involved, precisely by opposing the English household to the Spanish one. Whereas love and happiness reign as one in the English home, the narrator states that in the Spanish home:

> El eje de la sociedad doméstica no era el amor, que es el único elemento moralizante de la domesticidad; sus formas carecían de la ternura, que no es sino la expresión educatriz y genuina de ese amor; y todos los resortes por fin se concentraban en el del *miedo*. El albedrío se criaba sofocado, contrariado, extraviado. La falta de libertad legítima y de atmósfera moral viciaba en su raíz el estado de familia; y por eso era que bajo este despotismo exclusivo de la autoridad paterna (como bajo todos los otros despotismos), el vicio y la desmoralización se habían abierto mil sendas anchas y obscuras por donde buscar la saciedad. (191–92)

> [The crux of the domestic society was not love, which is the only moral element of domesticity; the home lacked tenderness, which is nothing else but the genuine and educational expression of that love. All the re-

sources were concentrated in *fear*. Free will was suffocated, obstructed, lost. The lack of legitimate freedom and morality corrupted the state of the family at its roots. Thus, under the exclusive despotism of paternal authority (as with every other despotism), vice and immorality had opened wide and obscure paths to satiety.]

Inasmuch as María has chosen and participated directly in the formation of her new family, she has actively become an intricate part of the political order. By reinforcing the link between the state and the home, this passage implicitly redefines women's space as an arena of love while assigning them a moralizing mission with political consequences. Men, as fathers, are to ensure the freedom of the home so that women may fulfill their duty, and through love teach the morals upheld by their spouses. This idealized home also establishes a gendered hierarchy, as women are to reproduce the morals and values first established and secured by men. By championing María's marriage to Henderson, López is also endorsing Juan Bautista Alberdi's project to incorporate the English within Argentine society to secure a prosperous future—a task that would be achieved, according to Alberdi, by uniting the Argentine women with the English men.[28] This layout of polarized confrontations and traumatic displacements is possible through the melodramatic plot that legitimizes extreme solutions such as López's.

Despite societal constraints, women's decisions can, in fact, prove to be a matter of life or death. Berenguela, the heroine in Ancona's novel, is incapable of opposing her mother's request to forget Leonel; she does not dare fight for what she truly wants. As a dutiful daughter, she embarks on a forced project that entails constructing a family other to the one she hoped for with Leonel. It will fail, however, for it lacks love. Perhaps in his desire to rectify this injustice, the narrator unites Berenguela and Leonel underground: the young hero commits suicide and leaves a request to be buried with his beloved. This ending in a way validates the need for younger generations to pursue their own goals and confront their parents or society when the burdens imposed are unjust and arbitrary. The young couple's tragic ending is in part due to the fact that Berenguela does not act in accordance to her feelings. She first accepts the arranged marriage to an older man she does not love. Then, although her widowhood offers her a second opportunity, she is coerced by her confessor to enter a convent despite her love and desire for Leonel. Faithful and determined, Leonel confronts every obstacle, yet he alone is unable to overcome colonial society's hypocritical constraints. Berenguela's passivity impedes, to a certain extent, the formation of an "equal" unity. Rather than projecting a promising future as López did, Ancona's ending underlines the harmful power embedded in society that must be reformed. The dismal ending of this melodrama can be read, in part, as the result of women's marginalization. Failure will ensue if women are bound to the borders of the narrative plot or political project; they must be within the center, participating in the cultural and political imaginings of the nation if it is to emerge triumphantly.

Reading Ancona's text as a fictionalization of women's roles in the national project simply mirrors the noteworthy position both white and *mestiza* women had in Yucatán during the process of modernization. As early as 1846, women acquired a significant visibility, when the first primary school for girls was established in the capital, Mérida.[29] In 1870 a feminist society was founded, La Siempreviva, which opened a new secondary school for women and published a newspaper written, edited, and printed by women. Although the reference to the equality of all citizens without gender distinction in Mexico was proclaimed in Article 24 of the 1814 Apatzingán constitution, it was only after 1850 that women's role and education began to be taken seriously; and it would take another fifty years for feminists actually to get results from their demands. Although political independence in Spanish America brought attention to the importance of women's roles in the domestic and political spheres, their possibility of action was severely constrained by the patriarchal contradictions governing the debates of nation building. Yet perhaps because of Yucatán's unique geography, resources, and historical development, women began to figure in the political changes relatively early compared to the rest of the country and continent. Not only was the concept of women's liberation first tried out here, but in 1916, the first two feminist congresses held in Mexico took place in Mérida.[30]

The fate of Conchita, Sierra O'Reilly's heroine in *El filibustero,* is even more disturbing than Berenguela's. Conchita confronts her family and societal rules by refusing to marry her cousin, who complies with all the "ideal" social qualifications. Instead, she chooses to remain faithful to her "foreigner" and is even willing to abandon Campeche and begin a new life with him, leaving her family behind. Only in the end, when she discovers that the true identity of her beloved is Diego *el mulato*, her father's assassin and the pirate she so terribly feared, does she realize the implications of her decision. Having to face her erroneous choice, she is driven to madness and is described years later as a "dirty, broken, and disheveled old lady" (48). Although Sierra O'Reilly does not expand on the significance of this ending, to the extent that madness occurs within a conflict of thoughts, Conchita's reaction exposes how women's positioning in the cultural imagining of the nation is full of contradictions.[31] She acts for love (as is her duty) but has chosen the wrong man to love; though there are concrete societal expectations for women, society does not prepare them to fulfill their demands.

Part of the problem for both Berenguela and Conchita is that they lack education. Berenguela's schooling is interrupted when her parents quickly marry her off. There is no reference concerning Conchita's education; she just lets herself be consumed by love despite not knowing anything about her "foreigner" and his values. In fact, she "never thought it was necessary to seriously think about the issue. Without knowledge, so young, without any experience, she only thought about the object of her idolatry" (22). Berenguela lets the wrong people decide for her, and Conchita makes the wrong decision. Hence, they are both punished.

In contrast, both Leonel and Diego let their actions be determined by love. Leonel becomes a pirate for love, and Diego is willing to renounce piracy for love. Their deaths, therefore, underline that men should be guided not by this passion but rather by principles. They may give their word to save the heroine, but men must never allow love to govern their soul. Love seems to be uncontrollable: Diego becomes "delirious, frenetic" (13), and Leonel "crazy, confident in the love of innocent hearts" (16). If piracy is a man's world, and seafaring is seen as a way of life that makes men (and names), then both Leonel and Diego distort the role of the pirate. Their emotions have undermined their masculinity. Pirates cannot be bound by women; their allegiance rests only with those sharing their cause, and it is a man's cause.[32] Pirates choose violence as a means of ensuring their freedom, but Leonel and Diego are forced to use violence. They are not truly seeking freedom for freedom's sake, but rather to be united with their beloved. This is perhaps why they cannot reach the unity they seek. Love is a consequence of a new state of being: it is the result of the development of a new political and cultural imagining; it is not the motivator of such a project. The failure of these plots is in part due to the instability of women's charges. Men need women so that they may fulfill their identity as founders, builders, and defenders of the nation. Consequently, women's fluctuating duties will thwart men's task. Perhaps Ancona and Sierra O'Reilly, both deeply committed to the Yucatec cause, felt the need to stress the importance of projecting the nation as a collective endeavor, placing women with a clearly defined role, so that the home and nation could prosper. The distressing endings of both their novels manifest what happens when this integration is not achieved. Without women's contribution, no national project can emerge successfully.

The representations of women in these novels reflect the difficulties society had defining their role. Acosta de Samper is the only writer who, aware of the contradictions assigned to women, presents a female character able to transcend the conflicts and position herself as a full-fledged citizen. In fact, Albertina de Leyva actually takes into her hands the political destiny of her country. Kidnapped by the English captain Robert Keith, who falls in love with her, Albertina consents to marry him and live in England to save her honor. The most traumatic aspect of this marriage is not that she is separated from her Spanish sweetheart and her father, but that against her will she has become "the wife of an Englishman, a declared enemy of Spain" (178). From the beginning of her narrative, Acosta de Samper underlines her heroine's patriotism, a patriotism that will take her outside the realm of the home.

As a member of the British fleet, Keith is involved in the plans to attack the Spanish colonies, something Albertina discovers by overhearing the discussion in her home. By placing the fictional story of Keith and Albertina at the intersection of the historical events, Acosta de Samper is able to give her heroine a unique role within history. Albertina steps out of the limits of the domestic realm and decides to notify the Spanish government of the English intentions; her reasoning is that before being the wife of an Englishman, she is Spanish and has certain responsibilities toward her country. Contractual agreements in this case are put behind patriotic feelings. National identity comes first.

Although Albertina first appears fragile and sick, once she recovers from her ailment, she is decidedly a strong-willed person. When Keith asks her early on if he has in any way offended her, Albertina responds matter-of-factly that he has not and adds, "Nor would a woman of my stature and nature permit you to do so" (168). Albertina does not let others decide for her; furthermore, she is proud of her own decisions. When she is forced to live among her enemies in England, Albertina's "patriotism grew passionately . . . and she would have gladly given her life to inform her father what was happening so that he could be prepared to resist the enemy in Cartagena" (179). Albertina casually inquires about the plans with Keith in order to obtain as much information as possible about the attack. Confident in the Spanish, she openly defies her husband and bets that this time they will not let the English seize Cartagena. Keith agrees to hand over the two medals he had made in honor of the future English triumph he was so sure would take place. The engraving states: "The English took Porto Bello with only six ships." Albertina keeps the medals, which she subsequently sends to the Spanish as proof of the English plans.

Once the Spanish receive her information, they are determined to overcome the English forces and quickly prepare Cartagena's defenses. Their actions in the end will award them a great victory over England. Albertina's collaboration with the Spanish forces transforms her into a patriot. Acosta de Samper intelligently structures this story, intertwining the domestic and public spheres to allow Albertina to behave in accordance with the gendered differences that characterized and constrained women (beautifully fragile, fainting often, innocent) while endowing her with a determination and participation in political events that place Albertina alongside the patriotic heroes of her time.

Through their portrayal of specific images of social relationships, pirate novels produce and enforce meaning, which is further enhanced by the melodramatic structure that highlights the moral connotations embedded within the social order represented. By focusing on the domestic realm and drawing on the interdependency between the family and the state, nineteenth-century novelists sought to construct a clearly visible social order that extended from the private sphere to the public one. For a nation to be progressive and democratic, order and freedom—at least for those participating in its project—and virtue must be the governing principles of the home. Nation and home are one, and according to Elizabeth Garrells, the historical novel clearly endorses this: "In its domestic scope, the historical novel advocates for the family; in its historical scope, it advocates for the homeland."[33] Hence, as pirates attack the nation and penetrate the domestic realm, the connections between family, nation, national alliances, and moral values become closely intertwined as they redefine the boundaries of the home.

Acosta de Samper takes the political interdependency between family and community one step further. By giving her heroines a voice that transcends the home and penetrates the political domain, she allows her female characters to participate actively within the public sphere. Rather than bringing the political within the home, she takes her heroines into the battlefields (as Clara Bustos in the second *cuadro* does) or gives them a political role (like Albertina de Leyva). These women step outside their assigned space precisely to uphold their duties as wives or daughters, but most importantly as Spanish wives and daughters. Acosta de Samper's representation of women implies that by carrying out their domestic duties, women can in fact be patriotic.[34]

Women's patriotism, however, does not mean they have to mirror men's civic responsibilities. In her writings, Acosta de Samper explicitly states her opposition to women participating in politics, preferring to confine their realm to the home, where they can exert their moral influence:

> La mujer no debe participar activamente en la política. Lejos de nosotros la idea de abogar por la absurda emancipación de la mujer, ni pretendemos pedir que ella aspire a puestos públicos, ni que se le vea luchando en torno a las mesas electorales, no, esa no es su misión, e indudablemente su constitución, su carácter y naturales ocupaciones no se lo permitirían jamás. Pero quedaría para ellas la parte más noble, la influencia moral en las cuestiones trascendentales y fundamentales de la sociedad . . . ella tiene el deber de comprender qué quieren y lo que aspiran los partidos, entonces ejercería su influencia.[35]

[Women must not actively participate in politics. The idea of advocating for women's emancipation seems absurd to us, neither do we ask them to aspire to public posts, nor that they fight in electoral centers; no, that is not their mission, and undoubtedly their physique, character, and natural occupations would never allow it. But they are left with the more noble part, the moral influence in meaningful and fundamental issues of society . . . women have the duty to understand what the political parties want and aspire, then they will be able to exert their influence.]

Without overtly challenging the traditional role assigned to women by men, Acosta de Samper advocates that women's domain be expanded to comply with their task of ensuring a specific national project. Women must be able to understand what the political parties want to transmit, whatever principles and moral values they have sanctioned. Thus women must be included within the political project. Furthermore, rather than waiting passively for this change to occur, Acosta de Samper believes women should take an active stand and position themselves in unison with men.

> No somos diosas ni esclavas, ni los hombres son ya héroes ni semidioses; debemos trabajar a su lado, aunque en diferentes caminos, y nuestra importancia y valor serán los que queremos.[36]

> [We are not goddesses or slaves, nor are men any longer heroes or demigods; we must work by their side, though along different paths. Our importance and worth will be what we determine them to be.]

Different, yet situated right next to men: this is women's new role. Echoing the reforms introduced by the Enlightenment, Acosta de Samper prompts women to get an education and spend their free time doing "algo útil," something useful. Acosta de Samper's message is directed to two different audiences. While reassuring men of their own supremacy, she reminds them that women have an important role in the building of the nation through their actions in the home. For this reason, they should be taken seriously and included within the political project. At the same time, her message to women cautiously undermines their subordinate status by stressing women's importance and self-worth within the home and consequently within society. Women must take charge of opening new doors for themselves and take on more responsibilities precisely to comply with their role as transmitters of societal values. By masking her discourse, Acosta de Samper advocates women's participation in the political events of her country. Women must understand to communicate. Their responsibility lies in stepping out of their seclusion and searching for new ways of participation; in doing so, women will implicitly force their realm to extend beyond that of the home. Ultimately, as Acosta de Samper states, women must make the decision to participate.

The character of Albertina illustrates Acosta de Samper's project distinctly. Albertina does not limit her role as a woman to being a self-sacrificing wife but forces herself to act as a loyal Spaniard and defend her country's interests. Albertina understands the rules of society concerning the place of women, which is why she decides to marry Keith. However, she is Spanish. Hence, her obligations are first and foremost to her country. Acosta de Samper's heroines fight to define themselves as women while taking on the responsibility of being true "citizens" both outside and inside the home. By giving them a voice, Acosta de Samper enables her heroines to construct themselves as subjects. This is her most important political gesture as a writer and as a woman.[37]

Through the differentiation of gender, these novels seek to order social life and consolidate the identity and values of an elite. Within that order, the place women are assigned is indeed contradictory. On the one hand, they are confined to the home, where they must mirror the ethics of their fathers or spouses, who will take charge of their political future. At the same time, these novels portray women as responsible for choosing their future husbands and the type of family they will form, since the home is the basis of society. Or at the very least, the novels expose a distressing future, when women are not given a distinct place in the national imagining. As primary caretakers of the home, women are essential to the whole system of nation building. Yet they are not allowed to act outside the domestic realm. Furthermore, the families women form are determined not by their own individual projects, but rather by their associations. In other words, the families are ultimately defined by men. Women are essentially placed at the center of the political project while being excluded from it. They articulate the melodramatic plot, but they must wait for others to resolve it. They are assigned a distinct place within the new sociopolitical order but have no freedom to act accordingly. Yet it is through melodrama that women are given more agency. These are a few of the political constraints imposed on women during the nineteenth century, the contradictions of "domestic ideology" that the melodramatic plot highlights so clearly.[38]

Whiting Out Race

One of the key factors present in these historical novels that articulates the endorsement of a particular sociopolitical order for Spanish America is undoubtedly difference, which is enhanced by the Manichaean worldview of melodrama. Through specific sets of differentiations—inclusions and exclusions, comparisons and contrasts—these novels construct a social hierarchy and world order that is geared toward defining a particular national identity. However, when looking at societal conformation in racial terms, most authors, despite their different political projects, echo a similar model in which whiteness is the embedded structuring element. In the same way as women are represented as one unified group without any apparent differences (except perhaps in Acosta de Samper's text), the racial conformation of the colonial society is barely alluded to in these novels. *Lo americano* is constantly invoked by these novelists, yet their texts rarely place as central characters individuals who do not belong to the *criollo* elite.

From the beginning of the Spanish conquest, whiteness was viewed as a symbol of superiority and became a determining element in the social positionings throughout the continent.[39] Spanish-born white males, or *peninsulares,* occupied the top of the societal ladder with all the legal privileges. They consequently held, until the independence from Spain, the highest positions in the two most important institutions: the Church and State. White *criollo* elite males followed, leaving the indigenous and black populations far behind, in both social and economic terms. These divisions, however, did not remain clear-cut and intact; and as previously stated, within each group, women continued to be subordinate to men. Spain's imperialist desires pushed for the forging of a "Hispanic" race that, at least theoretically, welcomed a union of Spaniards and other races.[40] As a result, a constellation of "races" soon populated the continent, creating a varied and complex hierarchical racial ordering in which whiteness, nevertheless, remained the distinguishing positive trait.[41] Men and women of European and Indian descent, the *mestizos,* ranked higher than the *pardos* or *mulatos.* Even lower were the pure blacks, and last of all the *zambos,* individuals of indigenous and black descent who were considered to have inherited the worst traits of both races. Of course, crossings between races did not stop here, and depending on the portion of Indian, black, and white blood a person had, each received a different label.[42]

The tendency to white out race reflects Spanish Americans' difficulty in addressing the dilemma regarding their country's racial configuration. Although racial heterogeneity characterized most societies, the need for a closer integration with the Northern European system encouraged the elite sectors to secure a closer connection to Europe in economic and political terms as well as social and cultural ones.[43]

In addition to skin color, there were other factors such as ethnic and religious identity. As Spain expanded her thirst for unification, ridding her land of infidels and populating the New World, any individual with a Jewish or Moorish ancestor was immediately set apart as the "other." But those who wished to be Hispanic simply had to prove their *pureza de sangre*, "purity of blood," which could involve a trial of faith, race, or national origin depending on the issue in question. The "purity of blood" during the colonial period in Spanish America meant more than anything else "purity of race," referring to the absence of Indian and especially African ancestry.[44] This form of renouncement or *auto de fé* is essentially a theatrical way of declaring oneself faithful to the "Hispanic Self."[45] Thus Spanish America was populated by a collection of voices and differences that were supposed to coexist and embrace each other to form one unified identity. Yet in practice, differences still remained patent and were important exclusionary factors.

The constellations of races, however, do not gain much access in these historical novels that claim to be apprehending and defining *el espíritu americano*. In fact, when looking at how these authors portray the societal conformation, it becomes clear that they are constructing a vision of America from an extremely elitist position, that of the white *criollos*. On the one hand, given the melodramatic structure of these texts, racial differences are used to highlight moral oppositions; on the other hand, racial differences within the same political spectrum are discreetly silenced and overlooked by the voice in charge of prescribing a unifying national model.

López's ideal for America, and particularly for Argentina, is reflected in the unity he projects in his novel between that *criollo* elite and the English. By staging *La novia del hereje* in the city of Lima, a stronghold of colonial Spain that was exploited for its riches by the ruling Spanish, "whom thousands of Blacks and Indians obeyed like slaves" (26), López is able to portray Spanish cruelty at work. Although he allows considerable space for *zambos, blacks,* and Indians to roam the streets of Lima weaving intricate plots for their masters, it is precisely these types of individuals, together with the corrupt Spanish authorities, who have transformed Lima into a city of turmoil and confusion. This is evident in the narrator's description of the central plaza:

> El alegre y bullicioso hablar de las negras y negros, el chirriar de la grasa hirviendo que preparaban para las frituras, la afluencia de los compradores y la diversidad de las castas, pues mezclados andaban el altivo castellano, con el cargado y francote catalán; el tosco gallego, con el insolente y afeminado zambo; el ardiente negro, con el indio humillado. Lima empezaba ya a ser entonces la famosa Babel americana. (32)

> [The loud and cheerful talk of blacks, the sizzling sound of boiling grease ready for frying, the crowding presence of buyers and disparate castes. Everyone was mixed together: the conceited Castilian with the annoying and candid Catalonian; the crude Galician with the insolent and effeminate *zambo;* the passionate black with the humbled Indian. Lima was already beginning to be the famous American Babel.]

Each class or caste is distinctly typified: Castilians are conceited; Catalans, emotional; Gallegos, coarse; *zambos,* insolent and effeminate; blacks, passionate; and Indians, belittled. This pandemonium of a society, the American Babel, where classes and races grotesquely overlap in a common territory, implicitly justifies the need for López's American heroine to seek a new home across the Atlantic. Thus, it is no surprise that María's new dwelling is placed amid a more dignified, regulated, and "civilized" society, as England is portrayed to be.

The noticeable inconsistencies depicting the secondary characters in *La novia del hereje* reflect López's racist views. Mercedes, for example, is described initially as a *zamba,* belonging to that class of shrewd individuals with a knack for taking advantage of situations and prospering (92–93). But as the novel advances, readers discover her noble "soul" as well as her noble lineage when we are told that her true name is Sinchiloya and that she is a daughter of the Inca empire. Another *zamba* is Juana, María's servant, who moves to England with her mistress, where she marries none other than Francis Drake.[46] López states that although Juana is dark skinned, she has harmonious features (38). In the end, we discover that Juana is the daughter of Mercedes, and therefore she too has a noble lineage. Class in *La novia del hereje* becomes a means of transcending racial limitations, which simultaneously refines specific features that, given the Northern European idealized model, would be undesirable. Finally, Mateo, a former servant, is "un indio ó mulato" (418) as if the terms were practically synonymous, or the differences did not matter. That *zambos* and Indians are indistinguishable "races" reflects the positioning these individuals have been assigned in the social conformation portrayed in the novel. They are completely secondary and, at best, can accompany the real heroes and heroines, who are white. Their primary function is to expose, through difference, the positive qualities of the endorsed national project visualized in the white heroes and heroines.

Blacks and Indians are similarly cast in Acosta de Samper's novel. However, as the author's interest is to highlight the virtues of the Spanish heritage, she distinguishes between the indigenous people (whose souls must be saved—and here lies the noble action of the Spanish) and blacks, who are portrayed in particularly negative terms. Neither Indians nor blacks have any importance in her narrative; the attention they receive is only to highlight and visibly contrast with the heroic and patriotic Spaniards. Blacks are referred to explicitly only a couple of times, and either they are criticized as cowards for refusing to fight with the same zeal as the Spaniards against the English forces, or else they are liars and traitors for trying to help the English or French forces against the Spanish in exchange for their freedom. Their disregard is based on the fact that when confronted with the enemy, "Muchos negros dijeron prontamente y con gusto todo lo que pudiera lastimar a sus amos, sin que hubiese necesidad de ponerles en tormento" [Many blacks quickly and with pleasure stated everything that might damage their masters, without needing to be tortured] (60).

Even Eligio Ancona and Sierra O'Reilly, who explicitly mention unfair treatment caused by difference of skin color in their novels, do so purely to expose the corruption of the white Spanish-born elite who governed their colonies and looked only after their own interests, not those of America. Only Sierra O'Reilly's hero, Diego *el mulato,* stands apart from the rest of the heroes. Even though he is an outcast for having a darker skin color, because he behaves in such a cruel and violent fashion, the white *criollo* elite that rejects him is, to a certain extent, proven right in doing so.

These texts refuse to address the racial differences of colonial society by masking them through aesthetic values. Clearly, the heroes and heroines in these melodramas embody specific ideals of beauty that are without exception marked by whiteness.[47] Beauty and goodness are the unifying characteristics that separate good from evil. As melodrama does not allow any difference between those individuals who are physically beautiful and those who are "spiritually" beautiful, aesthetic values distinguish good from bad in a totalizing way. Thus, the aesthetic categories and judgments articulated in these texts are clearly political ones.[48]

Whiteness is also associated with a political ideology that in turn endorses a specific national identity. By overlooking the existing differences that marked racial divisions, these texts seem to be creating a unified identity that would encompass all those aligned with that political project. Thus, even the faithful *zamba* Juana can aspire to a better life. Because she is devoted to her mistress and "gladly" accepts her position of subordination, she too is able to leave Lima and create a new family of her own in the same way as her mistress. In other words, all those supporting the ideological positionings of the *criollo* elite will also be benefited, regardless of their race. Of course, only the *criollo* elite will obtain the true benefits, particularly since the "others" are not even recognized. Portraying a strong image of unity was essential to convey a distinct and firm national identity. This explains why these authors, all of whom belonged to an intellectual white elite, chose to suppress the internal difficulties that existed in the colonies concerning racial differences in order to project a consolidated unity. And it is through melodrama's narrative structure and visual binary world conception that they are able to do so.

Through melodrama, the political consequences implied within the discussion of race and gender are reduced to unified moral and aesthetic terms, and with the genre's language of hyperboles and grandiose contrasts, virtue and corruption become explicitly visible. The melodramatic structure offers a Manichaean world in which the most extreme acts of violence and rupture may be unleashed, but in the end, order will be established and peace can be reassured. According to these novels, that peace will be secured only when the corrupt forces (however those forces might be defined) are completely eliminated. The number of melodramas articulating the debate of nation building underlines the power of the melodramatic mode in articulating the conflict and envisioning a world in which there can be only one virtuous project and, in addition, where everything else brings about disaster. These texts are not about reconciliation, whether political or familial. They are about one political project overcoming the other, one national identity suppressing the other, one domestic ideal replacing all others. This was how Spanish America began designing its future—as a battle between one voice commanding the other, one visual imagining overshadowing the other—and melodrama provided the ideal narrative form.

Conclusion

The debate about nation building in Spanish America emerges with its political emancipation. The sudden rupture and remapping of the continent left Spanish Americans caught between their colonial heritage and the modernizing influences of Northern Europe. Without a consensus as to the political program to be implemented, Spanish Americans began debating their future. United by a common language, the independent republics, as well as the territories that remained under Spanish control (Cuba and Puerto Rico), reached within their boundaries to assert their own uniqueness while defining themselves as an integral part of *América*. Whether politically independent or not, the need to define one's national identity became a crucial issue throughout the continent after postindependence; it was the first step toward securing a future.

In discussing what constitutes a nation, Ernest Renan concluded that the essential element is the creation of a strong sense of unity, which must come from sharing a past and envisioning a future together:

> To have common glories in the past and to have a common will in the present; to have performed great deeds together, to wish to perform still more—these are the essential conditions for being a people.[1]

Consequently, one could say that the past is the definitive element in nation building; it is a precondition for the construction of a future. Without a consolidated past, a firm and tangible project cannot be devised. A common past must be retrieved for a sense of wholeness to emerge. Only then can a community begin to "imagine" itself. Thus, it is in the past where the common bonds uniting a people lie. Reclaiming those bonds, however, implies not simply rescuing traditions and customs but rather a much more complex process of inscription and erasure. On the one hand, each community will highlight the valorous sacrifices made toward the consolidation of its place and identity; on the other hand, it will have to forget the traumatic and violent experiences entailed in securing that sense of heroism. As Renan states, "unity is always effected by means of brutality."[2] At the origin of all political formations lies a battle, often a violent one, for self-determination. It is this tension between heroism and brutality, between permanence and constant transformation, that the pirate illustrates so tellingly. A nation is not a fixed entity; it is constantly changing, being redefined even within its fixed political boundaries. And the pirate, with his heroic and cruel symbolisms, embodies both extreme components embedded in the metaphors of nation building.

During the period of national formation in Spanish America, literature played an important role in understanding the past and creating a sense of unity for the emerging nations. It grounded the experiences to be remembered while implicitly weeding out those that should be forgotten. In particular, the historical novel provided the ideal form to connect the past with the future. It enabled writers to reconstruct historical events that would underscore the sacrifices and battles a people had undergone. More importantly, through the historical novel, not only was the past retrieved, but its meaning and significance were illustrated through the fictional plot.

The great achievement of the historical novel as Scott canonized it was that it offered a comprehensive vision of society. Scott saw the past as fulfilled. The task of the writer was to recall the virtues, to distinguish them from the vices, of the past to meet the challenges of the new emerging social order. Scott had a tragic sense of the inevitability of progress. Although he was nostalgic for the heroic qualities of the past, he saw the "historical necessity" for their decline; it was part of the necessary process of transformation toward progress.[3]

Scott's vision of history was open-ended and free. No political or social group could claim to stand for social progress; progress was part of the constant evolutionary change. This gave him a certain distance in reconstructing the past (certainly not the chronological distance Anderson Imbert insisted on). Scott's historical view was essentially an aesthetic contemplation of change, governed by a necessary progress.[4] Thus his reconstructions of the past became examples of national greatness.

In Spanish America, however, writers could not look at the past in terms of a simple struggle of forces in an evolutionary process. Torn by civil wars that bloodied the continent, Spanish Americans looked back on the past to imagine their future. Rather than focusing on the past to highlight the progress Spanish America had made, writers were enmeshed in partisan divisions and used the past to illustrate their ideological positions. The past became the arena of contemporary political debates in which different social groups tried to present themselves as the emblem of progress. These forces could not come together; one had to displace the other. It was through the healing power of fiction that writers sought to mend the fragmented body of the nation dispersed throughout the continent.

The discussion of the past, however, did not have a conciliating effect. Those who sought to retrieve their Spanish heritage saw the conquest and colonization as a civilizing act brought on the Indians and an untamed nature. By contrast, those who saw Spain's presence as a menace to progress viewed the conquest as a devastating act of barbarism. Civilization and barbarism, freedom and dependency, modernization and backwardness—these became the structuring oppositions ordering the world.

To legitimize one interpretation of the past over another, writers in Spanish America tried to create a convincing portrait of that past by projecting an image of a unified community and grounding that image in history. In this sense, history had a foundational significance within the fictional narrative. History presented a "truth" and authorized the narrative as legitimate. To visualize its significance even further, history was emplotted through moral imperatives. This was the role of the melodramatic structure. Melodrama allowed writers to order their social world through distinct oppositions of good and evil, and to freeze the actors in symbolic relations to each other.[5] Thus, from a localized event and confrontation, absolutes could be drawn, displacing the bourgeois particular to the universal.[6]

Within the established social order, the role assigned to women, though distinctly defined, also appears fragmented, as they are positioned at the margins. As bearers of future generations, women are essential to the nation, yet they must comply wholeheartedly with their society's expectations. Those who do not fulfill their mandate go mad or find themselves erased from the spatial setting of the nation, as befalls a few of the heroines of the novels analyzed in this study. Women are locked into a central yet submissive role. They must help build the nation, but they cannot be patriots; they must just be mothers. It is in the gaps of these precepts that women can perhaps reclaim an "other" place for themselves, as patriots and mothers simultaneously, as Acosta de Samper's heroines do.

Read as a corpus, these texts, despite offering a world order constructed by imperatives, present a number of contradictions. It is in the fissures where the voices that have been silenced can be found; and it is there where the fragments of the nation can be pieced together. When discussing nation building in Spanish America, the same texts are often used to illustrate the terms in which the debate was articulated. In spite of having been written by well-known authors, the texts analyzed in this study have been disregarded by most literary critics. Mentioned only in passing—if at all—they are not considered part of the canon. Yet as a corpus they offer another reading of the nineteenth century. The importance of reshaping the canon is paramount because of its power to organize forms of knowledge. Not only do canons stabilize the past; they adapt that past to the present and project it toward the future. Through the canon, "a community defines and legitimizes its own territory by creating, reinforcing a tradition."[7] This study is part of an ongoing effort literary critics have recently embarked on to destabilize our understanding of the past and bring forth new texts and readings so that we may begin to reexamine the nineteenth century.

If we look at the historical narratives in which the pirate plays a central role in the reconstruction of the past, the shifts and inconsistencies between the different versions of what constituted progress are evident. The pirate embodied his own antagonists. From hero, to dangerous enemy, to a lost American roaming the seas in search of an identity, the pirate was constantly being resignified as Spanish Americans continued to imagine their past. The pirate in these narratives is at the crossroads of two world conceptions. The power of his image lies in his double and contradictory life. Through his irreverence, he defies the law and inverts all hierarchies.[8] His violent nature can be seen as a force to consolidate or sever a community. His mobility is his greatest asset, setting him free to embody the multiple imaginings, in this case, Spanish Americans had of themselves.

Perhaps it is precisely this mobility, this freedom, intertwined with the violent nature so deeply embedded in the traditional image of the pirate, that has spurred a number of contemporary portrayals of this historical figure. In spite of recent studies focusing on pirates' lives that reassess the established image such as those by Marcus Rediker and David Cordingly, the re-creations of pirate adventure stories continue to proliferate. Carmen Boullosa (Mexico), Laura Antillano (Venezuela), Jorge Eslava (Peru), and Alberto Vázquez-Figueroa (Spain) are just a few of the most recent writers in Latin America and Spain who re-create the pirates' legendary adventure stories.[9] But perhaps even more telling is the way pirate iconography tends to flourish during political crises in which the affirmation of a national identity is at stake and justifies an armed confrontation. One has only to recall the well-known films of Errol Flynn, the consummate swashbuckler hero who, under the mask of a great adventurous daredevil, takes on the dangerous and evil Spanish empire, assaulting their galleys and ultimately freeing the English prisoners (and the world) from Spain's treacherous exploitation. The subtext of war in these 1940 Hollywood films is underscored. As the United States was about to enter World War II, Hollywood looked to piracy to re-create a patriotic act and present Anglo-Saxon values as the only triumphant force capable of crushing the lethal desires of the Spanish.[10] The parallelism between the Spanish eagerness to expand their empire and the Nazi peril was evident.[11] More recently, during the 1982 Malvinas/Falkland war, the number of references in the Argentine popular press portraying the English as heretical pirates governed by their piratical queen—Margaret Thatcher—presented the exact opposite viewpoint but also placed the icon of the pirate as the structuring image.[12]

That the figure of the pirate still carries these strong connotations connected to heroism and violence evoked by popular culture certainly exposes the power and attraction that this Janus-like figure holds today. When violence becomes the structuring axis delimiting frontiers, the pirate seems to be the ideal figure to articulate the confrontation. His lack of political anchorage enables him to roam the seas, free to embody the enemy or the hero. Hence, behind the fascinating legends of these adventure stories lies the pirate sailing from shore to shore, amid the clashing waves of national confrontations: a metaphor for the brutal struggles of the collective imaginings of a nation.

Notes

Introduction

"My ship is my treasure / Freedom is my God / Strength and wind my laws / My only homeland, the sea." José de Espronceda, "Song of the Pirate." All translations, unless otherwise noted, are by the author.

1. Recent studies have focused on tracing the ways in which fact and fiction have merged to create the popular images of pirates: David Cordingly, *Life among the Pirates: The Romance and the Reality* (London: Little, Brown and Company, 1995); Jan Rogoziński, *Pirates! Brigands, Buccaneers, and Privateers in Fact and Fiction, and Legend* (New York: Da Capo Press, 1996).

2. In fact, there has been a resurgence of piracy on a global scale along the west coast of Africa, the northern coast of South America, as well as in the eastern Mediterranean, the Persian Gulf, and the South China Sea. In 1977 a warning was issued to Caribbean-bound vessels to beware of piracy and hijacking, especially in the Bahamas. See Jenifer Marx, *Pirates and Privateers of the Caribbean* (Malabar, Fla.: Krieger Publishing, 1992), 284–291. According to the International Maritime Bureau (IMB), a non-profit organization outside London, which monitors piracy worldwide, the number of attacks almost doubled in 1995 from the previous year, increasing from 92 to 170. For recent data on contemporary forms of piracy see William Sisson, "Blackbeard with an Automatic Rifle," *Soundings,* April 1996, 58–62.

3. Focusing on the *gauchesca,* Josefina Ludmer offers a brilliant analysis of the limits and modes of construction of a literary genre (*El género gauchesco: Un tratado sobre la patria* [Buenos Aires: Sudamericana, 1988], esp. 11–98).

4. Lord Byron, "The Corsair," in *The Poetical Works of Lord Byron* (London: Oxford University Press, 1960), 277–302.

5. José de Espronceda, "Canción del pirata," in *Obras Poéticas: "El Pelayo," poesías líricas, "El estudiante de Salamanca," "El diablo mundo"* (Mexico City: Editorial Porrúa, 1972), 24–25. Unless otherwise noted, all translations are by the author.

6. Michel de Certeau, *The Writing of History,* trans. Tom Conley (New York: Columbia University Press, 1988).

7. This is primarily due to the groundbreaking work of Monserrat Ordó-ñez and Gustavo Otero Muñoz. See *Soledad Acosta de Samper: Una nueva lectura* (Bogota: Fondo Cultural Cafetero, 1988).

8. Marcus Rediker, *Between the Devil and the Deep Blue Sea: Merchant Seamen, Pirates, and the Anglo-American Maritime World, 1700–1750* (Cambridge: Cambridge University Press, 1987), 292.

9. I am drawing on Eric Hobsbawm's analysis of social banditry. Although pirates are quite different from bandits, they share a position of marginality in relation to the rest of society and can be seen as a collective reaction to similar social and economic changes affecting life (Hobsbawm, *Bandits* [New York: Delacorte Press, 1969], 18).

10. Concerning the distribution of plunder, pirates awarded the captain and quartermaster between one and a half and two shares more than the rest of the crew. Everyone else received an equal share. In addition, there was a certain amount of money allotted for the reimbursement of the loss of an arm, leg, eye, and so forth as a form of insurance (each body part was worth a specific sum). Rankin includes in his study a set of regulations pirate were likely to sign before engaging in any trip and an insurance agreement (*The Golden Age of Piracy* [Williamsburg, Va.: Colonial Williamsburg, 1969], 31–32; Rediker, 254–87).

11. Rediker, 255.

12. Eric Hobsbawm, *Primitive Rebels: Studies in Archaic Forms of Social Movement in the 19th and 20th Centuries* (New York: Norton, 1965), 13–29.

13. Suzanne Desan, "Crowds, Community, and Ritual in the Work of E. P. Thompson and Natalie Davis," in *The New Cultural History*, ed. Lynn Hunt (Berkeley: University of California Press, 1989), 47–71.

14. In addition to the four historical novels discussed in this study, there exist other nineteenth-century texts that deal with piracy. There are minor references scattered throughout the narratives of Manuel Payno (*Un viaje a Veracruz en el invierno de 1843*) and Cirilo Villaverde (*Excursión a Vueltabajo*). *Cofresí*, by Alejandro Tapia y Rivera, and *El tesoro de Cofresí*, by Francisco Ortea (both centered on Roberto Cofresí, a well-known Puerto Rican pirate who was killed in 1825) and *El pirata del Guayas*, by the Chilean Manuel Bilbao, are novels in which the pirate is the central figure. Although I have found other references of "pirate novels," I have been unable to corroborate their existence, for the references are often contradictory or incomplete.

   A key aspect of this study is to look at the way authors have used historical events from the distant past to illustrate their discussion about national identity. Because references to the aforementioned novels do not reconstruct a distant past, they have not been included in the present corpus. Other texts have been referred to only tangentially, such as Carlos Echeverría's poem *Los piratas* (1891) and Vicente Riva Palacios's novel entitled *Los piratas del golfo* (1869). Although the latter reconstructs colonial life during the age of the buccaneers, the novel is overwhelmed with complicated subplots and presents a portrayal of piracy similar to the one offered by the Mexican novelists Justo Sierra O'Reilly and Eligio Ancona, discussed in depth in this study. *Carlos Paoli*, a short novel published in serialized form in 1877 by the obscure Venezuelan author Francisco Añez Gabaldón, portrays the life of a fictional Italian pirate along the coast of Santo Domingo in the early 1800s. The novel is set during a brief resurgence of the buccaneers, although its historical link is quite vague and it does not truly focus on the distant past. It does, however, offer a clear perspective of the cultural role society endorsed for women, as the hinge between the Spanish heritage of the past (her father) and the European model for the future (her lover).

15. Benedict Anderson, *Imagined Communities* (London: Verso, 1991).
16. The term "foundational fictions" is coined by Doris Sommer, who intelligently articulated an "erotics of politics" through her reading of what have traditionally been considered "representative" literary texts (*Foundational Fictions: The National Romances of Latin America* [Berkeley: University of California Press, 1991]).

Chapter 1   *Piracy in Spanish America: A History*

"A terrible case, sad and frightening / a traumatic event / a notable calamity / in certain ports of this New World / I sing with a hoarse and painful voice / that from its deepest depth / my meek chest sends to the tongue" (Juan de Castellanos, "The Discourse of Captain Francis Drake").

1. Cristóbal Real, *El corsario Drake y el imperio español* (Madrid: Editora Nacional, 1942), 7–8.
2. See *Webster's New World Dictionary*, 1988 ed.; *OED*, 1985 ed.
3. Justo Sierra, "Un año en el hospital de San Lázaro," in *Obras del Doctor Justo Sierra*, vol. 2 (Mexico City: Victoriano Agüeros, 1905), 105–6.
4. José Bravo Ugarte, *Historia de México, La Nueva España*, vol. 2, 3d ed. (Mexico City: Editorial Jus., 1953), 286.
5. *Le Petit Robert 1 Dictionnaire Alphabétique & Analogique de la Langue Française*, 1979.
6. *OED*. These Anglo-American filibusters made incursions to Cuba, Mexico, and Central America, as well as to the Sandwich Islands. The

most well known of these filibusters was undoubtedly William Walker, who occupied Granada and Nicaragua, where he became president for a short period in 1856. See Ralph Lee Woodward Jr., *Central America: A Nation Divided*, 2d ed. (New York: Oxford University Press, 1985), 136–46. The idea of obstruction is continued in today's use of the word, as it is most commonly used to designate the making of long speeches or the introduction of irrelevant material to obstruct the passage of a bill.

7. Christopher Lloyd, *Sir Francis Drake* (London: Faber and Faber, 1957), 81. Drake is said to have exploded when he found a letter from the king of Spain referring to him as a *corsario*. This occurred in Cartagena, in 1586, when Drake was attacking the Spanish colonies as a "commissioned high-ranking officer."

8. A clear example of this can be found in Soledad Acosta de Samper's use of the different terms as she reconstructs the piratical attacks on Cartagena by both English and French forces. See *Los piratas en Cartgena* (Colombia: Editorial Bedout, n.d.).

9. Philip Gosse, *The Pirate's Who's Who: Giving Particulars of the Lives and Deaths of the Pirates and Buccaneers* (Boston: Charles E. Lauriat, 1924), 15.

10. Not only did Spain assert its religious and political control, but furthermore, with the publication of Nebrija's *Gramática de la lengua castellana* in 1492, the first grammar of a modern European language, Spain found its "colonial pretext for the assimilation of otherness and others." For a discussion of the significance of the publication of this text and how it reflected Spain's expansionist policies see José Piedra, "Literary Whiteness and the Afro-Hispanic Difference," in *The Bounds of Race: Perspectives on Hegemony and Resistance*, ed. Dominick La Capra (Ithaca: Cornell University Press, 1991), 279.

11. Enrique de Gandía, *Historia de los piratas en el Río de la Plata* (Buenos Aires: Editorial Cervantes, 1936), 13.

12. Philip Ainsworth Means, *The Spanish Main: Focus of Envy, 1492–1700* (New York: Scribner's, 1935), 54.

13. See Allan Christelow, "Contraband Trade between Jamaica and the Spanish Main, and the Free Port Act of 1766," *The Hispanic American Historical Review* 22 (1942): 309–43.

14. The concept of envy is underlined by Means (47), and in chapter 3, "The Earliest English and French Intrusions in the Spanish Main: Envy of Spain Begins."

15. J. H. Parry, *The Spanish Seaborne Empire* (Berkeley: University of California Press, 1990), 46. The *Inter caetera* was complemented by two additional bulls awarded by the pope in 1501 and then in 1508. The concessions in these bulls made the Spanish sovereigns responsible for the introduction and maintenance of the Church in the New World, and for the conver-

sion of the Indians. Thus, the king was practically transformed into the secular head of the Church of the Spanish Indies (C. H. Haring, *The Spanish Empire in America* [San Diego: Harcourt Brace Jovanovich, 1975], 167).

16. For a description of Balboa's "discovery" see Carl Ortwin Sauer, *The Early Spanish Main* (Berkeley: University of California Press, 1966), 218–37.

17. See Justo Zaragoza, *Piraterías y agresiones de los ingleses y de otros pueblos de Europa en la América española desde el siglo XVI al XVIII* (Madrid: Manuel Hernández, 1883), 4.

18. For a description of the legal and commercial institutions governing the colonies see Clarence H. Haring, *Las instituciones coloniales de Hispanoamérica (siglos XVI a XVIII)* (San Juan: Instituto de cultura puertorriqueña, 1957), and *The Spanish Empire.*

19. C. H. Haring, *Buccaneers in the West Indies in the XVII Century* (Hamden, Conn.: Archon Books, 1966), 7.

20. Adolphe Roberts, *The French in the West Indies* (Indianapolis: Bobbs-Merrill, 1942).

21. Eric Williams, *From Columbus to Castro: The History of the Caribbean, 1492–1969* (New York: Vintage, 1984), 72.

22. Means, 19; Carlos Saiz Cidoncha, *Historia de la piratería en América española* (Madrid: San Martín, 1985), 20–22; Williams, 73.

23. Means, 58–75; Francisco Mota, *Piratas en el Caribe* (Havana: Casa de las Américas, 1984), 27–37.

24. Parry, 54.

25. Haring, *The Spanish Empire* 304.

26. For a detailed account of the fleet's route, see Haring, *Buccaneers,* 14–16, and *Spanish Empire,* 304–5.

27. Means, 56–58. James Williamson includes Rut's letter to Henry VIII in which he states that he and his men went to the Islands (referring to Santo Domingo) "as we were commanded at our departing." See James Williamson, *The Voyages of the Cabots and the English Discovery of North America under Henry VII and Henry VIII* (London: Argonaut Press, 1929), 104–5. Gonzalo de Oviedo confirms Rut's arrival but offers a different version of the outcome of the events. According to the chronicler, the English corsair managed to make a small trade, though he was denied permission, and then left. See Gonzalo Fernández de Oviedo y Valdés, *Historia general y natural de Indias, islas y tierra-firme del mar océano* (1535; Madrid: Imprenta de la real academia de la historia, 1851), lib. 19, cap. 13.

28. Hoffman, 64–65.

29. James Williamson, *Hawkins of Plymouth: A New History of Sir John Hawkins and of the Other Members of His Family Prominent in Tudor England* (New York: Barnes and Noble, 1969).

30. Helen Hill Miller, *Captains from Devon: The Great Elizabethan Seafarers Who Won the Oceans for England* (Chapel Hill: Algonquin Books of Chapel Hill, 1985), 26.

31. Bryan Bevan, *The Great Seamen of Elizabeth I* (London: Robert Hale, 1971), 16.

32. Juan Juárez Moreno, *Corsarios y piratas en Veracruz y Campeche* (Seville: Escuela de estudios hispano-americanos, 1972), 6.

33. David Quinn, *England's Sea Empire, 1550–1642* (London: George Allen and Unwin, 1983), 21.

34. Mendel Peterson, *The Funnel of Gold* (Boston: Little, Brown and Company, 1975), 132.

35. Julian Corbett, *Sir Francis Drake* (New York: Haskell House Publishers, 1968), 26.

36. For a detailed description of this trip see the Hakluyt Society, *The World Encompassed by Francis Drake* (New York: Burt Franklin, n.d.); Lloyd, 47–73.

37. See Neville William, *The Sea Dogs: Privateers, Plunder, and Piracy in the Elizabethan Age* (New York: Macmillan, 1975); and for Raleigh's activity in the Spanish Main, Means, chap. 6.

38. Felipe Fernández-Armesto defines this defeat as having "marked the rebirth" of the Spanish sea power; see *The Spanish Armada: The Experience of War in 1588* (Oxford: Oxford University Press, 1989), 269. Also on the Armada see Garrett Mattingly, *The Armada* (Boston: Houghton Mifflin, 1959).

39. Peter Gerhard, *Pirates of the Pacific, 1575–1742* (Lincoln: University of Nebraska Press, 1990), 101.

40. Peterson, 250.

41. For a more detailed description of Piet Heyn's actions see Peterson, 248–67; Mota, 91–95.

42. Haring, *Buccaneers,* 57.

43. Given that very little is known about the author and that the first edition was published in Dutch, most critics consider Exquemelin to be Dutch, although the Spanish translations present him as a French Huguenot. See Alexandre Olivier Exquemelin, *The Buccaneers of America: A True Account of the Most Remarkable Assaults Committed of Late Years upon the Coast of the West Indies by the Buccaneers of Jamaica and Tortuga, Both English and French. Wherein Are Contained More Especially the Unparalleled Exploits of Sir Henry Morgan, Our English Jamaican Hero, Who Sacked Porto Bello, Burnt Panama, etc.* (1684–1685; Glorieta, N. Mex.: Rio Grande Press, 1992). Depending on the translation, Exquemelin is spelled Esquemelin, Exquemeling, and Oexmelin, and his first name generally appears as Alexandre Olivier, although it can also appear as John.

44. James Burney, *History of the Buccaneers of America* (1816; London: George Allen and Company, 1912), 48–49.
45. Haring, *Buccaneers*, 66; Mota, 106; Burney, 50.
46. Rankin, 9.
47. Tomas Gage, *The English-American: A New Survey of the West-Indies, 1648* (London: Routledge, 1928).
48. Means defines these individuals as "unsavory elements from the gutters of London" (195), and Haring states that Jamaica was the "dumping-ground" for England's refuse population in *Buccaneers*, 126.
49. Rankin, 12; Peterson, 306.
50. For a detailed description of the events surrounding the English control of Jamaica and the reasons Lyttleton offered for maintaining the activities of the privateers, see Haring, *Buccaneers*, 85–112.
51. Exquemelin, 215. Philip Gosse disputes Exquemelin's portrait. Although he does acknowledge Morgan's "unseemingly" conduct and at times extreme actions such as abandoning his own men, leaving them without any ships or provisions, and taking all the plunder, Gosse does not mention Morgan's torture methods and highlights his brilliant military tactics, ultimately presenting him as "the greatest of all the 'brethren of the coast'" (*The Pirates' Who's Who*, 222–28).
52. Jan Rogoziński, *Pirates*, 229.
53. Gosse, 160; Peter Gerhard, 141; Peterson, 351.
54. See Peter Hulme, *Colonial Encounters: Europe and the Native Caribbean, 1492–1797* (London: Methuen, 1986).
55. Haring, *Buccaneers*, 272.
56. Williams, 136. The dramatic change the slave trade had in European economy is discussed by Williams, 136–55.
57. Among the pirates attacking the Caribbean during the eighteenth century, a few were American born, such as Diego Grillo (or Dieguillo), Diego de Avendaño, and Pedro José Armenteros y Poveda. Francisco Mota also mentions a number of corsairs active during the nineteenth century: Fitzgerald, Letrobe, and John Chase (English); Jean Rist and the Lafitte brothers (French); Thomas Taylor ("el yanqui"); José Copeda, Juan Manso, and José Gaspar (or Gasparilla) (Spanish) (Mota, 148–70).

Chapter 2   The Sea Monsters of the Colonial Era

"The young soul cries with compassion / his spirit alert and enlightened / seeing such an un-Catholic reign / govern this unfortunate nation / guided to the deep inferno / by a false and soulless beast: that great chatterbox and fierce monster / who was Martin Luder or mean Luther" (Juan de Castellanos, "The Discourse of Captain Frances Drake").

1. For an analysis of the colonial epic in Spanish America see Pedro Piñero Ramírez, "La épica hispanoamericana colonial," in *Historia de la literatura hispanoamericana*, vol. 1, *Epoca colonial*, coord. Iñigo Madrigal (Madrid: Cátedra, 1982), 161–88.

2. For a discussion of the different types of colonial discourse see Walter Mignolo, "Cartas, crónicas y relaciones del descubrimiento y la conquista," in Madrigal, vol. 1, 57–116.

3. See Isaac J. Pardo, *Juan de Castellanos: Estudio de las Elegías de varones ilustres de Indias* (Caracas: Universidad Central de Venezuela, 1961). Ten years after Castellanos, Lope de Vega Carpio wrote his renowned *La Dragontea* to glorify Spanish actions and exemplify "como acaban los enemigos de la Iglesia" (in *Obras Completas de Lope de Vega*, vol. 1 [Madrid: Consejo Superior de Investigaciones Científicas, 1965], 175–258).

4. Giovanni Meo-Zilio carefully reconstructs Castellanos's writing process in "Juan de Castellanos," in *Historia de la literatura hispanoamericana*, vol. 1, *Epoca colonial*, coord. Iñigo Madrigal (Madrid: Cátedra, 1982), 205–14. Concerning the historicity of his work, Castellanos claims to have used four types of documentation: (1) his own personal notes and recollections of past events, (2) *relaciones* written by friends that he personally requested, (3) notes written by other historians, and finally (4) previously published historical documents.

5. The collection was put together by Juan Bautista Muñoz. The history of this once lost part is reconstructed by Angel González Palencia in the prologue to the text itself. See Juan de Castellanos, *Discurso de el Capitán Francisco Draque* (1586–1587; Madrid: Instituto de Valencia de D. Juan, 1921), vii–xiii. All quotes from Castellanos's text belong to this edition. All translations are by the author. Hereafter cited in the text.

6. Robert Scholes and Robert Kellog, *The Nature of Narrative* (Oxford: Oxford University Press, 1966), 71.

7. I am drawing on Louis Montrose's discussion of the construction of Otherness in Walter Raleigh's *Discoverie*. Montrose identifies two specific types of discourse, which he terms the discourse of "morality" and that of "wonder" ("The Work of Gender in the Discourse of Discovery," *Representations* 33 [1991]: 25).

8. Rejecting Spain's monopoly, the queen of England stated, "by the law of nations such occupations could not hinder other princes from freely navigating those seas and transporting colonies to those parts where the Spanish did not actually inhabit; . . . prescription without possession availed nothing" (Williams, 72).

9. "Sagaz para darse cuenta de lo que le conviene. . . . Hábil para lograr lo

que quiere con engaños y ardides" (María Moliner, *Diccionario de uso del español* [Madrid: Gredos, 1983]).

10. Montrose, 25.

11. Martín del Barco Centenera, "La Argentina, o la conquista del Río de la Plata, poema histórico" 1602 in Pedro de Angelis, *Colección de obras y documentos relativos a la historia antigua y moderna de las provincias del Río de la Plata,* vol. 2 (Buenos Aires: Imprenta del estado, 1836), 1–312. All quotes are from this edition. All translations are by the author. Hereafter cited in the text. The original title was *Argentina y conquista del Río de la Plata, con otros acaescimientos de los Reynos del Perú, Tucumán y estado del Brasil.* See *Los fundadores: Martín del Barco Centenera, Luis de Tejeda y otros. Antología.* (Buenos Aires: Centro Editor, 1979), 42–46.

12. Richard Konetzke, *America Latina II La época colonial* (México: Siglo veintiuno, 1982), 205.

13. Fernando de los Ríos, "The Action of Spain in America," in *Concerning Latin American Culture* (New York: Columbia University Press, 1940), 53.

14. The Church in New Spain was far from a unified institution both in theological orientation and in patterns of action. During the first years after the Mexican conquest, the clergy relied on civil authorities to help preserve the faith. From 1522 a monastic Inquisition in which friar-inquisitors assumed episcopal powers operated in Mexico until the bishop Juan de Zumárraga received his bulls of consecration in 1532. The episcopal Inquisition remained in power until 1571, by when it had proven itself unsatisfactory to the State and the Church. This prompted Philip II to issue a royal *cédula* in 1569, creating two tribunals of the Holy Office in Mexico and Peru. Dr. Pedro Moya de Contreras was named the first inquisitor general of Mexico. For a history of the Mexican Inquisition see Richard E. Greenleaf, *The Mexican Inquisition of the Sixteenth Century* (Albuquerque: University of New Mexico Press, 1969).

15. John Oxenham, for example, one of Drake's captains, was caught in Panama but was tried and hanged in Lima.

16. Juan de Miramontes y Zuázola, *Armas Antárticas* (Caracas: Biblioteca Ayacucho, 1978). All translations are by the author. Hereafter cited in the text. For biographical information see Rodrigo Miró's introduction in *Armas Antárticas,* xxiv–xxvi.

17. Little is known about Drake's origins and early life. He was apparently born near Tavistock, approximately in 1540. His father, who was indicted in 1548 for stealing a horse, appears to have been a shearman and at other times a sailor. Drake's first recorded voyage was in 1566 with Captain John Lovell to the West Indies.

18. Clifford Geertz, *The Interpretation of Cultures: Selected Essays* (New York: Basic Books, 1973), 100.

19. Silvestre de Balboa, *Espejo de Paciencia* (La Habana: Instituto Cubano del Libro, 1976). For a critical study of the poem see Felipe Pichardo Moya, "Estudio crítico," *Cuadernos de Cultura*, Ministerio de educación, vol. 5, no. 4 (1942).

20. In fact, González Echevarría considers *Espejo de paciencia* to be the first Cuban poem. For a history of the different interpretations of the poem, see Roberto González Echevarría, "Reflexiones sobre 'Espejo de paciencia' de Silvestre de Balboa," *Nueva Revista de Filología Hispánica* 35 (1987): 571–90.

21. Mignolo, "Cartas, crónicas," 98.

22. See Cedomil Goic, "La novela hispanoamericana colonial," in Madrigal, vol. 1, 369–406. Goic summarizes the different arguments literary criticism has used to deny the existence of the novel in colonial Spanish America.

23. For an introduction to this discussion see Walter Mignolo, "El metatexto historiográfico y la historiografía indiana," *MLN* 96, no. 2 (1981): 358–402; Margarita Zamora, "Historicity and Literariness: Problems in the Literary Criticism of Spanish American Colonial Texts," *MLN* 102, no. 2 (1987): 334–46; Goic, "La novela hispanoamericana colonial."

24. Mignolo, "Cartas, crónicas," 98–99.

25. Juan Rodríguez Freyle, *El Carnero: Conquista y descubrimiento del Nuevo Reino de Granada de las Indias Occidentales del Mar Océano y fundación de la ciudad de Santa Fe de Bogotá primera de este reino donde se fundó la Real Audiencia y Cancillería, siendo la cabeza se hizo arzobispado. Cuéntase en ella su descubrimiento; algunas guerras civiles que había entre sus naturales; sus costumbres y gente, y de qué procedió este nombre tan celebrado* DEL DORADO. *Los generales, capitanes y soldados que vinieron a su conquista, con todos los presidentes, oidores y visitadores que han sido de la Real Audiencia. Los arzobispos, prebendados y dignidades que han sido de esta santa iglesia catedral, desde el año de 1539, que se fundó, hasta el de 1636, que esto se escribe; con algunos casos sucedidos en este Reino, que van en la historia para ejemplo, y no para imitarlos por el daño de la conciencia* (Caracas: Biblioteca Ayacucho, 1979). All translations are by the author. Hereafter cited in the text. It is interesting to note that most of the information concerning Rodríguez Freyle's life is scattered throughout his text.

26. María Casas de Faunce, *La novela picaresca Latino Americana* (Madrid: Planeta-Universidad, 1977).

27. José de Acosta, *La peregrinación de Bartolomé Lorenzo* (1586; Lima: Petro Perú, 1982). All translations are by the author. Hereafter cited in the text.

28. Hippolyte Delehaye, *The Legends of the Saints: An Introduction to Hagiography,* trans. V. M. Crawford (Norwood: Norwood Editions, 1974).

29. Louise Collazo, "El modelo hagiográfico en la *Peregrinación de Bartolomé Lorenzo*," unpublished paper, 19–20.
30. José Anadón traces the historical information on Bartolomé Lorenzo and his relationship with Acosta in *Historiografía literaria de América colonial* (Santiago de Chile: Universidad Católica de Chile, 1988), 21–49.
31. José Juan Arrom, prologue, in *Peregrinación de Bartolomé Lorenzo*, 15.
32. Forced to participate against his will in a campaign against a group of Indians, Bartolomé ends up caring for them and, more importantly, gets them baptized, thus transforming his expedition into a religious experience.
33. Peggy K. Liss, *Mexico under Spain, 1521–1556: Society and the Origins of Nationality* (Chicago: University of Chicago Press, 1984), 69; Konetzke, 226.
34. Haring, *Spanish Empire*, 172.
35. Manfred Barthel, *The Jesuits: History and Legend of the Society of Jesus* (New York: William Morrow, 1984), 37. The Jesuit order was founded by the basque Don Iñigo de Oñez y Loyola (San Ignacio de Loyola) and was officially approved as an order in 1540, by Pope Paul III. The Jesuits quickly became known for their extreme militance, serious discipline, and intellectual formation, as well as their overbearing missionary ambition. In 1566, the Consejo de Indias included the Jesuits among the official orders admitted in America.
36. Carlos Sigüenza y Góngora, *Infortunios que Alonso Ramírez, natural de la ciudad de San Juan de Puerto Rico padeciò, alli en poder de Ingleses Piratas que lo apresaron en las Islas Philipinas como navegando por si solo, y sin derrota, hasta varar en la Costa de Yucatan: Consiguiendo por este medio dar vuelta al Mundo*, otherwise known as *Infortunios de Alonso Ramírez* (1690; Madrid, 1902). All translations are by the author. Hereafter cited in the text.
37. *Infortunios* transcends the limits of the discursive categories precisely because of the ambiguity the first-person narrator creates. As Mabel Moraña states, *Infortunios* "twists and stretches the possibilities of the 'autobiographical pact'" ("Máscara autobiográfica y conciencia criolla en 'Infortunios de Alonso Ramírez,'" *Dispositio* 15, no. 40 [1990]: 107–17).
38. Alonso states: "Quiero que se entretenga el curioso. . . . Deducir máximas y aforismos que entre lo deleitable de la narración que entretiene cultiven la razón de quien en ello se ocupa, no será esto lo que yo aquí intente sino solicitar lástimas que, aunque posteriores á mis trabajos, harán por lo menos tolerable su memoria" [I want to entertain the curious. . . . To conclude maxims and aphorisms that might be found among the entertainment of the narration, to cultivate the mind, is not my in-

tention. I only want to solicit tears, even though they are after the fact, but they at least will make my memories more tolerable] (27–28).

39. The trajectory the narrator goes through, the importance hunger plays in the search for odd jobs, and the distinct presence of humor are other characteristics that link the text to the picaresque genre. See David Lagmanovich, "Para una caracterización de 'Infortunios de Alonso Ramírez,'" *Historia y crítica de la literatura hispanoamericana*, vol. 1, *Epoca colonial*, ed. Cedomil Goic (Barcelona: Editorial Crítica, 1988), 411–16.

40. See Kathleen Ross, *The Baroque Narrative of Carlos Sigüenza y Góngora* (Cambridge: Cambridge University Press, 1993); also Moraña.

41. David Lagmanovich believes that there is a certain ambiguity in Sigüenza y Góngora's description of the pirates, for although they are barbaric, Alonso is amazed that they shave every week, read the Bible, and pray on Sundays. According to Lagmanovich, this ambiguity is one of the key elements leading him to conclude that the nucleus of the narration is a true story ("allí reside una de las claves para concluir que, después de todo, el núcleo de la narración es una historia real") (414). This does not necessarily imply that the events actually occurred; indeed, whether or not the events happened is insignificant. The "ambiguity" characterizing the text should be looked at in conjunction with the textual production of the time and can be seen as the result of an incomplete cultural displacement. On one hand, the narrator transfers to the English everything the Spanish had previously attributed to the indigenous inhabitants. On the other, the English (who as Europeans physically resemble the Spanish and had become an impressive economic and political power) do not seem to be so different from the Spanish and in fact behave in a more "civilized" fashion than the indigenous peoples. Hence, it is not surprising that the portrayal of the English includes certain positive aspects, as in the work of other chroniclers.

42. Being able to overcome extraordinary obstacles through an unwavering religious belief in the Catholic doctrine and thus convert others was a sufficient justification to transform a personal narrative into a *relación*, as in the case of Alvar Núñez Cabeza de Vaca's account, *Naufragios* (1542). It should be noted that personal accounts did not receive any special attention unless they somehow concerned the king, the official addressee of these texts. In other words, the purpose of these narratives was to confirm a discovery or conquest. Sigüenza y Góngora's fictional account obviously does not comply with these requisites, but it is likely that this type of narrative nevertheless served as a model for his text. For a discussion of Nuñez Cabeza de Vaca's narrative technique see Nina Gerassi-Navarro, "'Naufragios' y hallazgos de una voz narrativa en la escritura

de Alvar Núñez Cabeza de Vaca," in *Conquista y contraconquista: La escritura del Nuevo Mundo (Actas XXVIII Congreso del Instituto Internacional de Literatura Iberoamericana)*, ed. Julio Ortega and José Amor y Vázquez (Mexico City: Colegio de México, Brown University, 1994), 175–86.

43. See the complete annotated version: Pedro de Solís y Valenzuela, *El desierto prodigioso y prodigio del desierto*, 3 vols., ed. Rubén Paez Patiño (Bogotá: Instituto Caro y Cuervo, 1977–1985). For a historical account of the manuscript, originally attributed to Solís y Valenzuela's brother, Bruno, see the introduction in vol. 1 by Jorge Páramo Pomareda (xi–lxxxii). All citations, however, are quoted from *"El desierto prodigioso y prodigio del desierto" de Pedro Solís y Valenzuela: primera novela hispanoamericana*, ed. Hector H. Orjuela (Bogotá: Instituto Caro y Cuervo, 1984). All translations are by the author. Hereafter cited in the text.

44. For a simplified plot description of this vast novel and an analysis of the different levels of writing and orality embedded within the text, see Flor María Rodríguez-Arenas, "Escritura y oralidad en 'El desierto prodigioso y el prodigio del desierto (hacia 1650) de Pedro Solís y Valenzuela,' " *Revista Iberoamericana* 172–73 (July–December 1995): 467–84.

Chapter 3 Defining National Identities through Piracy

"Like the wind flying free / through the immense planes of the sea / So the audacious corsairs dash / seeking the fight and the booty / Foaming waves, our homeland and reign / The red flag is our scepter / With a proud heart we confront / the perils and death" (Giuseppe Verdi).

1. The first two viceroyalties corresponded to the two indigenous empires: the Aztec and the Inca; they were the viceroyalty of New Spain, established in 1535 and that of Peru, established in 1542. The viceroyalty of Nueva Granada was created in 1717, and the last one was that of the Río de la Plata, created in 1776.

2. See Tulio Halperín-Donghi, *The Aftermath of Revolution in Latin America*, trans. Josephine de Bunsen (New York: Harper and Row, 1973).

3. In Argentina the centralists were generally liberals in economic and cultural terms, and the federalists were more inclined to defending the colonial traditions. However, in Venezuela, many conservatives defended liberalism in economic terms whereas the liberals were much more conservative, since they were mostly landowners. See Adrian C. Van Oss, "La América decimonónica," in *Historia de la Literatura Hispanoamericana: Del neoclacisimo al modernismo*, vol. 2 (Spain: Ediciones Cátedra, 1987), 11–53.

4. For a general introduction to the ideological discussions concerning na-

tion building during the nineteenth century in Spanish America, see Bradford Burns, *The Poverty of Progress: Latin America in the Nineteenth Century* (Berkeley: University of California Press, 1980); David Bushnell and Neill Macaulay, *The Emergence of Latin America in the Nineteenth Century* (New York: Oxford University Press, 1988); Germán Colmenares, *Las convenciones contra la cultura: Ensayos sobre la historiografía hispanoamericana del siglo XIX* (Colombia: Tercer Mundo Editores, 1987); Beatriz González Stephan, *La historiografía literaria del liberalismo hispanoamericano del siglo XIX* (La Habana: Casa de las Américas, 1987).

5. Leopoldo Zea, *El pensamiento latinoamericano* (Barcelona: Editorial Ariel, 1976).

6. Nicholas Shumway, in *The Invention of Argentina* (Berkeley: University of California Press, 1993), defines "guiding fictions" as those texts that consolidated a myth of peoplehood on which nations were subsequently built (7).

7. Ludmer, 27. Ludmer analyzes the voices and contrasting representations of the gaucho (patriotic figure/outlaw; popular figure/literate) before the consolidation of the Argentine state and reveals that once a specific ideological project is endorsed and implemented by the state, a hegemonic discourse is defined, which ultimately leads to the silencing of the gaucho.

8. As Germán Arciniegas states, the confusion over the name "América" is indeed unparalleled in the rest of the world. In English it generally refers to the United States, and "American" is the term individuals from the United States use to refer to themselves. In Spanish, however, *América* also refers to the whole continent. During the nineteenth century, Spanish Americans used "American" or *Americano* to refer to themselves. This is how the term will be used in this study. For an illuminating analysis on the development and different references the term "America" has come to designate, see Germán Arciniegas, *Latin America: A Cultural History*, trans. Joan MacLean (New York: Alfred A. Knopf, 1967).

9. Domingo Faustino Sarmiento (1811–1888) is perhaps the best-known, outspoken, prolific, and controversial author of his generation. He had an extremely public life: teacher, journalist, senator, minister, and even president of Argentina in 1868. As a diplomat, he traveled extensively throughout Europe and the United States, a country he admired. Among his major works are *Mi defensa* (1943); *Facundo: Civilización o barbarie* (1845); *Viajes* and *De la educación popular*, both published in 1849; *Recuerdos de provincia* (1850); and *Conflictos y armonías de las razas de América* (1884).

   Juan Bautista Alberdi (1810–1884) was one of the most influential

political Argentine doctrinaires of this generation. He strongly advocated progress and believed that this could be achieved by fomenting
European immigration. His works include numerous *artículos costum-
bristas* published under the pseudonym "Figarillo" in *La Moda*, in addition to histories, poems, plays, essays, and biographies, all illustrating
his political ideals concerning the future of Argentina. His *Bases y puntos
de partida para la organización política de la República Argentina* (1852) is undoubtedly his most important work and had a decisive role in guiding
the spirit of the legislators that set forth the constitution of 1853.

José Mármol (1817–1871), Argentine poet, is best known as the author
of his country's "first novel" *Amalia* (published as a book in 1855, though
its first appearance was in 1851 as a serialized novel in *La Semana*, in
Montevideo). The novel attacks the brutality of the Rosas regime and
Federalism in all its forms. Despite its overt partisanship, Mármol reconstructs a crucial period of Argentine history, and his novel is a renowned
example of social romanticism in Spanish America.

Esteban Echeverría (1805–1851) is the acclaimed precursor of romanticism in Argentina, and his poem *Elvira o la novia del Plata*, published
anonymously in 1832, marks the beginning of Argentina's literary emancipation. His works *La cautiva* (1837) and *El matadero* (1839) are crucial in
discussing social romanticism and the importance literature held in the
forging of a national spirit in Spanish America. His essay *Dogma socialista* (first published in 1839 and then in 1846 as *Dogma socialista de la
Asociación de Mayo precedido de una ojeada retrospectiva sobre el movimiento
intelectual en el Plata desde el año 37*), presents a sociopolitical analysis of
Argentina and articulates the essential ideals of the *generación del '37*.

10. Domingo Faustino Sarmiento, *Facundo: Civilización y barbarie* (1845;
Buenos Aires: Espasa-Calpe Argentina, 1970). Domingo Faustino Sarmiento, *Life in the Argentine Republic in the Days of the Tyrants; or, Civilization and Barbarism*, trans. Mrs. Horace Mann (New York: Hafner Press,
1868). Hereafter cited in the text; page references from the English translation.

11. For a close reading of the oppositions and contradictions of Sarmiento's
analysis see Noé Jitrik, *Muerte y transfiguración de Facundo* (Buenos Aires:
Centro Editor de América Latina, 1968).

12. For a valuable analysis of the role of writing in Sarmiento's study as
a way of mediating and "civilizing" the "barbarous" America see Julio
Ramos, *Desencuentros de la modernidad en América Latina: Literatura y política en el siglo XIX* (Mexico City: Fondo de Cultura Económica, 1989),
chap. 1. For a discussion of the role of literature and writing in general during the nineteenth century in Spanish America see Angel Rama,

La ciudad letrada (Hanover: Ediciones del Norte, 1984); Jean Franco, "La heterogeneidad peligrosa: Escritura y control social en vísperas de la independencia mexicana," *Hispamérica* 34–35 (1983): 3–34.

13. Vicente Fidel López, *La novia del hereje o la Inquisición de Lima* (Buenos Aires, 1854). There is a debate about when this text was first published and which version should be considered the definitive text. *La novia del hereje o la inquisición de Lima* was first published completely in serialized form in 1854 in *El Plata Científico y Literario* (Buenos Aires). In the "carta-prólogo" (letter-prologue) that precedes his novel, López states that he wrote the text when he was twenty-five years old, setting the original date back to 1840. He also mentions that the novel was published a few years prior, in Chile as a "folletín de un Diario," leading the public to believe that the novel itself had been published first in Chile. Further research has shown that only the first four chapters of the novel were actually published in 1843 in *El Observador Político* (Santiago de Chile), nos. 1–3 (24 July–16 August 1843). Hebe Beatriz Molina, "Algunas precisiones sobre la elaboración de 'La novia del hereje': Los folletines de 1843," *Revista de Literaturas Modernas* 19 (Universidad Nacional de Cuyo, Mendoza) (1986): 273–79; Molina, "Algunas precisiones sobre la elaboración de 'La novia del hereje': El texto definitivo," *Revista de Literaturas Modernas* 20 (1987): 201–7.

14. Among his writings, see *Evocaciones históricas*, which includes his autobiography, his essay "La gran semana de 1810," and "El conflicto y la entrevista de Guayaquil" (Buenos Aires: El Ateneo, 1929); *Curso de bellas letras* (Santiago de Chile, 1845); *Manual de historia de Chile* (Santiago de Chile, 1845); *Historia de la revolución argentina*, 4 vols. (Buenos Aires: Imprenta de Mayo, 1881); *Historia de la república argentina: Su origen, su revolución y su desarrollo político hasta 1852*, 10 vols. (Buenos Aires: Imprenta de Mayo, 1883–1893); *La loca de la guardia* (Buenos Aires, 1854). For a general study of the López family see Ricardo Piccirilli, *Los López: Una dinastía intelectual* (Buenos Aires: Editorial Universitaria de Buenos Aires, 1971).

15. Although these factors are determining, they are neither permanent nor stable elements in the definition of a nation. See Ernest Renan, "What Is a Nation?" trans. Martin Thom, in *Nation and Narration*, ed. Homi Bhabha (London: Routledge, 1990), 9–22.

16. Eric Hobsbawm differs with Anderson, claiming that the nation cannot be defined according to a particular criteria (either a common language, or past history, or cultural traits) because there will always be exceptions (*Nations and Nationalism since 1780: Programme, Myth, Reality* [Cambridge: Cambridge University Press, 1990], 9). For a comparison of both authors see Hilda Sábato, "¿Qué es una nación?" *Punto de vista* 41 (1991): 29–34.

17. For a discussion of the ways in which colonial discourse produced the "other" as savage see Peter Hulme, *Colonial Encounters: Europe and the Native Caribbean, 1492–1797* (London: Methuen, 1986).
18. Miguel Cané, quoted in Ricardo Piccirilli, *Los López, Una dinastía intelectual: Ensayo histórico literario, 1810–1852* (Buenos Aires Eudeba, 1972), 75.
19. Ludmer, 143.
20. Soledad Acosta de Samper, *Los piratas de Cartagena* (1886; Colombia: Editorial Bedout, n.d.). All translations are by the author. Hereafter cited in the text.
21. Although Cartagena was attacked numerous times by pirates during the colonial period, Drake's assault was so devastating that even today his name in the coastal area of Colombia instills fear. In this region, when children misbehave, they will often hear that instead of the more commonly known *cuco, coco,* or bogeyman, it is Drake who will come to get them.
22. Geertz, *The Interpretation of Cultures,* 104.
23. The Colombian constitution of 1863 also guaranteed free trade, abolition of slavery, freedom of expression, and freedom of the press, in addition to a federalist system of independent states. It is considered the most liberal document in the West at the time.
24. Núñez was first elected president for the period 1880 to 1882 and was reelected president in 1884. In 1887, he was driven to exile in Costa Rica.
25. Although the Battle of Boyacá marks the beginning of the republican period (1819–1832), it is in 1821 that the first constituent congress took place and enacted the liberal reforms. Subsequently, Colombia (which at the time included Venezuela and Ecuador) would undergo numerous name changes: Nueva Granada (1832–1857), the Confederación Granadina (1857–1963), Estados Unidos de Colombia (1863–1886), and finally, the República de Colombia (1886 to the present). See David Bushnell, *The Making of Modern Colombia: A Nation in Spite of Itself* (Berkeley: University of California Press, 1993).
26. For more on *costumbrismo* see Carlos José Reyes, "El costumbrismo en Colombia," in *Manual de literatura colombiana,* vol. 1 (Bogota: Procultura: Planeta, 1988), 175–246; Raymond Leslie Williams, *The Colombian Novel, 1844–1987* (Austin: University of Texas Press, 1991).
27. For a brief introduction on the role women had in Colombia during the nineteenth century see Flor María Rodríguez-Arenas, "Mujer, tradición y novela en el siglo XIX," in *¿Y las mujeres? Ensayos sobre literatura colombiana,* ed. María Mercedes Jaramillo, Angela Inés Robledo, and Flor María Rodríguez-Arenas (Colombia: Universidad de Antioquia, 1991), 77–87.
28. An example of Acosta de Samper's tenacity concerning her religious

and ideological convictions is the fact that in 1855, when she married José María Samper (lawyer, journalist, soldier, and prominent liberal politician), she continued to be outspoken of her beliefs despite her husband's political disagreements. For a detailed bibliography of her work see Flor María Rodríguez-Arenas, "Soledad Acosta de Samper, pionera de la profesionalización de la escritura femenina colombiana en el siglo XIX: 'Dolores', 'Teresa la limeña' y 'El corazón de la mujer (1869),'" *¿Y las Mujeres?* 133–75; Montserrat Ordóñez, *Soledad Acosta de Samper: Una nueva lectura* (Bogotá: Ediciones Fondo Cultural Cafetero, 1988).

29. Carlos Saénz Echeverría, *Los piratas* (Chile: Cervantes, 1891). All translations are by the author. Hereafter cited in the text. Acosta de Samper quotes Justo Zaragoza's book *Piraterías y agresiones de los ingleses y de los otros pueblos de Europa en la América Española desde el siglo XVI al XVIII* (Madrid: Imprenta de Manuel C. Hernández, 1883), 3.

30. Eric Hobsbawm, *Nations and Nationalism since 1780: Programme, Myth, Reality* (Cambridge: Cambridge University Press, 1990), 68.

31. The construction of a closed field or space through which a particular culture represents another it considers to be a menace is developed in Edward Said's *Orientalism* (New York: Vintage Books, 1979).

32. Hayden White, "The Forms of Wildness: Archaeology of an Idea," in *Tropics of Discourse: Essays in Cultural Criticism* (Baltimore: Johns Hopkins University Press, 1987), 151.

33. Flor María Rodríguez-Arenas, *Hacia la novela: La conciencia literaria en Hispanoamérica (1792–1848)* (Santafé de Bogotá: Códice, 1993). For a discussion of the relationship between nation and state in addition to Hobsbawm and Anderson see Ernest Gellner, *Nations and Nationalism* (Ithaca: Cornell University Press, 1983).

34. For an introduction to Yucatán's economic developments during independence see Alejandra García Quintanilla, "En busca de la prosperidad y la riqueza: Yucatán a la hora de la Independencia," *Siglo XIX* 1 (1986): 165–87.

35. Bradford Burns, *Latin America: A Concise Interpretive History* (Englewood Cliffs, N.J.: Prentice Hall, 1994), 163.

36. Bushnell, 71–80.

37. Read, 140.

38. Ancona's historical novels are *El filibustero* (1864), *La cruz y la espada* (1866), *Los mártires de Anáhuac* (1870), *El conde de Peñalva* (1879), and *Memorias de un Alférez* (1879). His last novel, *La mestiza* (1891), is not historical.

39. Eligio Ancona, *El filibustero* (Mérida: Leonardo Cervera, 1864), vi. The term *Yucatec* is of particular interest. *Webster's New World Dictionary* (1988) defines *Yucatec* as "a member of a North American Indian people of the

Yucatán Peninsula" or "the Mayan language of this people." The *OED* (1985) does not provide any definition, not even of *Yucatán*. But in Spanish, in the *Diccionario ideológico de la lengua española,* Julio Casares (1988) defines *yucateco* as a person originally from the Yucatán, (something or someone) belonging to this country of America, or the language of the *yucatecos.* It does not, however, make any allusion to the indigenous people. This is important because Ancona uses the term *Yucatec* to refer to a native from the Yucatán (meaning an American born in the Yucatán), without implying any reference to the indigenous culture.

40. *Encomendero* was the individual in charge, during the colonial period, of the *encomienda,* a group of indigenous laborers who, in return for religious education and protection (which they did not seek voluntarily), were assigned specific work and expected to pay taxes.

41. Barbillas, or *El Bigotes,* as he was otherwise known, does not appear to have committed violent raids. Yet he is known for his fearlessness, as he dared enter the legislative sessions of the *cabildo* in Campeche (Juan Juárez Moreno, 402).

42. Pierre Macheray, *A Theory of Literary Production* (London: Routledge, 1986), 85–89.

43. Marte R. Gómez, prólogo, in *Segundo libro del diario de mi viaje a los Estados Unidos,* by Justo Sierra O'Reilly (Mexico City: Manuel Porrúa, 1953), 9–23.

44. Emilio Abreu Gómez, *Clásicos, románticos, modernos* (Mexico City: Ediciones Botas, 1934), 102.

45. Timothy Brenan presents the division between exile and nationalism as one between loser and winner. See "The national Longing for Form," in *Nation and Narration,* ed. Homi Bhabha (London: Routledge, 1990), 61.

46. Justo Sierra O'Reilly, *El filibustero* (1841–1842; Mexico City, 1932), 11–12. Translations are by the author. Hereafter cited in the text.

47. The critical silence of women in this process will be discussed in chapter 5.

48. Soledad Acosta de Samper, *Biografías de hombres ilustres ó notables, relativas a la época del Descubrimiento, Conquista y Colonización de la parte de América denominada actualmente EE. UU. de Colombia.* (Bogotá: La Luz, 1883), 2.

Chapter 4   Nation Building and the Historical Novel

1. Michel Foucault, *The Order of Things: An Archaeology of the Human Sciences* (New York: Vintage Books, 1973), xxiii.

2. Christina Crosby carefully looks at the relation between women and

history by analyzing the way "man" constituted himself as the historical subject and placed "women" outside, in the category of "the other,"
in *The Ends of History: Victorians and "the Woman Question"* (New York:
Routledge, 1991).

The nineteenth century did not present just one "mode" of historical
thought. Hayden White studies the different phases of historical consciousness during this period in *Metahistory: The Historical Imagination in
Nineteenth-Century Europe* (Baltimore: Johns Hopkins University Press,
1975).

3. Concha Meléndez, *La novela indianista en Hispanoamérica (1832–1889)* (San
   Juan de Puerto Rico: Editorial Cordillera, 1970). Meléndez catalogues as
   novela indianista "all novels in which Indians and their traditions are portrayed with fondness" *(con simpatías)* (11).

4. John Lloyd Read, *The Mexican Historical Novel, 1826–1910* (New York: Instituto de las Españas, 1939), 1. Read cites the *cantares de gesta*, the *Anales
   toledanos*, the *romances*, the novels of chivalry as examples of the "blending of facts of history into an artistic expression." In addition, he includes
   the Spanish chronicles describing the New World as the most important
   antecedent and provides a detailed description of these chronicles and
   their role in the formation of the historical novel in nineteenth-century
   Mexico. In his discussion of the historical novel, Amado Alonso distinguishes two complementary ways of treating history. On the one hand,
   there is history per se, defined as the succession of actions that together
   form a unity, and on the other hand there is archaeology, the cultural
   and social characteristics of a particular period during which a specific action takes place. This diachronic and synchronic division allows
   Alonso to classify the treatment of history from Herodotus and Caesar
   to the nineteenth century. But Alonso does not cite the sixteenth- and
   seventeenth-century Spanish chronicles that Read considers so important as antecedents of the historical novel (Amado Alonso, *Ensayo sobre
   la novela histórica* [Madrid: Gredos, 1984], 5–81).

5. Avrom Fleishman, *The English Historical Novel: Walter Scott to Virginia
   Woolf* (Baltimore: Johns Hopkins University Press, 1971), 39.

6. Alonso, 32–33.

7. For a detailed list of the Spanish translations of Walter Scott's work see
   José F. Montesinos, *Introducción a una historia de la novela en España en el
   siglo XIX* (Madrid: Castalia, 1982), 239–44.

8. Alonso, 36.

9. For Del Monte's analysis of the historical see Anderson Imbert, "Notas
   sobre la novela histórica en el siglo XIX," in *Estudios sobre escritores de
   América* (Buenos Aires: Raigal, 1954), 30–31.

10. In discussing the historical novel, Heredia states: "Género malo en sí

mismo, género eminentemente falso. . . . la novela es una ficción y toda ficción es mentira. ¿Llamaremos *mentiras históricas* las obras de Walter Scott?" [It is a bad genre in itself, eminently false. . . . the novel is fiction, and every fiction is a lie. Shall we call Walter Scott's work *historical lies?* (quoted in Anderson Imbert, 33).

11. Alessandro Manzoni, *On the Historical Novel,* trans. Sandra Bermann (Lincoln: University of Nebraska Press, 1984), 81.

12. Michel de Certeau, *Heterologies: Discourse on the Other,* trans. Brian Massumi (Minneapolis: University of Minnesota Press, 1986), 200.

13. *Aristotle's Theory of Poetry and Fine Art,* trans. and ed. S. H. Butcher (n.p.: Dover Publications, 1951), 35.

14. Hayden White, "Historical Text as Literary Artifact," in *Tropics of Discourse: Essays in Cultural Criticism* (Baltimore: Johns Hopkins University Press, 1978), 85.

15. Roland Barthes, "The Discourse of History," in *The Rustle of Language,* trans. Richard Howard (Berkeley: University of California Press, 1989). Barthes states: "A fact never has any but a linguistic existence (as the term of discourse), yet everything happens as if this linguistic existence were merely a pure and simple 'copy' of *another* existence, situated in an extra-structural field, the 'real.' This discourse is doubtless the only one in which the referent is addressed as external to the discourse, though without its ever being possible to reach it outside this discourse" (139). Also see Félix Martínez-Bonati, "Representación y ficción," *Revista Canadiense de Estudios Hispánicos* 6, no. 1 (1981): 67–89.

16. Fleishman, 4.

17. López, *La novia del hereje,* 19.

18. Lukács, 42.

19. See Enrique Anderson Imbert, "Notas sobre la novela histórica en el siglo XIX," in *Estudios sobre escritores de América* (Buenos Aires: Raigal, 1954), 40.

20. Anderson Imbert, 40.

21. Alonso, 81.

22. Alexis Márquez Rodríguez, *Historia y ficción en la novela venezolana* (Caracas: Monte Avila, 1991), 22.

23. Emile Benveniste, *Problems in General Linguistics,* trans. Mary Elizabeth Meck (Coral Gables, Fla.: University of Miami Press, 1971), 206.

24. Benveniste states: "We shall define historical narration as the mode of utterance that excludes every 'autobiographical' linguistic form. The historian will never say *je* or *tu* or *maintenant,* because he will never make use of the formal apparatus of discourse, which resides primarily in the relationship *je: tu;*" (206).

25. José Mármol, *Amalia* (Buenos Aires: Ediciones Estrada, 1944), n.p.

26. Márquez Rodríguez, 24.
27. Manzoni, 65.
28. Alonso, 23.
29. Lukács, 41.
30. Fleishman, 15.
31. Lukács, 42.
32. Lukács, 63.
33. Márquez Rodríguez, 32–33.
34. Until recently *Jicotencal* was considered the first historical novel written in Spanish, though further research has conferred that place to *Ramiro, conde de Lucena*, originally thought to be published in 1828 by the Spanish author Rafael de Húmara y Salamanca. Mercedes Baquero Arribas claims that the latter novel was in fact published in 1823. In her essay, she also analyzes the differences between *Jicotencal* and another historical novel *Xicotencal, príncipe americano* by Salvador García Brahamonte published in Valencia in 1831, often confused with the novel published in Philadelphia. See her "La conquista de América en la novela histórica del romanticismo español: El caso de 'Xicotencal, príncipe americano,'" *Cuadernos Hispanoamericanos*, June 1990, 125–32.
35. Noé Jitrik, "De la historia a la escritura: Predominios disimetrías, acuerdos en la novela histórica latinoamericana," in Balderston, *The Historical Novel*, 17.
36. Harry Shaw, *The Forms of Historical Fiction: Sir Walter Scott and His Successors* (Ithaca: Cornell University Press, 1983). Shaw stresses the dependency of the historical novel on the history of the novel as a whole. Thus, he concludes, the historical novel will undoubtedly reflect the aesthetic and cultural presuppositions of the novel at a specific time (23).
37. López, *Manual de la historia argentina*, vol. 1 (Buenos Aires: La Facultad, 1920), xxxi.
38. Vicente Fidel López, *Memoria* (Buenos Aires, 1943), quoted by Luis Soto Ruiz, *Novela histórica hispanoamericana: Tema del pirata* (Milwaukee: Marquette University), 98.
39. This is the structuring argument of Doris Sommer's analysis in *Foundational Fictions: The National Romances of Latin America* (Berkeley: University of California Press, 1991).
40. James Burney, *A Chronological History of the Discoveries in the South Sea or Pacific Ocean* (London: Luke Hansard, 1803), 298–99. Burney dates Oxenham's activities in Panama during 1575. According to Burney, although a number of men collaborating with Oxenham were taken prisoners by the Spanish, it was "some time" before Oxenham was caught. Burney does not specify the precise date and only states that Oxenham was

interrogated in Panama and then executed. He does not mention Oxenham's transfer to Lima, where, according to a number of sources, he was actually hanged. See Christopher Lloyd, *Sir Francis Drake* (London: Faber and Faber, 1957), 62; Mendel Peterson, *The Funnel of Gold* (Boston: Little, Brown, 1975), 154. Lloyd and Peterson claim that Oxenham was already imprisoned when Drake arrived in Lima in 1578. According to Juan de Castellanos, who uses this event to prove Drake's selfishness, Drake did not even try to meet Oxenham, much less try to rescue him from the hands of the Spanish.

41. See chapter 5, note 38, in this volume.

42. Rogelio Pérez Perdomo, "Law and Urban Explosion in Latin America," in *Rethinking the Latin American City,* ed. Richard M. Morse and Jorge Hardoy (Baltimore: Johns Hopkins University Press, 1992), 144.

43. Soledad Acosta de Samper, *Biografías de hombres ilustres ó notables* (Bogota: Imprenta de "La Luz," 1883), 3–4.

44. For a brief biography see Santiago Samper Trainer, "Soledad Acosta de Samper: El eco de un grito," *Las mujeres en la historia de Colombia,* vol. 1, dirección académica, Magdala Velásquez (Bogota: Presidencia de la República de Colombia y grupo editorial Norma, 1995), 132–55; Montserrat Ordóñez, "Soledad Acosta de Samper: Una nueva lectura," *Nuevo texto crítico* 4 (1989): 50.

45. Mieke Bal, *Narratology: Introduction to the Theory of Narrative,* trans. Christine van Boheemen (Toronto: University of Toronto Press, 1985), 100–104.

46. Haring, *Buccaneers,* 262–66.

47. In his analysis of *Los piratas de Cartagena,* Luis Soto-Ruiz lists the sources he claims Acosta de Samper stated she used for the reconstruction of Admiral Vernon's attack on Cartagena. This assertion appears to be included within the text itself, but Acosta de Samper only mentions in passing the English historian Hervey, though she does not cite his work directly. In another instance, she prefers to summarize the general opinion of English historians without providing any specific name. See Luis Soto-Ruiz, *Novela histórica hispanoamericana: Tema del pirata* (Milwaukee: Marquette University), 225 n. 44.

48. Rodríguez-Arenas focuses on the literary techniques Acosta de Samper uses to transform her narrative and present a unique portrait of women, significantly different from those presented by men during the nineteenth century, without rejecting the traditional narrative conventions of the time. See Jaramillo, 133–75.

49. Donald McGrady, *La novela histórica en Colombia, 1844–1959* (Bogota: Editorial Kelly, 1969), 144; Soto-Ruiz, 210.

50. A year after declaring its independence, Mexico became a monarchy

when Agustín de Iturbide, commander in chief of the armed forces, crowned himself emperor in 1822. Iturbide was soon overthrown by general Antonio López de Santa Anna, and in 1824, the first formal constitution was finally adopted. Nevertheless, internal battles continued between monarchists and republicans, and between the *criollo* elites and the Indian and mestizo masses. In 1846 Mexico went to war with the United States (1846–1848), and more armed conflicts followed: the Caste War in the Yucatán (1847–1850), the Revolution of Ayutla (1853–1855), the Wars of Reform, and the French occupation (1864–1867), which ended with Maximilian's execution and former president Benito Juárez's return to power.

51. Ignacio Manuel Altamirano, *La literatura nacional*, vol. 1 (Mexico City: Editorial Porrúa, 1949), 13–14.

52. Ledda Arguedas, "Ignacio Manuel Altamirano," in Madrigal, vol. 2, 194.

53. Fernando Calderón (1809–1845) is one of Mexico's first romantic poets and dramatists. Although he showed a concern for the Amerind racial spirit, much of his poetry was strongly influenced by the works of the French poet Lamartine and the Spanish author Espronceda. José Heriberto García de Quevedo (1819–1871) was a Venezuelan dramatist, poet, and novelist, who moved to Madrid at the age of thirty.

54. Eligio Ancona, *Historia de Yucatán, desde la época más remota hasta nuestros días*, 2d ed. (Barcelona: Jaime Roviralta, 1889), 4.

55. Diego López de Cogolludo, *Los tres siglos de la dominación española en Yucatán, ó sea historia de esta provincia, desde la conquista hasta la independencia*, 2 vols. (Mérida: Imprenta de Castillo y Compañía, 1845).

56. Wolfgang Iser, "Interaction between Text and Reader," in *The Reader in the Text: Essays on Audience and Interpretation*, ed. Susan R. Suleiman and Inge Crosman (Princeton, N.J.: Princeton University Press, 1980), 106–19.

57. Ancona made his antagonism toward the Inquisition the central aspect of another historical novel, *La hija del judío*. In comparing all of Ancona's historical novels, John Read considers *Los mártires de Anáhuac* (1870) superior in both technique and historical accuracy. See John Lloyd Read, *The Mexican Historical Novel* (New York: Instituto de la Españas en los Estados Unidos, 1939), 148–53.

58. Read, 145.

59. Mota, 303.

60. Diego López de Cogolludo, *Historia de Yucatán* (1688; Mexico City: Editorial Academia Literaria, 1957), 596–602. The title of the second edition was *Los tres siglos de la dominación española en Yucatán, ó sea historia de esta provincia, desde la conquista hasta la independencia*, 2 vols. (Mérida: Imprenta de Castillo y Compañia, 1845). Sierra O'Reilly included a pro-

logue praising López de Cogolludo's work and a number of appendixes. For a detailed description of Sierra O'Reilly's edition see the edition cited of the *Historia de Yucatán*.

61. Stephens's work, entitled *Incidents of Travel in Yucatan*, was originally published in 1843.

62. Philip Gosse, *The Pirates' Who's Who: Giving the Particulars of the Lives and Deaths of the Pirates and Buccaneers* (Boston: Charles Lauriat, 1924), 115.

63. Juan Juárez Moreno, 12–18. Mota corroborates this date and also bases his brief comments on López de Cogolludo, 292–93.

64. López de Cogolludo does mention it, however. He claims that Diego was baptized in Havana, which is why he describes him as a "criollo de la Havana" and also states that Galván was his godfather. Juan Juárez Moreno bases his description of Diego *el mulato* on López de Cogolludo's narration.

65. Gage, 352.

66. López de Cogolludo, 658.

67. Soto-Ruiz, 83.

68. According to López de Cogolludo, the offense was an unjust slap Captain Domingo Rodríguez Calvo gave Diego in Campeche. This is why the chronicler states that Diego tried to find the captain during his attack on Campeche to "cut his ears and nose off, and not kill him" and thus obtain his revenge (598).

69. In addition, it reinforces the melodramatic characteristics of the text, which are discussed in chapter 5.

Chapter 5   The Force of Melodrama

"Melodrama is essentially considered the 'persona non grata' of literary history. Dismissed by all, drama of excess, it has become a synonym of bad taste" (J. M. Thomasseau).

1. Peter Brooks, *The Melodramatic Imagination: Balzac, Henry James, Melodrama, and the Mode of Excess* (New York: Columbia University Press, 1985); Michael R. Booth, *English Melodrama* (London: Herbert Jenkins, 1965); Robert Heilman, *Tragedy and Melodrama: Versions of Experience* (Seattle: University of Washington Press, 1968); Ira Hauptman, "Defending Melodrama," *Themes in Drama: Melodrama* (Cambridge: Cambridge University Press, 1992), 281–89; William R. Morse, "Desire and the Limits of Melodrama," in *Themes in Drama: Melodrama*, 17–46; Martha Vicinus, " 'Helpless and Unfriended': Nineteenth-Century Domestic Melodrama," *New Literary History: A Journey of Theory and Interpretation* 13,

no. 1 (1981): 127–43. More recently, melodrama has been reevaluated through its connection with film and television. For an excellent historical introduction to melodrama and its development in cinema see Christine Gledhill's "The Melodramatic Field: An Investigation," in *Home Is Where the Heart Is: Studies in Melodrama and the Woman's Film*, ed. Christine Gledhill (London: British Film Institute, 1987), 5–42. The essays in this volume provide a superb critical framework for discussing melodrama and the "woman's film." See also *Imitations of Life: A Reader on Film and Television Melodrama*, ed. Marcia Landy (Detroit: Wayne State University Press, 1991).

2. See Earl F. Bargainnier, "Melodrama as Formula," *Journal of Popular Culture* 9 (1975): 726–33. For a brief history of melodrama see Pierre Reboul, "Peuple Enfant, Peuple Roy, ou Nodier, Mélodrame et Révolution," *Revue des Sciences Humaines* 162 (1976): 251.

3. Booth, 14.

4. Brooks, 32.

5. Jesús Martín-Barbero, *De los medios a las mediaciones: Mediaciones, cultura y hegemonía* (Mexico City: Gustavo Gili, 1987), 129.

6. It should be noted that the politics and morality of melodrama were intensely debated during the nineteenth century. Its supporters found that it was useful in educating the mass public with bourgeois values. Those against it claimed that melodrama would be responsible for undermining the social hierarchy essential to maintain stability and happiness from a bourgeois perspective. See Gabriell Hyslop, "Pixérécourt and the French Melodrama Debate: Instructing Boulevard Theatre Audiences," in *Themes in Drama: Melodrama* (Cambridge: Cambridge University Press, 1992), 61–85.

7. Brooks, xiii.

8. Gledhill, 21.

9. Although Sommer stresses the link with history and nation building throughout the texts she analyzes, they are not all historical novels, nor do they all pertain to the nineteenth century.

10. Sommer, 7.

11. During the latter part of the century, however, melodramas became much more truculent, and the "good" heroes did in fact succumb.

12. The underlining idea is that dramatizations have an important role in educating audiences. In fact, the imposition of a particular value system through the theater has a considerably long tradition in Spanish America. During the colonial period, theater was used by the Spanish as a means of enforcing the spiritual colonization of the indigenous people. The Spanish quickly appropriated the basic structure of pre-Hispanic

theater and adapted it to spread the Christian doctrine. The results were such that María Sten asserts, "The theatre was for the spiritual conquest what horses and gunpowder were for the military conquest" (*Vida y muerte del teatro náhuatl: El Olimpo sin Prometeo* [Mexico City: Secretaría de Educación Pública, 1974], 8).

13. Heilman, 96.

14. Donald McGrady, *La novela histórica colombiana, 1844–1959* (Bogotá: Editorial Kelly, 1962), 43–44.

15. Heilman, 03.

16. A similar depiction is presented of Brazo de Acero, the hero in Riva Palacio's novel, who goes off with the English pirate Henry Morgan, hoping to create a new nation free of Spanish tyranny. Brazo de Acero stands out among the British pirates for his black eyes, olive-skinned complexion, and bushy dark beard.

17. Booth, 18.

18. In discussing this aspect of melodrama in the United States, Heilman states that the psychological rewards are so immediate and intense that "we unconsciously try to make reality conform to the melodramatic pattern" (104).

19. López continues sculpting his heroine all the way down to her feet, detailing her body parts: "De su cintura suelta y delgada se desprendían las formas más redondas y más airosas que se pueden imaginar. Su pecho saliente y abovedado sostenía un cuello torneado y esbelto, coronado por la bella cabeza, que, inclinada un tanto al lado izquierdo, completaba el aire extraordinario de gracia modesta que dominaba en su figura encantadora" [From her loose and slender waist came the most round and elegant shapes imaginable. Her noticeably curved chest held a sculpted and elongated neck, crowned by her beautiful head, which, slightly tilted to the left, completed that extraordinary air of modest grace that dominated her enchanting figure].

20. J. Hillis Miller, *Topographies* (Stanford: Stanford University Press, 1995), 21.

21. Joan Scott underlines how gender is a constitutive element of social relationships in *Gender and the Politics of History* (New York: Columbia University Press, 1988). Scott identifies four interrelated elements that shape these relationships: culturally available symbols; their interpretations and meanings; the application of these interpretations into political, economic, domestic, social, and educational institutions; and finally the subjective identity of the gendered persons in society (42–43).

22. Elaine Scarry, *The Body in Pain: The Making and Unmaking of the World* (New York: Oxford University Press, 1987), 207. In this particular chap-

ter, Scarry articulately analyzes the power relationship between God and human beings, focusing on the significance of the separation between the body and the voice. This analysis also applies to the relationship between men and women, where the same hierarchical division is reproduced in the interaction established between the two genders.

23. Marysa Navarro, "Women in Pre-Columbian and Colonial Latin America," in *Restoring Women to History: Teaching Packets for Integrating Women's History into Courses on Africa, Asia, Latin America, the Caribbean, and the Middle East* (Bloomington: Organization of American Historians, 1988), 1–40.

24. Johanna S. Mendelson, "The Feminine Press: The View of Women in the Colonial Journals of Spanish America, 1790–1810," in *Latin American Women: Historical Perspectives,* ed. Asunción Lavrín (Westport, Conn.: Greenwood Press, 1978), 198–218. For a history of women's vote in Latin America see Jane Jaquette, "Female Participation in Latin America," in *Sex and Class in Latin America,* ed. June Nash and Helen Icken Safa (New York: Praeger Publishers, 1976), 221–44. See also Anna Macías, *Against All Odds: The Feminist Movement in Mexico to 1940* (Westport, Conn.: Greenwood Press, 1982).

25. Mary Louise Pratt, "Women, Literature, and National Brotherhood," in *Women, Culture, and Politics in Latin America: Seminar on Feminism and Culture in Latin America* (Berkeley: University of California Press, 1990), 51.

26. As Linda Kerber notes on the ambiguities of female citizenship in the United States, though women's relationship to the nation seemed vicarious, "it was impossible for women, like male civilians, to ignore the highly charged political atmosphere in which they lived." Linda Kerber, "May All Our Citizens Be Soldiers and All Our Soldiers Citizens: The Ambiguities of Female Citizenship in the New Nation," in *Women, Militarism, and War: Essays in History, Politics, and Social Theory,* ed. Jean Bethke Elshtain and Sheila Tobias (Savage, Md.: Rowman and Littlefield, 1990), 93.

27. For a brief summary concerning the way marriage affected the different sections of society during the colonial period see Navarro, 28–33. Susy Bermúdez notes that during the period of the liberal administration in Colombia (1853–1856), although a number of legislative reforms concerning marriage were introduced, the basic concept of family, which was in fact grounded on marriage, was not questioned. This would not occur until the end of the century. See Susy Denise Bermúdez, "Debates en torno a la mujer y a la familia en Colombia, 1850–1886," *Texto y contexto: Mentalidades e instituciones en la Constitución de 1886* 10 (Bogotá, January–April 1987): 116.

28. According to Alberdi, "No son las leyes que necesitamos cambiar; son las cosas. Necesitamos cambiar nuestras gentes incapaces de libertad, por otras gentes hábiles para ella, sin abdicar el tipo de nuestra raza original, y mucho menos el señorío del país; suplantar nuestra actual familia argentina, por otra igualmente argentina, pero más capaz de *libertad*, de *riqueza* y *progreso*. ¿Por conquistadores más ilustrados que la España, por ventura? Todo lo contrario; conquistando en vez de ser conquistados. La América del Sud posee un ejército a este fin, y es el encanto que sus hermosas y amables mujeres recibieron de su origen andaluz, mejorado por el cielo espléndido del nuevo mundo. Removed los impedimentos inmorales, que hacen estéril el poder del *bello sexo americano* y tendréis realizado *el cambio de nuestra raza* sin la pérdida del idioma ni del tipo nacional primitivo" [We do not need to change our laws, we need to change certain things. We need to change our people who are incapable of handling freedom, for others with greater dexterity, without abdicating our original race and much less the nobility of our country. We must substitute our current Argentine family for another equally Argentine but much more capable of *freedom, richness,* and *progress.* Perhaps for more illustrious conquerors than the Spanish? By no means! On the contrary; we must conquer instead of being conquered. South America possesses an army for this: the enchantment our beautiful and able women have received from their Andalusian origins, improved by the splendid sky of the New World. Remove all immoral impediments that sterilize the *beautiful American sex* and you will have *the needed change in our race* without the loss of our language or of our original national type] (Alberdi, *Las Bases,* 163–64; emphasis added).
29. Macías, 61.
30. For a history of the feminist movement in Mexico and Yucatán's particular role see Macías, especially the introduction and chapter 3.
31. Shoshana Felman provides an interesting analysis of madness, underlining that "it can only occur within a world of conflict, within a conflict of thoughts" (*Writing and Madness (Literature/Philosophy/Psychoanalysis)*, trans. Martha Noel Evans and Soshana Felman, with the assistance of Brian Massumi [Ithaca: Cornell University Press, 1985], 36).
32. In his analysis of the experience of two female freebooters, Marcus Rediker explores the ways in which gender markers such as physical strength, personal initiative, and, most importantly, courage among pirates were appropriated by women at sea. Women pirates were, in fact, an exception, and most captains drew up articles that specifically banned them from their ships. Nevertheless, recent studies have shown that occasionally women were found aboard naval, whaling, privateering, and pirate

vessels, more commonly masked by cross-dressing, but not always. See Marcus Rediker, "Liberty beneath the Jolly Roger: The Lives of Anne Bonny and Mary Read, Pirates," in *Iron Men, Wooden Women: Gender and Seafaring in the Atlantic World, 1700–1920,* ed. Margaret S. Creighton and Lisa Norling (Baltimore: Johns Hopkins University Press, 1996); Linda Grant De Pauw, *Seafaring Women* (Boston: Houghton Mifflin, 1982).

33. Elizabeth Garrells, " 'El espíritu de la familia' en 'La novia del hereje' de Vicente Fidel López," *Hispamérica* 46–47 (1987): 5.

34. Barbara Bardes and Suzanne Gossett, *Declarations of Independence: Women and Political Power in Nineteenth-Century American Fiction* (New Brunswick: Rutgers University Press, 1990), 22.

35. Acosta de Samper, *La mujer* 59 (1851), quoted in Bermúdez, 127.

36. Acosta de Samper, *La mujer,* 20 May 1879, quoted in Bermúdez, 130.

37. In analyzing Acosta de Samper's novels, Flor María Rodríguez Arenas notes that the Colombian author discussed important issues concerning the cultural role assigned to women through her female characters. Rather than echoing the ideals of modern society generally set forth by men, Acosta de Samper transformed her heroines into spokespersons for women "so that women could resist the fossilization of the traditional structures that trapped, repressed and condemend them." Rodríguez Arenas goes on to affirm that Acosta de Samper "used her work to advance a plan of action so that the women of her time could see that alternatives in fact did exist to fight against their insignificant position" ("Siglo XIX," 142–43).

38. Crosby, *The Ends of History,* 90.

39. Bushnell and Macaulay, 5. Although there was a considerable correlation between wealth and the whiteness of one's skin, Bushnell and Macaulay stress that race should not be considered an economic factor, for there were certain trade-offs between degrees of skin color and economic or cultural characteristics. Thus, a wealthy black would probably be perceived more as a *mulato,* and an educated *mestizo* essentially as a *criollo.* Hence, according to the authors, "racial differences never exactly coincided with socioeconomic ones, even though they did, on the whole, reinforce the latter—and vice versa" (6).

40. See José Piedra's illuminating essay "Literary Whiteness and the Afro-Hispanic Difference," in *The Bounds of Race: Perspectives on Hegemony and Resistance,* ed. Dominick La Capra (Ithaca: Cornell University Press, 1991), 128–310.

41. In view of the discussion surrounding the definition of "race," numerous critics have chosen to place the word in brackets to underscore that "race" is "a metaphor for something else and not an essence or a thing

in itself, apart from its creation by an act of language," as Henry Louis Gates Jr. has defined it. See Henry Louis Gates Jr., "Talkin' That Talk," in *"Race," Writing, and Difference,* ed. Henry Louis Gates Jr. (Chicago: University of Chicago Press, 1986), 402.

42. In her recent book, Mary Louise Pratt has included a table from W. B. Stevenson's *Narrative of Twenty Years Residence in South America* (1825) in which he charts the mixture of different castes with their common names. Stevenson makes a point of stating that his classification of colors has been done according to appearance and not of caste because "I have always remarked, that a child receives more of the colour of the father than of the mother" (vol. 1, 286), quoted by Pratt in *Imperial Eyes: Travel Writing and Transculturation* (London: Routledge, 1992), 152.

43. Richard Graham, introduction to *The Idea of Race in Latin America, 1870–1940,* ed. Richard Graham (Austin: University of Texas Press, 1990).

44. Navarro, 26.

45. Piedra, 286. According to the author, the trial was a "staged" event. To gain public attention in defending their rights, many prominent black citizens, for example, accused themselves of crimes that could be proven untrue during those trials.

46. In discussing this marriage, Elizabeth Garrells accurately notes that on one hand, Drake marries up to the extent that he is a plebeian and his origin is obscure. On the other hand, Juana, although she proves to be the daughter of a noble Inca, has dark skin. Hence in marrying a white Englishman, she marries up, particularly for the *generación del '37,* who defined the Englishman as "the most perfect of all men," as Juan Bautista Alberdi once stated (18–20).

47. As already noted, except for Henderson, the whiteness marking the heroes and heroines in these texts reflects a distinct Spanish origin with their dark hair and eyes, and slightly darker skin color.

48. Walter Benn Michaels, "The Souls of White Folk," in *Literature and the Body: Essays on Populations and Persons,* ed. Elaine Scarry (Baltimore: Johns Hopkins University Press, 1988), 204.

Conclusion

1. Ernest Renan, "What Is a Nation?" in *Nation and Narration,* ed. Homi Bhabha (London: Routledge, 1990), 19.

2. Renan, 11.

3. It is precisely for this reason that Lukács does not consider Scott a romantic author.

4. Fleishman, 50.
5. Crosby, 89.
6. Roland Barthes, *Mythologies,* trans. Annette Lavers (New York: Hill and Wang, 1972).
7. Walter Mignolo, "Canons a(nd) Cross-Cultural Boundaries (Or, Whose Canon Are We Talking About?)" *Poetics Today* 12, no. 1 (spring 1991): 128.
8. In this sense, piracy can be related to the carnival. See Mikhail Bakhtin, *Rabelais and His World,* trans. Hélène Iswolsky (Bloomington: Indiana University Press, 1984).
9. Carmen Boullosa, *Son vacas, somos puercos: filibusteros del mar Caribe* (Mexico: Ediciones Era, 1991); Jorge Eslava, *Descuelga un pirata* (Lima: Seglusa y Colmillo Blanco Editores, 1994); Alberto Vázquez Figueroa, *Piratas* (Spain: Plaza y Janés, 1996); Laura Antillano, *Tuna de Mar* (Caracas: Fundarte, 1991).
10. Among the films portraying pirate adventures during the late 1930s and early 1940s, the most notorious are *The Buccaneer* (1938), *The Sea Hawk* (1940), *The Black Swan* (1942), and *The Spanish Main* (1945).
11. This becomes even more obvious if one takes into account that Howard Koch, the Warner Brothers' scriptwriter who also authored *The Sea Hawk* —perhaps Flynn's best-known pirate film—was notorious for his committed antifascism.
12. Thatcher, in fact, made the cover of the weekly magazine *Tal Cual,* dressed as a pirate, eye patch and all, with the headline "Pirate, Witch, and Assassin." See *Tal Cual* (Buenos Aires, Argentina), 30 April 1982.

Bibliography

Abreu Gómez, Emilio. *Clásicos, románticos, modernos*. Mexico City: Ediciones Botas, 1934.

Acosta, José de. *La peregrinación de Bartolomé Lorenzo*. Lima: Petro Perú, 1982.

Acosta de Samper, Soledad. *Biografías de hombres ilustres ó notables, relativas a la época del descubrimiento, conquista y colonización de la parte de América denominada actualmente EE. UU. de Colombia*. Bogota: La Luz, 1883.

———. *Los piratas de Cartagena*. Colombia: Edit. Bedout, 1886.

Alberdi, Juan Bautista. *Bases y puntos de partida para la organización política de la República Argentina*. Buenos Aires: Centro Editor de América Latina, 1979.

Alonso, Amado. *Ensayo sobre la novela histórica: El modernismo en "La Gloria de Don Ramiro."* 1942. Madrid: Gredos, 1984, 5–81.

Altamirano, Ignacio Manuel. *La literatura nacional: Revistas, ensayos, biografías y prólogos*. Vol. 1. Mexico City: Editorial Porrúa, 1949.

Althusser, Louis. *For Marx*. Trans. Ben Brewster. London: Verso, 1990.

Ancona, Eligio. *El filibustero*. Mérida: Leonardo Cervera, 1864.

Anderson, Benedict. *Imagined Communities: Reflections on the Origin and Spread of Nationalism*. London: Verso and New Left Books, 1983.

Anderson Imbert, Enrique. "Notas sobre la novela histórica en el siglo XIX." In *Estudios sobre escritores de América*, 26–46. Buenos Aires: Editorial Raigal, 1954.

———. *Historia de la literatura hispanoamericana: La colonia, cien años de República*. Vol. 1. Mexico City: Fondo de Cultura Económica, 1962.

Arac, Jonathan, and Harriet Ritvo, eds. *Macropolitics of Nineteenth-Century Literature: Nationalism, Exoticism, Imperialism*. Philadelphia: University of Pennsylvania Press, 1991.

Arciniegas, Germán. *Latin America: A Cultural History*. Trans. Joan MacLean. New York: Alfred A. Knopf, 1967.

Arguedas, Ledda. "Ignacio Manuel Altamirano." In Madrigal, 193–201.

Arrom, José Juan. Prologue to *Peregrinación de Bartolomé Lorenzo*, by José de Acosta, 9–26.

Bal, Mieke. *Narratology: Introduction to the Theory of Narrative*. Trans. Christine van Boheemen. Toronto: University of Toronto Press, 1985.

Balboa, Silvestre de. *Espejo de Paciencia*. Havana: Editorial Pueblo y Educación, 1976.

Balderston, Daniel, ed. *The Historical Novel in Latin America: A Symposium.* Gaithersburg, Md.: Ediciones Hispamérica, 1986.

Baquero Arribas, Mercedes. "La conquista de América en la novela histórica del romanticismo español: El caso de 'Xicotencal, príncipe americano.'" *Cuadernos Hispanoamericanos* 480 (1990): 125–32.

Barco Centenera, Martín del. "La Argentina, o la conquista del Río de la Plata, poema histórico" in Pedro de Angelis, *Colección de obras y documentos relativos a la historia antigua y moderna de las provincias del Río de la Plata.* Vol. 2. Buenos Aires: Imprenta del estado, 1836.

Bardes, Barbara, and Suzanne Gossett. *Declarations of Independence: Women and Political Power in Nineteenth-Century American Fiction.* New Brunswick: Rutgers University Press, 1990.

Bargainnier, Earl F. "Melodrama as Formula." *Journal of Popular Culture* 9 (1975): 726–33.

Barthel, Manfred. *The Jesuits: History and Legend of the Society of Jesus.* Trans. and adapt. Mark Howson. New York: William Morrow, 1984.

Barthes, Roland. *Mythologies.* Trans. Annette Lavers. New York: Hill and Wang, 1982.

———. "The Discourse of History." In *The Rustle of Language,* trans. Richard Howard, 127–41. Berkeley: University of California Press, 1989.

Bejarano, Jesús Antonio, comp. *El siglo XIX en Colombia visto por historiadores norteamericanos.* Bogotá: La Carreta, 1977.

Bello, Andrés. "Modo de escribir la historia." In *Obras Completas.* Caracas: Fundación Casa de Andrés Bello, 1981.

Benjamin, Walter. *Illuminations.* Trans. Harry Zohn. New York: Schocken Books, 1985.

Bentley, Eric. *The Life of the Drama.* New York: Atheneum, 1967.

Bermúdez, Susy Denise. "Debates en torno a la mujer y a la familia en Colombia, 1850–1886." *Texto y contexto: mentalidades e instituciones en la constitución de 1886* 10 (January–April 1987): 111–44.

Bevan, Bryan. *The Great Seamen of Elizabeth I.* London: Robert Hale, 1971.

Beveniste, Emile. *Problems in General Linguistics.* Trans. Mary Elizabeth Meck. Coral Gables, Fla.: University of Miami Press, 1971.

Bhabha, Homi, ed. *Nation and Narration.* London: Routledge, 1990.

Booth, Michael R. *English Melodrama.* London: Herbert Jenkins, 1965.

Braudy, Leo. *Narrative Form in History and Fiction: Hume, Fielding, and Gibbon.* Princeton: Princeton University Press, 1970.

Bravo Ugarte, José. *Historia de México: La Nueva España.* 3d ed. 2 vols. Mexico City: Editorial Jus., 1953.

Brenan, Timothy. "The National Longing for Form." In Bhabha, 44–70.

Brooks, Peter. *The Melodramatic Imagination: Balzac, Henry James, Melodrama, and the Mode of Excess.* New Haven: Yale University Press, 1976.

Brown, David. *Walter Scott and the Historical Imagination.* London: Routledge, 1979.

Brushwood, John. *Genteel Barbarism: Experiments in Analysis of Nineteenth-Century Spanish-American Novels.* Lincoln: University of Nebraska Press, 1981.

Burney, James. *A Chronological History of the Discoveries in the South Sea or Pacific Ocean.* London: Luke Hansard, 1803.

———. *History of the Buccaneers of America.* 1816. London: George Allen, 1912.

Burns, Bradford. *The Poverty of Progress: Latin America in the Nineteenth Century.* Berkeley: University of California Press, 1980.

Bushnell, David, and Neill Macaulay. *The Emergence of Latin America in the Nineteenth Century.* Oxford: Oxford University Press, 1988.

Butcher, S. H., ed. and trans. *Aristotle's Theory of Poetry and Fine Art.* Dover Publications, 1978.

Byron, George. "The Corsair." In *Tales and Poems,* 127–204. Philadelphia: Carey and Hart, 1849.

Canal Feijóo, Bernardo, ed. *Los fundadores: Martín del Barco Centenera, Luis de Tejeda y otros.* Antología. Buenos Aires: Centro Editor, 1979.

Carilla, Emilio. *El romanticismo en la América hispánica.* 2 vols. Madrid: Gredos, 1967.

Casares, Julio. *Diccionario ideológico de la lengua española.* 2d ed. Barcelona: Gustavo Gili, 1988.

Castellanos, Juan de. *Discurso de el Capitán Francisco Draque.* Madrid: Instituto de Valencia de D. Juan, 1921.

Certeau, Michel de. *Heterologies: Discourse on the Other.* Trans. Brian Massumi. Minneapolis: University of Minnesota Press, 1986.

———. *The Writing of History.* Trans. Tom Conley. New York: Columbia University Press, 1988.

Chartier, Roger. *Cultural History: Between Practices and Representations.* Trans. Lydia G. Cochrane. Ithaca: Cornell University Press, 1988.

Chatman, Seymour. *Story and Discourse: Narrative Structure in Fiction and Film.* Ithaca: Cornell University Press, 1986.

Cheyfitz, Eric. *The Poetics of Imperialism: Translation and Colonization from "The Tempest" to "Tarzan."* Oxford: Oxford University Press, 1991.

Christelow, Allan. "Contraband Trade between Jamaica and the Spanish Main, and the Free Port Act of 1766." *Hispanic American Historical Review* 22 (1942): 309–43.

Collazo, Louise. "El modelo hagiográfico en la 'Peregrinación de Bartolomé Lorenzo' del Padre José de Acosta." Unpublished manuscript.

Colmenares, Germán. *Las convenciones contra la cultura: Ensayos sobre la historiografía hispanoamericana del siglo XIX.* Colombia: Tercer Mundo Editores, 1987.

Cooper, James Fenimore. *Sea Tales: "The Pilot," "The Red Rover."* 1849. New York: Library of America, 1991.

Corbett, Julian. *Sir Francis Drake.* New York: Haskell House, 1968.

Cordingly, David. *Life among the Pirates: The Romance and the Reality.* Great Britain: Little, Brown, 1995.

Crosby, Christina. *The Ends of History: Victorians and "the Woman Question."* New York and London: Routledge, 1991.

Cusac, Marian. *Narrative Structure in the Novels of Sir Walter Scott.* The Hague: Mouton, 1969.

Cvitanovic, Dinko, and Nilsa M. Alzola de Cvitanovic. "Narración histórica, didactismo y expresión literaria en 'La novia del hereje.'" *Revista interamericana de bibliografía: Inter-American Review of Bibliography* 36 (1986): 145–50.

Davoine, Jean-Paul. "L'Epithète mélodramatique." *Revue des Sciences Humaines* 162 (1976): 183–92.

Day, Geoffrey. *From Fiction to the Novel.* London: Routledge and Kegan Paul, 1987.

Dekker, George. *The American Historical Romance.* Cambridge: Cambridge University Press, 1990.

Delehaye, Hippolyte. *The Legends of the Saints: An Introduction to Hagiography.* Trans. V. M. Crawford. Norwood, Pa.: Norwood Editions, 1974.

Desan, Suzanne. "Crowds, Community, and Ritual in the Work of E. P. Thompson and Natalie Davis." In *The New Cultural History,* ed. Lynn Hunt, 47–71. Berkeley: University of California Press, 1989.

Duby, Georges. "Ideologies in Social History." Trans. David Denby. In *Constructing the Past: Essays in Historical Methodology,* ed. Jacques Le Goff and Pierre Nora. Cambridge: Cambridge University Press, 1987.

Espronceda, José de. "La canción del pirata." In *Obras poéticas: "El Pelayo," poesías líricas, "El estudiante de Salamanca." "El diablo mundo,"* 24–25. 1839. Mexico City: Editorial Porrúa, 1972.

Exquemeling, Alexandre Olivier. *The Buccaneers of America: A True Account of the Most Remarkable Assaults Committed of Late Years upon the Coast of the West Indies by the Buccaneers of Jamaica and Tortuga Both English and French Wherein Are Contained More Especially the Unparalleled Exploits of Sir Henry Morgan, Our English Jamaican Hero, Who Sacked Porto Bello, Burnt Panama, etc.* 1684–1685; Glorieta, N. Mex.: Rio Grande Press, 1992.

Faunce, María Casa de. *La novela picaresca Latino Americana.* Madrid: Planeta-Universidad, 1977.

Felman, Shoshana. *Writing and Madness (Literature/Philosophy/Psychoanalysis).* Trans. Martha Noel Evans and Soshana Felman with the assistance of Brian Massumi. Ithaca: Cornell University Press, 1985.

Fernández-Armesto, Felipe. *The Spanish Armada: The Experience of War in 1588.* Oxford: Oxford University Press, 1989.

Fiedler, Leslie A. *Love and Death in the American Novel.* Cleveland: Meridian Books, 1962.

Fleishman, Avrom. *The English Historical Novel: Walter Scott to Virginia Woolf.* Baltimore: Johns Hopkins University Press, 1971.

Foucault, Michel. *The Archaeology of Knowledge and the Discourse on Language.* Trans. A. M. Sheridan Smith. New York: Pantheon Books, 1972.

———. *The Order of Things: An Archaeology of the Human Sciences.* New York: Vintage Books, 1973.

Franco, Jean. "Un viaje poco romántico: Viajeros británicos hacia Sudamérica, 1818–28." *Escritura* (January–June 1979): 129–42.

———. "La heterogeneidad peligrosa: Escritura y control social en vísperas de la independencia mexicana." *Hispamérica* 12, nos. 34–35 (1983): 3–34.

Frankl, Victor. *El "Antijovio" de Gonzálo Jiménez de Quesada y las concepciones de realidad y verdad en la época de la contrarreforma y del Manierismo.* Madrid: Ediciones Cultura Hispánica, 1963.

Frye, Northrop. *Anatomy of Criticism: Four Essays.* Princeton: Princeton University Press, 1973.

———. *The Secular Scripture: A Study of the Structure of Romance.* Cambridge: Harvard University Press, 1976.

Gage, Tomas. *The English-American: A New Survey of the West Indies, 1648.* London: Routledge, 1928.

Gandía, Enrique de. *Historia de los piratas en el Río de la Plata.* Buenos Aires: Editorial Cervantes, 1936.

García Quintilla, Alejandra. "En busca de la prosperidad y la riqueza: Yucatán a la hora de la independencia." *Siglo XIX* 1 (1986): 165–87.

Garrels, Elizabeth. "El espíritu de la familia en 'La novia del hereje' de Vicente Fidel López." *Hispamérica* 16, nos. 46–47 (1987): 3–24.

Gates, Henry Louis, Jr. "Talkin' That Talk." In Gates, *"Race," Writing, and Difference,* 402–9.

———, ed. *"Race," Writing, and Difference.* Chicago: University of Chicago Press, 1986.

Geertz, Clifford. *The Interpretation of Cultures.* New York: Basic Books, 1973.

———. *Local Knowledge: Further Essays in Interpretive Anthropology.* New York: Basic Books, 1983.

Gellner, Ernest. *Nations and Nationalism.* Ithaca: Cornell University Press, 1983.

Gerassi-Navarro, Nina. " 'Naufragios' y hallazgos de una voz narrativa en la escritura de Alvar Núñez Cabeza de Vaca." In *Conquista y contraconquista: La escritura del Nuevo Mundo (actas XVIII Congreso, Instituto Internacional de Literatura Iberoamericana),* 175–85. Mexico City: Colegio de México, 1994.

Gerhard, Peter. *Pirates of the Pacific, 1575–1742.* Lincoln: University of Nebraska Press, 1990.

Gillman, Susan. "The Mulatto, Tragic or Triumphant? The Nineteenth-Century American Race Melodrama." In Samuels, 221–43.

Gledhill, Christine. "The Melodramatic Field: An Investigation." In *Home Is Where the Heart Is: Studies in Melodrama and the Woman's Film,* ed. Christine Gledhill, 5–42. London: British Film Institute, 1987.

Goic, Cedomil. "La novela hispanoamericana colonial." In Madrigal, vol. 1, 369–406.

———, ed. *Historia y crítica de la literatura hispanoamericana.* 3 vols. Barcelona: Editorial Crítica, 1988.

González Echevarría, Roberto, comp. *Historia y ficción en la narrativa Hispano-americana (coloquio de Yale).* Venezuela: Monte Avila, 1985.

González Palencia, Angel. Prologue to *Discurso de el Capitán Francisco Draque, que compuso Joan de Castellanos,* vii–cxviii. Madrid: Instituto de Valencia de D. Juan, 1921.

González Stephan, Beatriz. *La historiografía literaria del liberalismo hispano-americano del siglo XIX.* Havana: Casa de las Américas, 1987.

Gosse, Philip. *The Pirate's Who's Who: Giving Particulars of the Lives and Deaths of the Pirates and Buccaneers.* Boston: Charles E. Lauriat Company, 1924.

———. *The History of Piracy.* London: Longmans, Green, 1934.

Greenleaf, Richard E. *The Mexican Inquisition of the Sixteenth Century.* Albuquerque: University of New Mexico Press, 1969.

Grimsted, David. *Melodrama Unveiled: American Theater and Culture, 1800–1850.* Chicago: University of Chicago Press, 1968.

Groot, José Manuel. *Historia eclesiástica y civil de Nueva Granada escrita sobre documentos auténticos.* 2 vols. Bogota: Casa Editorial de M. Rivas y Cía, 1889.

Halperín-Donghi, Tulio. *The Aftermath of Revolution in Latin America.* Trans. Josefine de Bunsen. New York: Harper and Row, 1973.

Hampden, John. *Francis Drake: Privateer.* Tuscaloosa: University of Alabama Press, 1972.

Haring, Clarence Henry. *Las instituciones coloniales de Hispanoamérica (siglos XVI a XVIII).* San Juan: Instituto de cultura puertorriqueña, 1957.

———. *The Buccaneers in the West Indies in the XVII Century.* Hamden, Conn.: Archon Books, 1966.

———. *The Spanish Empire in America.* San Diego: Harcourt Brace Jovanovich, 1975.

Hauptman, Ira. "Defending Melodrama." In *Themes in Drama: Melodrama,* 281–90. Cambridge: Cambridge University Press, 1992.

Heilman, Robert Bechtold. *Tragedy and Melodrama: Versions of Experience.* Seattle: University of Washington Press, 1968.

Hobsbawm, Eric J. *Primitive Rebels: Studies in Archaic Forms of Social Movement in the 19th and 20th Centuries*. New York: Norton, 1965.

———. *Bandits*. New York: Delacorte Press, 1969.

———. *Nations and Nationalism since 1780: Programme, Myth, Reality*. Cambridge: Cambridge University Press, 1990.

Hollis, Christopher. *The Jesuits: A History*. New York: Macmillan, 1968.

Hulme, Peter. *Colonial Encounters: Europe and the Native Caribbean, 1492–1797*. London. Methuen, 1986.

Hunt, Lynn, ed. *The New Cultural History*. Berkeley: University of California Press, 1989.

Hyslop, Gabriell. "Pixérécourt and the French Melodrama Debate: Instructing Boulevard Theatre Audiences." In *Themes in Drama: Melodrama*, 61–85. Cambridge: Cambridge University Press, 1992.

Iser, Wolfgang. "Interaction between Text and Reader." In *The Reader in the Text: Essays on Audience and Interpretation*, ed. Susan R. Suleiman and Inge Crosman, 106–19. Princeton: Princeton University Press, 1890.

Jameson, Frederic. *The Political Unconscious: Narrative as a Socially Symbolic Act*. Ithaca: Cornell University Press, 1981.

Jaquette, Jane. "Female Participation in Latin America." In *Sex and Class in Latin America*, ed. June Nash and Helen Icken Safa, 221–44. New York: Praeger Publishers, 1976.

Jaramillo, María Mercedes, Angela Inés Robledo, and Flor María Rodríguez-Arenas. *¿Y las mujeres? Ensayos sobre literatura colombiana*. Colombia: Universidad de Antioquia, 1991.

Jitrik, Noé. *Muerte y transfiguración de Facundo*. Buenos Aires: Centro Editor de América Latina, 1968.

———. "De la novela histórica a la escritura: Predominios disimetrías, acuerdos en la novela histórica latinoamericana." In Balderston, 13–29.

Juárez Moreno, Juan. *Corsarios y piratas en Veracruz y Campeche*. Seville: Escuela de Estudios Hispano-Americanos, 1972.

Kamen, Henry. *The Spanish Inquisition*. London: Weidenfeld and Nicolson, 1965.

Kerber, Linda K. "May All Our Citizens Be Soldiers and All Our Soldiers Citizens: The Ambiguities of Female Citizenship in the New Nation." In *Women, Militarism, and War: Essays in History, Politics, and Social Theory*, ed. Jean Bethke Elshtain and Sheils Tobias, 89–103. Savage, Md.: Rowman and Littlefield, 1990.

Konetzke, Richard. *América Latina II: la época colonial*. Mexico City: Siglo XXI, 1982.

Kristeva, Julia. *Strangers to Ourselves*. Trans. Leon S. Roudiez. New York: Columbia University Press, 1991.

La Capra, Dominick, ed. *The Bounds of Race: Perspectives on Hegemony and Resistance.* Ithaca: Cornell University Press, 1991.

Lagmanovich, David. "Para una caracterización de 'Infortunios de Alonso Ramírez.'" In Goic, *Historia,* vol. 1, 411–16.

Landy, Marcia, ed. *Imitations of Life: A Reader on Film and Television Melodrama.* Detroit: Wayne State University Press, 1991.

Lane, Kris. *Pillaging the Empire: Piracy in the Americas, 1500–1750.* New York: M. E. Sharpe, 1998.

Langbauer, Laurie. *Women and Romance: The Consolations of Gender in the English Novel.* Ithaca: Cornell University Press, 1990.

Lascelles, Mary. *The Story-Teller Retrieves the Past: Historical Fiction and Fictitious History in the Art of Scott, Stevenson, Kipling, and Some Others.* Oxford: Clarendon Press, 1980.

Las mujeres en la historia de Colombia. Vols. 1 and 3. Ed. Magdala Velásquez. Bogota: Presidencia de la República de Colombia y Grupo editorial Norma, 1995.

Lavrín, Asunción. "In Search of the Colonial Woman in Mexico: The Seventeenth and Eighteenth Centuries." In Lavrín, *Latin American Women,* 23–59.

———, ed. *Latin American Women: Historical Perspectives.* Westport, Conn.: Greenwood Press, 1978.

Leal, Luis. "'El Siglo de Oro' de Balbuena: Primera novela americana." *Kentucky Romance Quarterly* 23, no. 3 (1976): 327–34.

Liss, Peggy. *Mexico under Spain, 1521–1556: Society and the Origins of Nationality.* Chicago: University of Chicago Press, 1984.

Lloyd, Christopher. *Sir Francis Drake.* London: Faber and Faber, 1957.

Londoño, Patricia. "El ideal femenino del siglo XIX en Colombia: entre flores, lágrimas y ángeles." In *Las mujeres en la historia de Colombia,* vol. 3, 302–29.

López de Cogolludo, Diego. *Historia de Yucatán.* 1688. Mexico City: Editorial Academia Literaria, 1957.

López, Vicente Fidel. *La novia del hereje o la Inquisición de Lima.* 1845–1850. Buenos Aires: La cultura argentina, 1917.

———. *Manual de la historia argentina.* Buenos Aires: "La Facultad" de Juan Roldán, 1920.

———. *Evocaciones históricas.* Buenos Aires: El Ateneo, 1929.

Lucena Salmoral, Manuel. *Piratas, bucaneros, filibusteros y corsarios en América: Perros, mendigos y otros malditos del mar.* Spain: Mapfre, 1992.

Ludmer, Josefina. *El género gauchesco: Un tratado sobre la patria.* Buenos Aires: Sudamericana, 1988.

Lukács, Georg. *The Historical Novel.* Trans. Hannah and Stanley Mitchell. Boston: Beacon Press, 1963.

———. *Theory of the Novel: A Historico-Philosophical Essay on the Forms of Great Epic Literature.* Trans. Anna Bostock. Cambridge: MIT Press, 1985.

Macheray, Pierre. *A Theory of Literary Production.* Trans. Geoffrey Wall. London: Routledge, 1989.

Macías, Anna. *Against All Odds: The Feminist Movement in Mexico to 1940.* Westport, Conn.: Greenwood Press, 1982.

Madrigal, Iñigo, coord. *Historia de la literatura hispanoamericana.* 2 vols. Madrid: Cátedra, 1982, 1987.

Manzoni, Alessandro. *Del romanzo storico; On the Historical Novel.* Trans. Sandra Bermann. Lincoln: University of Nebraska Press, 1984.

Marcouz, Paul J. "Guilbert de Pixérécourt: The People's Conscience." In *Themes in Drama: Melodrama,* 47–59. Cambridge: Cambridge University Press, 1992.

Mármol, José. *Amalia.* Buenos Aires: Clásicos Argentinos, 1944.

Márquez Coronel, Coriolano. *El pirata o la familia de los condes de Osorno.* Buenos Aires: Imprenta de la Bolsa, 1863.

Márquez-Rodríguez, Alexis. *Historia y ficción en la novela venezolana.* Venezuela: Monte Avila, 1990.

Martín-Barbero, Jesús. *De los medios a las mediaciones, cultura y hegemonía.* Mexico City: Gustavo Gili, 1987.

Martínez-Bonati, Félix. "Representación y ficción." *Revista canadiense de estudios hispánicos* 6, no. 1 (1981): 67–89.

Marx, Jenifer. *Pirates and Privateers of the Caribbean.* Malabar, Fla.: Krieger, 1992.

Matthews, Brander. "The Historical Novel." In *The Historical Novel and Other Essays,* 3–28. New York: Charles Scribner's Sons, 1901.

McGrady, Donald. *La novela histórica en Colombia, 1844–1959.* Bogota: Editorial Kelly, 1969.

Means, Philip Ainsworth. *The Spanish Main: Focus of Envy, 1492–1700.* New York: Charles Scribner's Sons, 1935.

Meléndez, Concha. *La novela indianista en Hispanoamérica (1832–1889).* Madrid: Imprenta Hernando, 1934.

Melo, Jorge Orlando, and Alsonso Valencia Llano. *Reportaje de la Historia de Colombia: 158 documentos y relatos de testigos presenciales sobre hechos ocurridos en 5 siglos.* 2 vols. Bogota: Planeta Colombiana Editorial, 1989.

Mendelson, Johanna S. "The Feminine Press: The View of Women in the Colonial Journals of Spanish America, 1790–1810." In Lavrín, *Latin American Women,* 198–218.

Meo-Zilio, Giovanni. "Juan de Castellanos." In Madrigal, vol. 1, 205–14.

Michaels, Walter Benn. "The Souls of White Folk." In Scarry, *Literature and the Body,* 185–209.

Mignolo, Walter. "El Metatexto Historiográfico y la historiografía indiana." *MLN* 96 (1981): 358–402.

————. "Cartas, crónicas y relaciones del descubrimiento y la conquista." In Madrigal, vol. 1, 57–116.

————. "Canons a(nd) Cross-Cultural Boundaries (Or, Whose Canon Are We Talking About?)." *Poetics Today* 12, no. 1 (spring 1991): 1–28.

Miller, Helen Hill. *Captain from Devon: The Great Elizabethan Seafarers Who Won the Oceans for England.* Chapel Hill: Algonquin Books, 1985.

Miller, J. Hillis. *Topographies.* Stanford: Stanford University Press, 1995.

Miramón, Alberto. "Piratas, corsarios y bucaneros." *Boletín de historia y antigüedades* 29 (1942): 16–33.

Miramontes y Zuázola, Juan de. *Armas Antárticas.* Caracas: Biblioteca Ayacucho, 1978.

Miró, Rodrigo. Introducción. In *Armas Antárticas,* by Juan de Miramontes y Zuázola, ix–xxx. Caracas: Biblioteca Ayacucho, 1978.

Molina, Hebe Beatriz. "Algunas apreciaciones sobre la elaboración de 'La novia del hereje': Los folletines de 1843." *Revista de Literaturas Modernas* 19 (Universidad Nacional de Cuyo, Mendoza, 1986): 273–79.

————. "Algunas precisiones sobre la elaboración de 'La novia del hereje': El texto definitivo." *Revista de Literaturas Modernas* 20 (Universidad Nacional de Cuyo, Mendoza, 1987): 201–7.

Moliner, María. *Diccionario de uso del español.* Madrid: Gredos, 1983.

Montesinos, José F. *Introducción a una historia de la novela en España en el siglo XIX.* Madrid: Castalia, 1982.

Montrose, Louis. "The Work of Gender in the Discourse of Discovery." *Representations* 33 (1991): 1–41.

Moraña, Mabel. "Máscara autobiográfica y conciencia criolla en *Infortunios de Alonso Ramírez.*" *Dispositio* 15, no. 40 (1990): 107–17.

Morse, William. "Desire and the Limits of Melodrama." In *Themes in Drama: Melodrama,* 17–30. Cambridge: Cambridge University Press, 1992.

Mota, Francisco. *Piratas en el Caribe.* Havana: Casa de las Américas, 1984.

Moya, Felipe Pichardo. "Estudio crítico." *Cuadernos de cultura* 4, 5th series (1942).

Navarro, Marysa. "Women in Pre-Columbian and Colonial Latin America." In *Restoring Women to History: Teaching Packets for Integrating Women's History into Courses on Africa, Asia, Latin America, the Caribbean, and the Middle East,* 3–40. Bloomington, Ind.: Organization of American Historians, 1988.

Ordóñez, Montserrat. "Soledad Acosta de Samper: Una nueva lectura." *Nuevo texto crítico* 4 (1989): 49–55.

Oviedo y Valdés, Gonzalo Fernández. *Historia general y natural de Indias, islas y tierra-firme del mar océano.* 1535. Madrid: Imprenta de la Real Academia de la Historia, 1851.

Pagden, Anthony. *European Encounters with the New World: From Renaissance to Romanticism.* New Haven: Yale University Press, 1993.

Pardo, Isaac. *Juan de Castellanos: Estudio de las "Elegías de varones ilustres de Indias."* Caracas: Universidad Central de Venezuela, 1961.

Pares, Richard. *War and Trade in the West Indies, 1739–1763.* London: Thomas Nelson, 1963.

Parry, J. H. *The Spanish Seaborne Empire.* 1960. Berkeley: University of California Press, 1990.

Payne, Manuel. *Un viaje a Veracruz en el invierno de 1843.* Xalapa: Universidad Veracruzana, 1984.

Pérez Perdomo, Rogelio. "Law and Urban Explosion in Latin America." In *Rethinking the Latin American City,* 144–48.

Pérez Valenzuela, Pedro. *Historia de piratas: Los aventureros del mar en la América Central.* Guatemala: Centro América, 1936.

Peterson, Mendel. *The Funnel of Gold.* Boston: Little, Brown, 1975.

Piccirilli, Ricardo. *Los López, Una dinastía intelectual: Ensayo histórico literario, 1810–1852.* Buenos Aires: Edit. Universitaria de Bs.As., 1972.

Piedra, José. "Literary Whiteness and the Afro-Hispanic Difference." In *The Bounds of Race: Perspectives on Hegemony and Resistance,* ed. Dominick La Capra, 278–310. Ithaca: Cornell University Press, 1991.

Pirates: Terror on the High Seas—from the Caribbean to the South China Sea. Atlanta: Turner Publishing, 1996.

Pratt, Mary Louise. "Women, Literature, and National Brotherhood." In *Women, Culture, and Politics in Latin America: Seminar on Feminism and Culture in Latin America,* 48–73. Berkeley: University of California Press, 1990.

———. *Imperial Eyes: Travel Writing and Transculturation.* London: Routledge, 1992.

Preminger, Alex. *Princeton Encyclopedia of Poetry and Poetics.* Princeton: Princeton University Press, 1990.

Quinn, David. *England's Sea Empire, 1550–1642.* London: George Allen and Unwin, 1983.

Rahill, Frank. *The World of Melodrama.* University Park: Pennsylvania State University Press, 1967.

Rankin, Hugh F. *The Golden Age of Piracy.* Williamsburg: Holt, Rinehart and Winston, 1969.

Ramírez, Pedro Piñero. "La épica hispanoamericana colonial." In Madrigal, vol. 1, 161–88.

Ramos, Julio. *Desencuentros de la modernidad en América Latina: Literatura y política en el siglo XIX.* Mexico City: Fondo de Cultura Económica, 1989.

Read, John Lloyd. *The Mexican Historical Novel, 1826–1910.* New York: Instituto de la Españas, 1939.

Real, Cristóbal. *El corsario Drake y el imperio español.* Madrid: Editora Nacional, 1942.

Reboul, Pierre. "Peuple Enfant, Peuple Roy, ou Nodier, Mélodrame et Révolution." *Revue des Sciences Humaines* 162 (1976): 247–56.

Rediker, Marcus. *Between the Devil and the Deep Blue Sea: Merchant Seamen, Pirate, and the Anglo-American Maritime World, 1700–1750.* Cambridge: Cambridge University Press, 1987.

———. "Liberty beneath the Jolly Roger: The Lives of Anne Bonny and Mary Read, Pirates." In *Iron Men, Wooden Women: Gender and Seafaring in the Atlantic World, 1700–1920,* ed. Margaret S. Creighton and Lisa Norling, 1–35. Baltimore: Johns Hopkins University Press, 1996.

Renan, Ernest. "What Is a Nation?" Trans. Martin Thom. In Bhabha, 9–22.

Restoring Women to History: Teaching Packets for Integrating Women's History into Courses on Africa, Asia, Latin America, the Caribbean, and the Middle East. Bloomington, Ind.: Organization of American Historians, 1988.

Rethinking the Latin American City. Ed. Richard M. Morse and Jorge E. Hardoy. Baltimore: Johns Hopkins University Press, 1992.

Ríos, Fernando de los. "The Action of Spain in America." In *Concerning Latin American Culture,* 49–78. New York: Columbia University Press, 1940.

Rippy, Fred. "Anglo-American Filibusters and the Gadsden Treaty." *The Hispanic American Historical Review* 5, no. 2 (1922): 155–80.

Riva Palacio, Vicente. *Los piratas del golfo.* 2 vols. 1869. Mexico City: Editorial Porrúa, 1946.

Robert, Paul. *Le Petit Robert 1: Dictionnaire Alphabétique et Analogique de la Langue Française.* Paris: Société du Nouveau Littré, 1979.

Roberts, Adolphe. *The French in the West Indies.* Indianapolis: Bobbs-Merrill, 1942.

Rodó, José Enrique. *Obras Completas.* Madrid: Aguilar, 1957.

Rodríguez-Arenas, Flor María. "Siglo XIX: Soledad Acosta de Samper." In *¿Y las mujeres? Estudios de literatura colombiana.* Medellín: Universidad de Antioquia, 1991.

———. *Hacia la novela: La conciencia literaria en Hispanoamérica (1792–1848).* Santafé de Bogotá: Códice, 1993.

Rodríguez Freyle, Juan. *El carnero.* Venezuela: Biblioteca Ayacucho, 1979.

Rogoziński, Jan. *A Brief History of the Caribbean: From the Arawak and the Carib to the Present.* New York: Meridian, 1994.

———. *Pirates! Brigands, Buccaneers, and Privateers in Fact, Fiction, and Legend.* New York: Da Capo Press, 1996.

Ross, Kathleen. *The Baroque Narrative of Carlos Sigüenza y Góngora: A New World Paradise.* Cambridge: Cambridge University Press, 1993.

Sábato, Hilda. "¿Qué es una nación?" *Punto de vista* 41 (1991): 29–34.

Sáenz Echeverría, Carlos. *Los piratas: Leyenda histórica.* Chile: Imprenta Cervantes, 1891.

Safford, Frank. *Aspectos del siglo XIX en Colombia*. Colombia: Hombre Nuevo, 1977.

Sahlins, Marshall. *Islands of History*. Chicago: University of Chicago Press, 1987.

Said, Edward. *Orientalism*. New York: Vintage Books, 1979.

Samper Trainer, Santiago. "Soledad Acosta de Samper: El eco de un grito." In *Las mujeres en la historia de Colombia*, vol. 1, 122-55.

Samuels, Shirley, ed. *The Culture of Sentiment: Race, Gender, and Sentimentality in Nineteenth-Century America*. New York: Oxford University Press, 1992.

Sarmiento, Domingo Faustino. *Facundo: Civilización y barbarie*. Buenos Aires: Espasa-Calpe, 1970.

Scarry, Elaine. *The Body in Pain: The Making and Unmaking of the World*. New York: Oxford University Press, 1987.

———, ed. *Literature and the Body: Essays on Populations and Persons*. Baltimore: Johns Hopkins University Press, 1990.

Scholes, Robert, and Robert Kellog. *The Nature of Narrative*. Oxford: Oxford University Press, 1966.

Scott, Joan. *Gender and the Politics of History*. New York: Columbia University Press, 1988.

Scott, Walter. *Essays on Chivalry, Romance, and the Drama*. London: Frederick Warne, 1887.

———. *The Pirate*. 1821. 2 vols. Boston: Houghton Mifflin, 1923.

Sharp, William. "Structure of Melodrama." In *Themes in Drama: Melodrama*, 281-90. Cambridge: Cambridge University Press, 1992.

Shaw, Harry. *The Forms of Historical Fiction: Sir Walter Scott and His Successors*. Ithaca: Cornell University Press, 1983.

Shumway, Nicolas. *The Invention of Argentina*. Berkeley: University of California Press, 1993.

Sierra O'Reilly, Justo. *El filibustero*. 1841-1842. Mexico City, 1932.

———. *Un año en el hospital de San Lázaro*. Vol. 2 of *Obras del Doctor Justo Sierra*. Mexico City: Victoriano Agüeros, 1905.

Sigüenza y Góngora, Carlos de. *Infortunios de Alonso Ramírez*. 1690. Madrid: Imprenta de la viuda de Gabriel Pedraza, 1902.

Smith-Rosenberg, Carroll. "Domesticating 'Virtue': Coquettes and Revolutionaries in Young America." In Scarry, *Literature and the Body*, 160-84.

Solís y Valenzuela, Pedro de. *El desierto prodigioso y prodigio del desierto*. 2 vols. Edición de Rubén Pérez Patiño. Introduction, study, and notes by Jorge Páramo Pomareda, Manuel Briceño Jáuregui, and Rubén Pérez Patiño. Bogota: Instituto Caro y Cuervo, 1977, 1984.

Sommer, Doris. *Foundational Fictions: The National Romances of Latin America*. Berkeley: University of California Press, 1991.

Soto-Ruiz, Luis. "Novela histórica hispanoamericana: Tema del pirata." Ph.d. diss., University of Michigan, 1958. Milwaukee: Marquette University, 1977.

Sten, María. *Vida y muerte del teatro náhuatl: El Olimpo sin Prometeo*. Mexico City: Secretaría de Educación Publica, 1974.

Stephens, John L. *Incidents of Travel in Yucatan*. 2 vols. 1843. New York: Dover Publications, 1963.

Suárez-Radillo, Carlos Miguel. *El teatro neoclásico y costumbrista hispanoamericano: Una historia crítico-antológica*. 2 vols. Spain: Ediciones Cultura Hispánica, 1984.

Taylor, Paul. "Spanish Seamen in the New World during the Colonial Period." *Hispanic American Historical Review* (1922): 631–61.

Therborn, Goran. *The Ideology of Power and the Power of Ideology*. London: Verso Editions, 1980.

Thomasseau, Jean-Marie. *Le Mélodrame*. Paris: Presses Universitaires de France, 1984.

Todorov, Tzvetan. *Nous et les autres: Reflexion française sur la diversité humaine*. Paris: Seuil, 1989.

Una nueva lectura: Soledad Acosta de Samper. Bogota: Fondo Cultural Cafetero, 1988.

Unzueta, Fernando. *La imaginación histórica y el romance nacional en Hispanoamérica*. Lima-Berkeley: Latinoamericana editores, 1996.

Van Oss, Adrian. "La América decimonónica." In Madrigal, vol. 2, 11–53.

Vega Carpio, Lope Félix de. *La Dragontea*. Vol. 1 of *Obras Completas de Lope de Vega*, 175–258. Madrid: Consejo Superior de Investigaciones Científicas, 1965.

Vicinus, Martha. " 'Helpless and Unfriended': Nineteenth-Century Domestic Melodrama." *New Literary History: A Journey of Theory and Interpretation* 8, no. 1 (1981): 127–43.

Vidal, Hernán. *Literatura hispanoamericana e ideología liberal: Surgimiento y crisis*. Buenos Aires: Ediciones Hispanoamérica, 1976.

Villaverde, Cirilo. *Excursión a Vueltabajo*. Consejo Nacional de Cultura, 1961.

Watt, Ian. *The Rise of the Novel: Studies in Defoe, Richardson, and Fielding*. Berkeley: University of California Press, 1967.

White, Hayden. *Metahistory: The Historical Imagination in the Nineteenth Century*. Baltimore: Johns Hopkins University Press, 1973.

———. "The Forms of Wildness: Archaeology of an Idea." In *Tropics of Discourse: Essays in Cultural Criticism*, 150–82. Baltimore: Johns Hopkins University Press, 1987.

———. *The Content of the Form: Narrative Discourse and Historical Representation*. Baltimore: Johns Hopkins University Press, 1989.

Williams, Eric. *From Columbus to Castro: The History of the Caribbean, 1492–1969*. New York: Vintage, 1984.

Williams, Nelville. *The Sea Dogs: Privateers, Plunder, and Piracy in the Elizabethan Age*. New York: Macmillan, 1975.

Williams, Raymond Leslie. *The Colombian Novel, 1844–1987*. Austin: University of Texas Press, 1991.

Williamson, James A. *The Voyages of the Cabots and the English Discovery of North America under Henry VII and Henry VIII*. London: Argonaut Press, 1929.

————. *Hawkins of Plymouth: A New History of Sir John Hawkins and of the Other Members of His Family Prominent in Tudor England*. New York: Barnes and Noble, 1969.

Woodward, Ralph Lee, Jr. *Central America: A Nation Divided*. 2d ed. New York: Oxford University Press, 1985.

The World Encompassed by Sir Francis Drake. 1854. New York: Burt Franklin, n.d.

Zamora, Margarita. "Historicity and Literariness: Problems in the Literary Criticism of Spanish American Colonial Texts. *MLN* 102, no. 2 (1987): 334–46.

Zamudio, José Zamora. *La novela histórica en Chile*. Buenos Aires: Francisco de Aguirre, 1973.

Zaragoza, Justo. *Piraterías y agresiones de los Ingleses y de otros pueblos de Europa en la América española desde el siglo XVI al XVIII deducidas de las obras de D. Dionisio de Alsedo y Herrera*. Madrid: Imprenta de Manuel C. Hernández, 1883.

Zea, Leopoldo. *El pensamiento latinoamericano*. Barcelona: Ariel, 1976.

Index

Nina Gerassi-Navarro is Associate Professor,
Department of Spanish and Italian,
Mount Holyoke College.

Library of Congress Cataloging-in-Publication Data

Gerassi-Navarro, Nina.
Pirate novels : fictions of nation building in Spanish
America / Nina Gerassi-Navarro.
p.   cm.
Includes bibliographical references and index.
ISBN 0-8223-2360-5 (alk. paper). — ISBN 0-8223-2393-1
(pbk. : alk. paper)
1. Spanish American fiction—19th century—History
and criticism.   2. Historical fiction, Spanish
American—History and criticism.   3. Pirates in
literature.   4. Nationalism and literature—Latin
America.   I. Title.
PQ7082.N7G36   1999
863—dc21   99-25491